San Francisco Nights

The Psychedelic Music Trip, 1965–1968

BY
GENE SCULATTI AND DAVIN SEAY

SIDGWICK & JACKSON
LONDON

First published in Great Britain in 1985
by Sidgwick and Jackson Limited

Originally published in the United States
of America by St Martin's Press, Inc.

ISBN 0-283-99277-8

Printed in Great Britain by
R. J. Acford, Industrial Estate, Chichester, Sussex
for Sidgwick and Jackson Limited
1 Tavistock Chambers, Bloomsbury Way
London WC1A 2SG

Contents

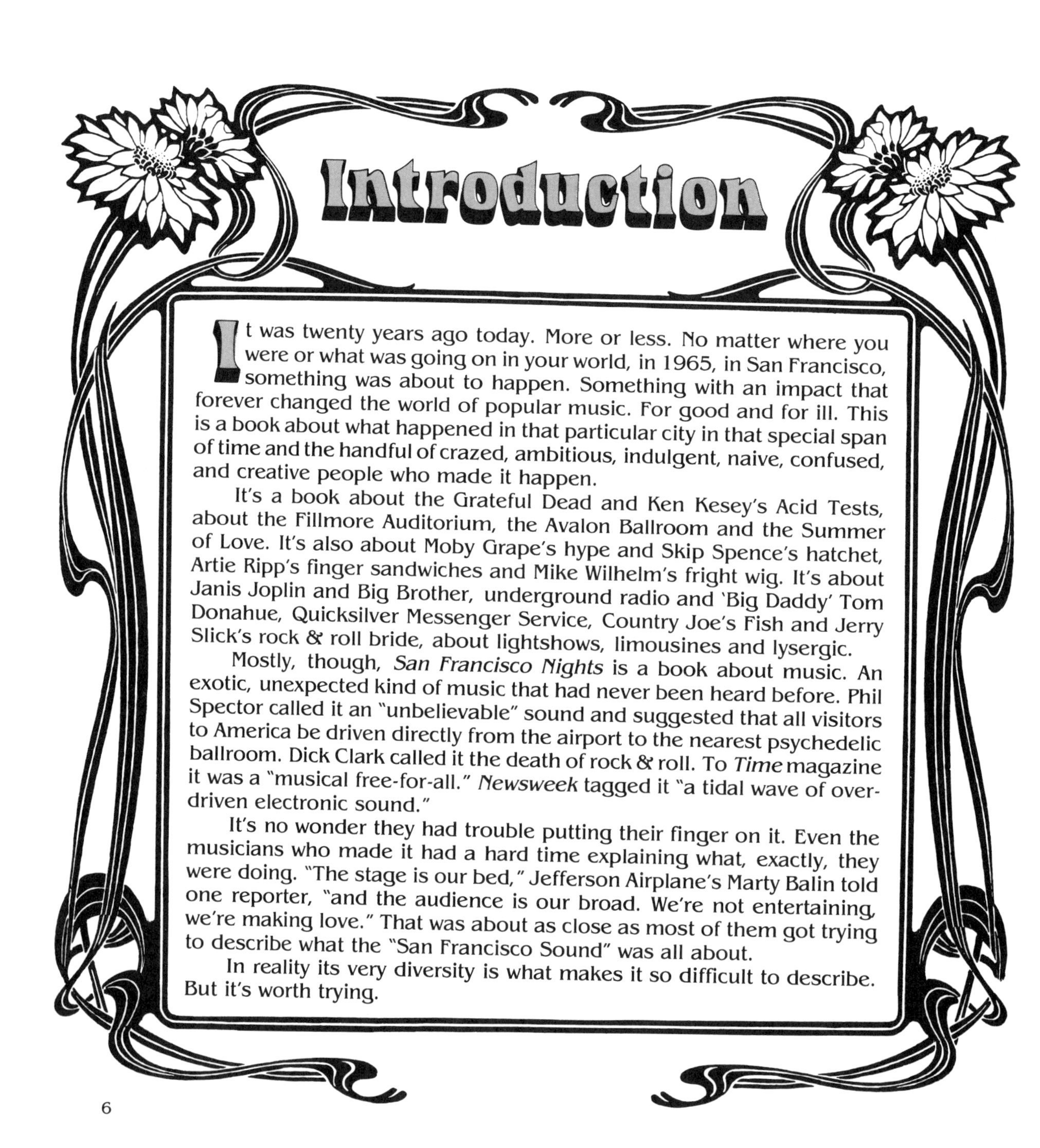

Introduction

It was twenty years ago today. More or less. No matter where you were or what was going on in your world, in 1965, in San Francisco, something was about to happen. Something with an impact that forever changed the world of popular music. For good and for ill. This is a book about what happened in that particular city in that special span of time and the handful of crazed, ambitious, indulgent, naive, confused, and creative people who made it happen.

It's a book about the Grateful Dead and Ken Kesey's Acid Tests, about the Fillmore Auditorium, the Avalon Ballroom and the Summer of Love. It's also about Moby Grape's hype and Skip Spence's hatchet, Artie Ripp's finger sandwiches and Mike Wilhelm's fright wig. It's about Janis Joplin and Big Brother, underground radio and 'Big Daddy' Tom Donahue, Quicksilver Messenger Service, Country Joe's Fish and Jerry Slick's rock & roll bride, about lightshows, limousines and lysergic.

Mostly, though, *San Francisco Nights* is a book about music. An exotic, unexpected kind of music that had never been heard before. Phil Spector called it an "unbelievable" sound and suggested that all visitors to America be driven directly from the airport to the nearest psychedelic ballroom. Dick Clark called it the death of rock & roll. To *Time* magazine it was a "musical free-for-all." *Newsweek* tagged it "a tidal wave of over-driven electronic sound."

It's no wonder they had trouble putting their finger on it. Even the musicians who made it had a hard time explaining what, exactly, they were doing. "The stage is our bed," Jefferson Airplane's Marty Balin told one reporter, "and the audience is our broad. We're not entertaining, we're making love." That was about as close as most of them got trying to describe what the "San Francisco Sound" was all about.

In reality its very diversity is what makes it so difficult to describe. But it's worth trying.

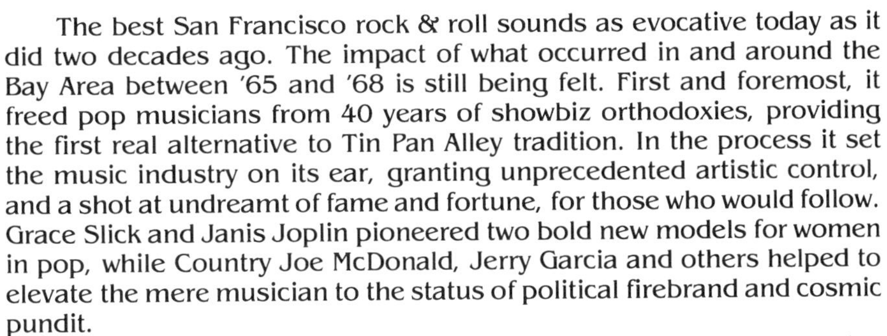

The best San Francisco rock & roll sounds as evocative today as it did two decades ago. The impact of what occurred in and around the Bay Area between '65 and '68 is still being felt. First and foremost, it freed pop musicians from 40 years of showbiz orthodoxies, providing the first real alternative to Tin Pan Alley tradition. In the process it set the music industry on its ear, granting unprecedented artistic control, and a shot at undreamt of fame and fortune, for those who would follow. Grace Slick and Janis Joplin pioneered two bold new models for women in pop, while Country Joe McDonald, Jerry Garcia and others helped to elevate the mere musician to the status of political firebrand and cosmic pundit.

San Francisco also led to musical and professional excesses which proved Dick Clark's dire pronouncement at least partially right. From the first Fillmore guitar freak-outs to lyrics passed off as "poetry", rock would never again be unselfconscious. Its innocence was lost. The effect of pop music on the culture-at-large was suddenly significant.

Yet, aside from its aesthetic and sociological significance, San Francisco's psychedelic age was a great time, full of thrills and surprises, optimism and oddities. But more than anything else, it makes a whale of a tale, with heroes and villains, comedy and tragedy. For us, being there when it happened was a once-in-a-lifetime trip. Twenty years later, with this book, we've tried to make that trip again.

Everyone who was there or anyone who has wished they were, is invited to climb on.

Grateful acknowledgement is due any number of generous friends and fellow travelers. Among the many: Chuck Thegze, who remembered it all but "wanted to know more"; John Javna, for the introductions; Bob Miller, our editor at St. Martin's; and Bob Merlis, for the room with a view and so much more. Special thanks are also in order to Liz Lufkin, who conducted the interviews with Bill Graham and Marty Balin, and to John Platt who furnished the bulk of material on the London scene. Also, thanks to Michael Ochs for kindnesses above and far beyond; Harry Chester and friends, for their best work yet; Rick Griffin, for same; Ken Barnes, the world's foremost pop expert who was never more than a phone call away, and the Trend-setters, Mike Daly and Ron Nagle, for art, information, and "Elephant Walk." Also: Raechel Donahue for pix that clicked; Carl Scott for the Autumn of his years; Larry Caffo for soul and inspiration; Mike Prichard for his conclusions; Dick Blackburn for re-opening the doors; Ronn Spencer for art's sake; Steve Keyser for tracking the Dinosaurs; Peter Albin for great ribs and reminiscence; Chet Helms in the back room of Atelier Dore; John Cipollina for his eloquence on guitar and history. And to George "That's exactly how it happened" Hunter, who started it all.

And all the rest: Paul Grein at *Billboard,* Gary Goodrow, Jeff Gold, Jim Bickhart, Jim Trombetta, Pete Frame, Mrs. Evelyn Cipollina and Antonia, Natalie Nielson, Cynthia Bowman, Clyde Bakkemo, Joe Smith, Artie "The Ripper" Ripp, Debbie Clark, Bill Graham, Grelun Landon, Nadine Condon, Barry Hansen, Neely Plumb, Erik Jacobsen, David Freiberg, Ed Denson and Howard Larman, Gene Anthony, Herb Greene, Ruta Fox, Philly Joe McEwen, Tom Vickers, Jack Casady, Paul Kantner, Darby Slick, David Rubinson, Luria Castell, Jean Gleason, Michael Rachoff, Dennis Nolan, Pete Welding, Dennis McNally and Jerry Garcia, Howard and Diana Seay, Gordon Skene, and Chuck Krall. Our sincere thanks also to the Hamerschlagg Archives and the Jordan Collection for allowing generous access to their collection of Bay Area Memorabilia. And to our wives, Marsha "Taighde agus Clóscríobh" Meyer and Diane "Don't glorify drugs" Seay . . .

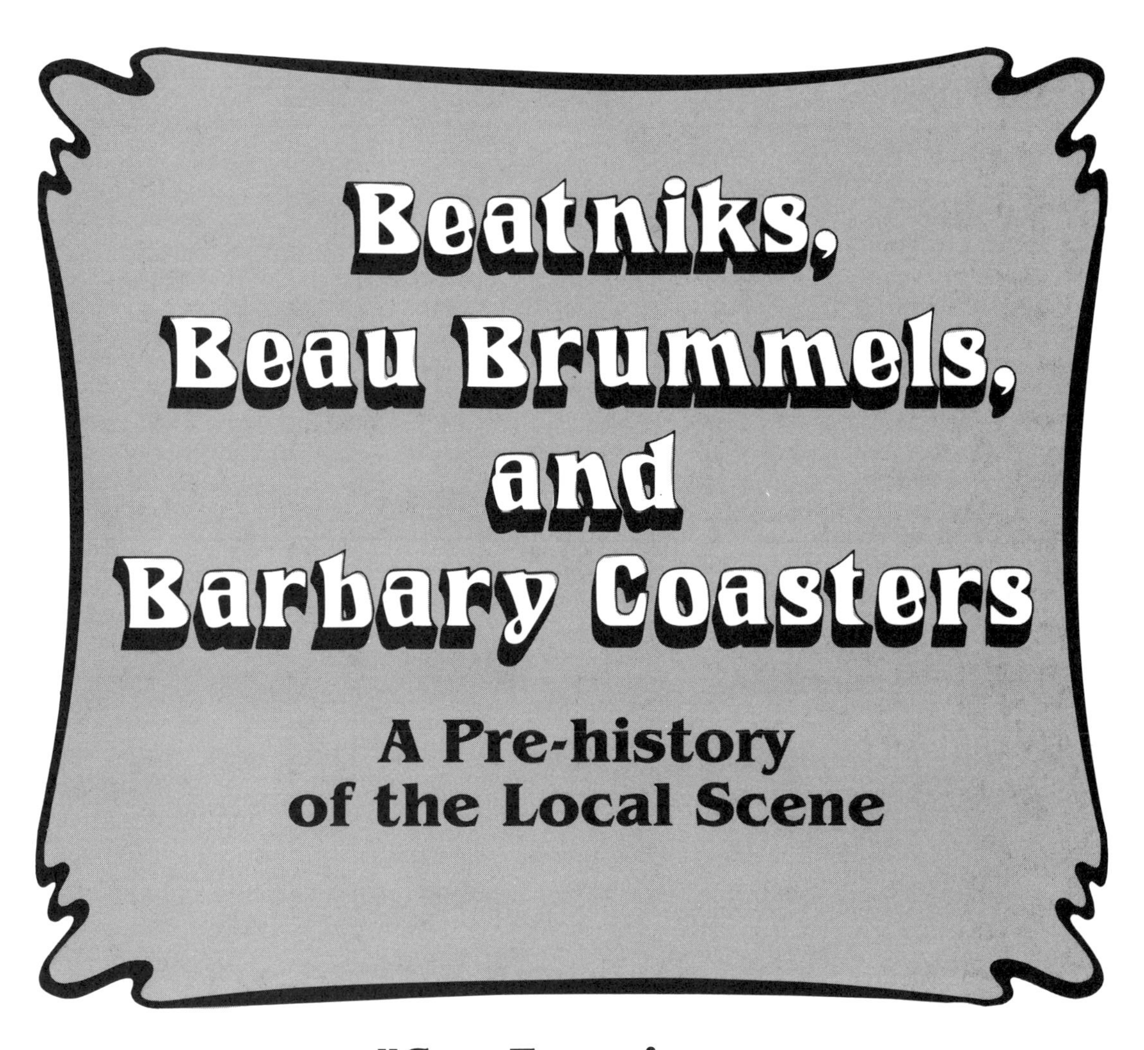

"San Francisco, now there's a grown-up, swinging town" —Frank Sinatra

Back in 1966, music columnist Ralph Gleason's declaration that San Francisco had become the new Liverpool sounded like the worst sort of verbal overkill, one more example of the kind of hyperbole Frisco boosters have too often indulged in. Long before "White Rabbit," the city had been addicted to peering at itself through the looking-glass. And it generally liked what it saw: a cosmopolitan jewel glittering on a gold-crazed frontier, a rich, rowdy, eminently tolerant town with liberty and license for all. Before it was Liverpool, it was the Paris of the West or Baghdad-by-the-Bay or the swinging, suitably enigmatic "City That Knows How."

If San Francisco's wild reputation at times seems contrived or overdone, there's little doubt that it was a valid claim when first staked. Social critic Clifton Fadiman likened the town (and California in general) to an overgrown mining camp. "For a mining camp, however small and rude, is large and sophisticated in the sense that its entire inner life points straight toward tomorrow and all the tomorrows. Hence it loves chances, risks, novelty, change, loud music, colorful false fronts; whatever moves, deceives, plays jokes on stodgy reality; whatever pays off big or flops with a bang, whatever can be quickly destroyed and replaced."

The description fit the Frisco of 1849 to a "T." Overnight, the gold rush transformed Padre Serra's dusty mission hamlet into a boomtown, filled with thousands of brawling Irish, Indians, Germans, Mexicans, Chinese and Chilean. They made fortunes in days, squandering them on diamond rings, gold-headed canes and hundred buck bacon-and-egg breakfasts. When they ran out of things to buy, many went to dentists to have their perfectly good teeth replaced with costly gold ones, better for smiling the flashy grin of success. "The people of San Francisco," wrote the New York **Evening Post** correspondent after his visit of '49, "are mad, stark raving mad."

Within a year, the gold rush was history, another wise-ass prank played on "stodgy reality." But it left the city something to remember, a soiled souvenir called the Barbary Coast, which was to contribute heavily to the San Francisco myth for the next 70 years. By the time it closed down for good, the notorious dockside quarter had survived the 1906 earthquake, and continuous assaults by rope-toting vigilantes and the Salvation Army.

The Ape-man and the Maltese Falcon

The Coast welcomed all vices, though it had its specialties; opium dens, lewd stageshows, prostitution, the shaghai'ing of whiskey-wrecked sailors, prowling murderous gangs with names like the Hounds and the Sydney Ducks. The area was overrun with pimps, pickpockets, card sharks and fake colonels, tong chiefs and crooked cops. There were brothels and dancehalls and exotic combinations of the two—Bull Run, the Bella Union, Rosebud, Jupiter, Dutch Emma's and Bert's New Idea Melodeon. And there was Abe Warner's Cobweb Palace, a funked-out saloon whose bizarre interior suggests a sensory-overload that would have made an easy match for the Fillmore or the Avalon at their freakiest. The cavernous room boasted thousands of nude paintings, cages of live monkeys and birds (including a parrot that cursed in four languages), and cobwebs—covering the walls, lighting fixtures, even the liquor bottles stocked behind the bar.

By the turn of the century, the town had gained a lot of attention for its tolerance, even endorsement, of the oddballs in its midst. San Franciscans took great pride in such characters as Oofty Goofty (a self-proclaimed Borneo "ape-man" who tarred himself with horsehair and lived in a cage), 300-lb. camp songstress Big Bertha, and Emperor Norton I, an addled millionaire-turned-pauper who one day declared himself ruler of the city and proved it by printing his own money and handing it out to his "subjects."

Frisco's first king-freak:
Emperor Norton I.

Courtesy California Historial Society, San Francisco
Photograph: Houseworth, San Francisco

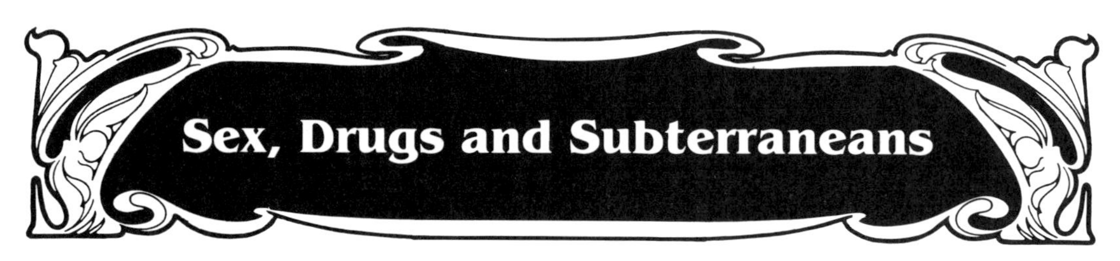

Sex, Drugs and Subterraneans

San Francisco's was an atmosphere that nurtured the muse in a number of more established names as well: Mark Twain, Ambrose Bierce, Frank Norris, Dashiell Hammett, Caruso, Valentino, Ansel Adams, Joe DiMaggio. Legendary prizefighter John L. Sullivan slugged it out with "Gentleman" Jim Corbett at a Grand Opera House exhibition, Kid Ory's was the house band over at the Cliff House, and down on Haight St. Charlie Chaplin gave free performances at the Chutes Theatre. Hollywood discovered San Francisco in the Thirties and Forties, using it as the setting for **The Maltese Falcon,** Cagney's **Frisco Kid** and Gable's **San Francisco,** various Charlie Chan pictures, Hitchcock's **Vertigo** and **The Birds, Bullitt** and the Dirty Harry epics.

But it was in the Fifties that the city got its last real shipment of bonafide crazies, from New York and Boston and all the hung-up hometowns between the coasts. And the way San Francisco reacted to **this** group of eccentrics was indicative of nothing so much as how deeply and irrevocably the anything-goes mining camp itself had changed. If the Beats' search was for satori instead of glittering nuggets, they pursued it with no

Beatniks as joke fodder

Courtesy Editors Archives

less abandon than the Forty-niners. Life was one big rush through the realm of the senses, a marathon of sex and cheap transports—riding the rails, guzzling jug wine, grass, speed, sometimes smack. The epiphanies were endless too. One could dig Paul Desmond or Gerry Mulligan flying free down at the Blackhawk or Basin St. West, reread the zen masters till the words flew off the page, stay up for days talking, thinking, typing till it all came out.

At first, San Francisco loved the Beats. Allen Ginsberg shocked the stuffy poetry establishment when he debuted the scathing "Howl" at a Six Gallery reading one November night in '55. Then came Kerouac's wild prose dance, and Burroughs, Corso, Diane DiPrima and Kenneth Patchen. By 1958, the newsmagazines were simultaneously proclaiming Frisco the hip headquarters of an international artistic revolution and as "weirdo capital of the world." And the good press was great for business. Tourists ogled bohos outside the Co-Existence Bagel Shop and through the windows of City Lights Books. Nineteen-sixty brought the film version of **The Subterreaneans** (starring George Peppard as Kerouac) and soon the Grey Line tour buses were shuttling up and down Columbus Avenue, cruising for crazies.

Three years later, the Beat Scene was old news, the tail of a parade that had passed into history. Having served their purpose, the "beatniks" were hustled off the front pages and relegated to the odd joke in Herb Caen's **Chronicle** columns. Those few who hadn't split for greener pastures found themselves a conspicuous presence and increasingly the target of police harassment. "Whatever can be quickly destroyed and replaced . . ."

Scotch & Soda and Bennett's "Heart"

Clearing the way for the next spectacle seemed to be what San Francisco had on its mind. Conveniently, the act was warming up just down the Broadway-Columbus midway, having been dreamt up minutes before by Davey Rosenberg, a local press agent. At Rosenberg's suggestion, Carol Doda, a cocktail waitress at the Condor nightclub, took the stage one night in a "topless" bathing suit and performed a mildly suggestive dance called the Swim. Overnight, the old jazz dives folded or fell to their knees and North Beach was awash in sidewalk barkers and silicone playmates, topless bars and restaurants, even topless shoe-shine stands. **Barbary redux.**

Unlike the Beat phenomenon, the topless fad had no messy social repercussions. It was safe, a well-designed, functional false front that—along with such subsequent items as the Milk-Moscone murders, gay pride parades and the Indian takeover of Alcatraz island—did wonders to shore up San Francisco's wicked reputation.

All the peepshow permissiveness, though, could not conceal the fact that the city was not really practicing what it preached. San Francisco's liberal personality was dealt a heavy blow in 1960 when news cameras caught the S.F.P.D. beating protesters at the House Unamerican Activities Committee hearings at City Hall.

And, in the city where the 1964 Republican convention would nominate Barry Goldwater for President, Wild Bill Hearst's flagship San Francisco **Examiner** routinely attacked anyone espousing views to the left of Teddy Roosevelt.

What's more, many San Franciscans were happy to distance themselves from the old mining camp legacy, no matter how noble or exciting it may once have been. With sprawling Los Angeles aggressively setting the style for jet-age metropolises, Frisco's gas-lit past suddenly seemed a bit embarrassing. Before long, San Francisco was tying itself up in freeways and urban renewal projects. In the Western Addition area, dozens of stately Victorian mansions were razed, their gilt and ginger-bread buried in the rush to progress. Downtown, work started on the city's first skyscrapers and over on Van Ness Ave. the new Jack Tar Hotel seemed to symbolize everything ultramodern. Forget the hoary spoilsports who tagged it "the box Disneyland came in." The all-steel, turquoise and white apparition was an omen of tomorrow's seamless facade. Which meant that San Francisco pretty much held the same aspirations as any mid-sized American burg of the day; growth, prestige, respect from its peers. It had fought for and got its own pro baseball team. It had a voter-approved rapid transit plan in place, and, by 1962, it even had its own schmaltzy anthem in Tony Bennett's "I Left My Heart In San Francisco." Comedienne Phyllis Diller was starting to break big out of the Bay Area, and a former band singer from San Jose, Merv Griffin, was beginning the first season of his new NBC afternoon talkshow.

One thing San Francisco had never had was a fully functioning pop music scene. After going strong in the late Fifties, the town's two homegrown hitmakers had hit dry spells. Crooner Johnny Mathis had turned to xeroxing copies of his earlier ballad smashes ("Gina", "What Will My Mary Say") while the crewcut Kingston Trio was veering from commercial folk music to outright novelty material ("Reverend Mr. Black," "Scotch And Soda").

And there were sporadic hits—jazz pianist Vince Guaraldi's clever "Cast Your Fate to the Wind" and Pete Seeger's version of Malvina Reynolds' smug anti-suburbia tract "Little Boxes." To say nothing of local chartmakers like Little "E" & the Mellotone Three's "Candy Apple Red Impala" or "Oliver Twist," a dance fad cash-in by the then unpublished sandpaper-larynxed poet Rod McKuen. And there were albums by the Smothers Brothers and the Limeliters, and occasional R&B hits out of the East Bay; Jimmy McCracklin's "Think" and "The Walk", Johnny Fuller's much-covered "Haunted House" and K.C. Douglas' "Mercury Blues."

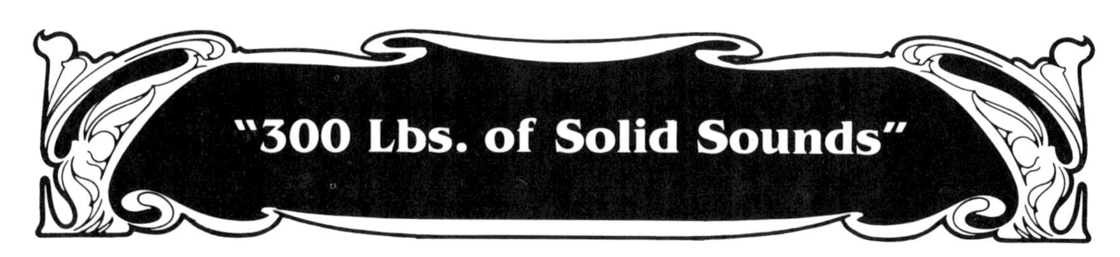

"300 Lbs. of Solid Sounds"

Until the late Sixties, there was never more than a handful of mom-and-pop recording studios in the Bay Area, usually sound-proofed with egg cartons and operating out of the back rooms of music stores. The only record labels were located in Oakland and Berkeley—Chris Strachwitz's Arhoolie Records specialized

Courtesy Carl Scott

in blues and old timey music while Max Weiss' Fantasy cut only jazz (Brubeck, Desmond, vibist Cal Tjader) and, when he was out of jail, Lenny Bruce. Anyone looking for a place to stage a rock 'n' roll revolution could hardly have picked a worse site than San Francisco.

Enter Tom Donahue and Bobby Mitchell.

Fleeing the payola scandals that shook the East Coast in 1959 and '60, disc jockeys "Big Daddy" Donahue ("300 pounds of solid sounds") and the "Mighty Mitch" rocked and rolled into town in 1961, finger-snapping and looking for action. They found it first at KYA, a tepid Top Forty outlet they turned around in a matter of weeks. Overriding station management to boldly program their own shows, Donahue and Mitchell shot KYA's playlist full of gritty R&B and struck up a close relationship with audiences, using irreverent broadcast styles. Big Daddy opened his shows by announcing he was "here to blow your mind and clean up your face" while Mitchell often admonished his teenage listeners "Don't come to the hop tonight unless you take a bath!"

Having become radio kingpins, Donahue and Mitchell in 1963 decided to duplicate their success with a move into concert promotion. Never mind that the pair had no experience in the field, they'd simply call on their record biz friends for help. At the series of sold-out concerts at the 18,000-seat Cow Palace that followed, Phil Spector helped by conducting an orchestra of crack L.A. session musicians. Various record company presidents, grateful for the obvious promotional benefits, donated the talent—the Beach Boys, Marvin Gaye, the Ronettes, Four Seasons, Righteous Bros., "Little" Stevie Wonder, Dee Dee Sharp, Martha & the Vandellas, Roy Orbison, Jan & Dean, Dionne Warwick and others. At one show, Muhammad Ali (when he was still known as "Cassius Clay") recited poetry between acts.

The Bay Area's answer to Britain: Autumn Records hitmakers, the Beau Brummels

Courtesy: Hamerschlagg Archives

Flushed with success, the following year Mitchell and Donahue took the plunge into the record business itself, opening Autumn Records out of a warehouse in the city's garment district. Their first single flopped, but the second, Bobby Freeman's surf-ish salute to the North Beach dance craze "C'mon And Swim", became a national hit the summer of '64. Written and arranged by Autumn's $100-a-week go-fer Sly Stone (then "Sylvester Stewart"), the record was followed by a string of Sly-produced local hits by the Mojo Men, the Vejtables and others. Later that year, a hooker Big Daddy knew pulled his coat to a band she'd seen at a club in San Mateo who "really have the English sound down." Before long, Autumn had the Beau Brummels in the studio cutting "Laugh Laugh" and "Just A Little."

It seemed as if Big Daddy and Mitch had practically conjured their mini-empire out of thin air. Here they were, happening simultaneously on three fronts—reigning as boss jocks, cutting more hits, negotiating to bring the Beatles to San Francisco. And, no less importantly, they had fired the imagination of hundreds of aspiring pop stars throughout the Bay Area. By 1965, many had caught the fever so bad that, in a spectacle which mimicked the events taking place across the Bay on the U.C. Berkeley campus, fledgling musicians were showing up outside the Cow Palace shows with picket signs, demanding Donahue and Mitchell sign them to Autumn Records.

In the midst of all this, through connections with the Premier Talent agency in New York, the two deejays agreed to book an up-and-coming British band called the Rolling Stones into the Civic Auditorium one weekend in mid-May.

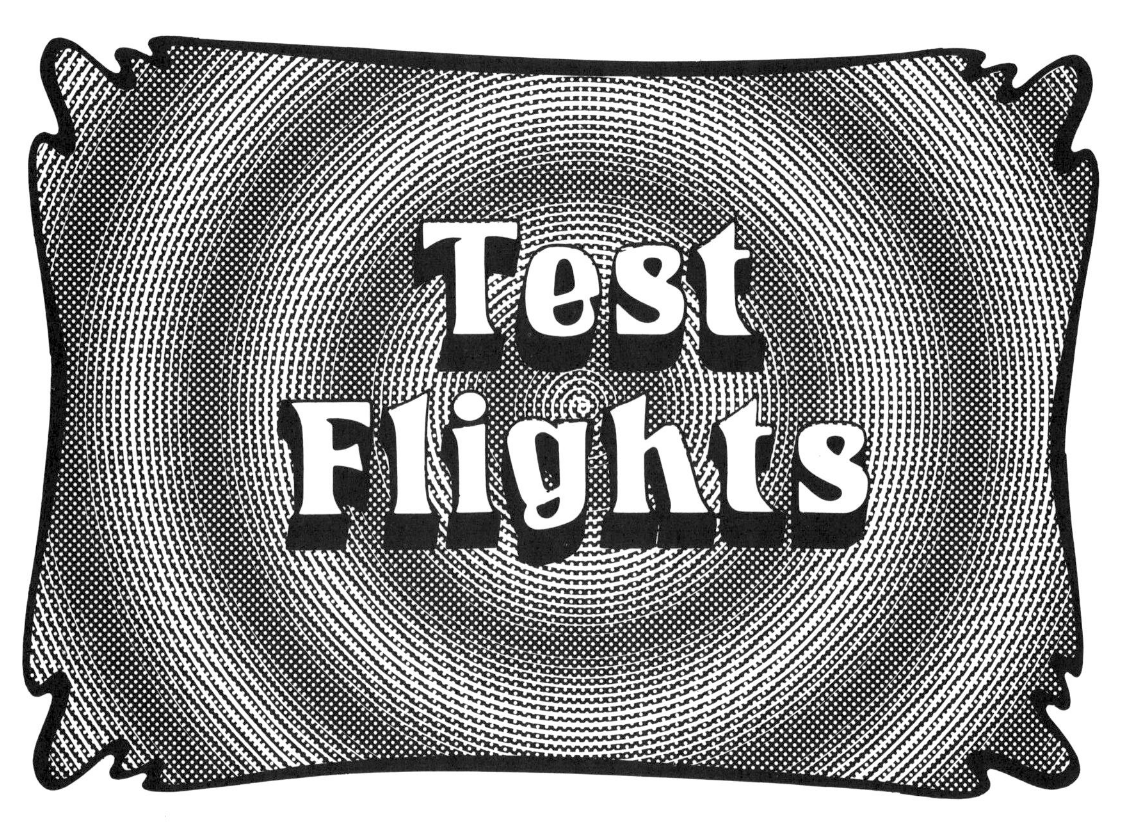

By the spring of '65 the sharp, short jolts of change that had been sending shocks through the pop music establishment since the Beatles secured the beachhead of the British invasion, had become a single, sustained musical overload. The year had kicked off with promising omens for Mitchell and Donahue's Autumn Records demi-empire. "Laugh Laugh" and "Just A Little" were Top Twenty hits from the Beau Brummels and proof that the English didn't have a monopoly on nasal Edwardian affectations. But if the Beatles and all the mop-top foppery that followed was challenging Brill Building business-as-usual, Hibbing, Minnesota's favorite son was defying basic hit-making conventions.

Bob Dylan, fresh from turning the folk music world on its staid ear (and being drummed out of the ranks of the acoustically faithful for his trouble) had just released his first electric album *Bringing It All Back Home* and promptly landed on the pop charts with an impossibly dense in-joke called "Subterranean Homesick Blues." It wasn't long after that a former folkie named David Crosby stopped by KYA to bring Donahue an acetate copy of the first in what proved to be an endless succession of rock and pop Dylan covers. The Byrds' "Mr. Tambourine Man" was all jet-stream twelve-strings and three-part harmonies and Big Daddy knew the sound of tomorrow when he heard it. Endless spins of the acetate took the song to Number One in the Bay Area by May.

Everything seemed to be happening at once and none of it looked the least bit familiar. Spike-heeled girl groups, the harmonic blondness of surf music, airbrushed dreamboats of Italo-American extraction, it was all being subtly but surely outclassed by a growling folkie with a mouth organ wired to his neck.

Hordes of Limeys and their earnest American emulators were suddenly the ones weakening pubescent female knees. June/Moon/Spoon had given way to Love Minus Zero/No Limit while all the careful homogenization of pop music that had been going on since the late Fifties was being upended by ragged upstarts celebrating the butt-shaking pleasure of the Real Stuff.

And no one took to that task with more vengeful glee than the Rolling Stones. It was all there in the adjectives: The Fab Four were just that—exuberant, whimsical, mum'n'dad-pleasing. The Liverpudlian one-liners and cherubic smiles helped take the edge off those shaggy haircuts and occasional flashes of animal magnetism. But the Stones—dirty, ugly, unkempt—were way too much, far too soon. "I want to hold your hand," chirped The Beatles. "All I really want to do," pleaded Sonny to Cher, "is, baby, be friends with you." "I'm a king bee," hissed Mick Jagger, slithering around the stage with fists full of maracas, "buzzin' around your hive."

The Stones were riding high just then with their second Top Ten hit, "The Last Time," a keening tribal chant anchored to an echoing, elliptical riff and recorded, it seemed, in a cave. It was a sign of sounds to come. The band had landed on American charts a few times before thanks to rave-up reworkings of "Time Is On My Side" and "Not Fade Away." "The Last Time" was something different. It ripped through tinny car speakers like something big, distorted and out of control. The Stones were on a roll. In the midst of a barnstorming U.S. tour, the band had hit a string of third-rate one-nighters—towns like Clearwater, Florida, and Birmingham, Alabama—before barreling into Los Angeles on May 13th to cut their next single, "Satisfaction."

Bedlam at the Civic

The following night found them playing before the less-than-capacity crowd that had answered the summons of Mitchell and Donahue, pitching their show relentlessly over KYA. The concert was produced by Big Daddy's wife Raechel when Donahue's attention began to wander elsewhere. "From a promotion standpoint it was a complete failure," recalls Carl Scott, a longtime Donahue friend, who worked at the Autumn complex as an underpaid booking agent at the time. "Hardly anyone showed up. It was really too early for the Stones. Nobody knew who they were."

Almost nobody. In amongst a smattering of prescient adolescents, the mildly curious and the simply misplaced were a handful of people with nothing better to do than take all the seething, unfocused energy of the time and manhandle it into a scene. For the Rolling Stones, May 14th, 1965 was one more lay-over on a treacherous road to the top. But for a gaggle of miscreant locals it was the cue they'd been waiting for. "At The Rolling Stones show, they were all there but they didn't recognize each other," was the way Tom Donahue later remembered the night.

Shindig and Satisfaction

"The Stones concert was a big deal," remembers Ron Nagle, "probably one of the most moving experiences of my life. Right there in the Civic Auditorium people were rolling down the isles, black and whites together . . . it was unbelievable. Charlie Watts got yanked off his stool. Real bedlam. The Byrds were on the bill, Paul Revere and the Raiders. The Mojo Men did 'Off The Hook' . . . funny for a Stones concert." The bill that evening was rounded out by a local band with the unlikely name of Gary Bazooka and the Parachutes.

"There were maybe 500 people down there," says George Hunter. "It was pretty amazing. We had some idea of who the Stones were. We maybe even paid to get in."

George Hunter and Ron Nagle. They were to cross paths again, a few weeks after that fateful night when they'd both watched, dazed and delighted, as England's Newest Hit Makers clawed at the status quo. The two had never met, but their reputations preceded them up and down the city's hilly ascents to the black heart of the Fillmore ghetto, to a one-time ice and roller skating rink known as The Primalon.

"Yeah, the Stones show was important," says Hunter, "but in a way it wasn't important as the Terrazzo Brothers. That was the first show we saw that was an expression of the new business that was on its way."

The Terrazzo Brothers!? The new business!? It must have taken some kind of super-attuned sixth sense to intercept that vibe, to check out a quartet of rank amateurs and know, unmistakably, that you were listening to faint, wavering signals from the New Age.

The Stones had blown town two weeks before, on their way to San Ber'doo, Long Beach, 'Diego and a slot on *Shindig* debuting "Satisfaction." Shortly thereafter, a haphazard collection of local artists, among them such future luminaries as Ron Davis and Ernie Palomino, decided to throw a party, for reasons unknown. It may have had something to do with the pervasive atmosphere of brotherhood permeating The Primalon, which, since its ice rink days, had been subdivided into cubicles—studios rented by a sundry collection of starving artist types.

The Trend of Things to Come

A date was set, May 30th, and the requisite supply of red wine and Ritz crackers was laid in. All that was missing was the evening's entertainment. Enter Ron, Larry, John and Bob, aka The Terrazzo Bros., aka The Mystery Trend.

Ron Nagle was a Frisco native, S.F. State ceramics grad and, at the time, a

Mystery Trend publicity shot. Courtesy Mike Daly

fledgling songwriter and keyboardist who badly wanted into what was happening all around him on the radio. He roomed in a storefront in the Castro district with Larry Bennett, a bass-playing college chum with a coffee pot tattooed on one arm from his Marine days. Bennett and the oddball collection of quasi-musicians recruited from the San Francisco Art Institute were the raw material for Nagle's nascent musical ambitions. There was John Luby, the bonafide jazz drummer and Bob Cuff, the Kinks freak. "It was like a license to get up there and act weird. It was the art school mentality. A lot of English groups had come out of art schools just like us and the only guys around the city who had long hair then were artists too . . ."

Artists in the audience. Artists on stage. It was a self-contained and self-nurturing incubation fostering all sorts of quirky pretexts to "act weird." The as-yet-unnamed band began a sporadic series of rehearsals, working up Fifties R&B and blues arcana like Buster Brown's "Fannie Mae," "It's Too Late" by Tarheel Slim and Little Ann, Sonny Boy Williamson's "Don't Start Me Talkin' ", the Penguins' "Hey, Senorita," along with some skewered Nagle originals like "Ducts," "Rickets," and the suitably enigmatic "Other Side of the Room." By the time the Primalon party-planners approached them, they were ready as they were ever going to be.

"It was the first big dance, really," recalls Mike Daly, another S.F. State friend of Nagle's and later the band's manager, "before anything else on the scene. About a thousand people showed up. It was a really big crowd." The show earned the Terrazzo Brothers—named, for reasons unknown, after a type of chipped marble flooring—ten dollars. Enough, remembers Nagle, to buy beer all around. "The people dug us and we were playing just horrible, horrible stuff." It was not unlike, according to Nagle, some of the band's later shows. "We had a mood piece called 'Casbah,' " he laughs. "We were good at mood pieces. That was the song that taught me that audiences had absolutely no discretion about what they were hearing. We had a lead guitarist then, Larry West, a Jeff Beck type, who we'd found at the Blue Unicorn coffee house coming down from speed. He'd put the capo on his guitar one fret off, so he'd be playing in one key and I couldn't transpose, so I'm playing in another key and the other guitar player is playing his own key. So the song was actually being played in three different keys. Complete cacaphonic bedlam and they loved it!"

The Divine Right to Weirdness

Why not? The draw, after all, wasn't proficiency, virtuosity, or even the rudiments of tunesmithing. "We heard there was a dance," says George Hunter. "Nagle and those guys. Pretty interesting, I mean, there was nothing to compare it to at that point. Nagle had this Fender Rhodes piano and whoever was singing was doing a variation of Jagger with tambourine and maracas. It may not have been the best performance in the world, but it was real significant."

No, what those people liked best about events like the Rolling Stones at the Civic or the Terrazzo Brothers at the Primalon was, well . . . each other. To-

Mystery Trend live (Ron Nagle at the piano)

Courtesy Mike Daly

gether. In a lump. Reinforcing their individual, divine right to weirdness.

They were, together, a group of insolent mutations, drawing the strength from (and biting the hand of) all the self-conscious scenes that had preceeded them—folk purity, beatnik nihilism, political righteousness, all blending with the smug boredom of ungrateful middle class youth looking for a good time. All this rock & roll frenzy, these poses and snotty attitudes, may have been all right for teen-agers, caught in the grip of rebellious hormones, but these guys, for the most part, were in their twenties, college students or better. They were almost adults, for God's sake, and should have been thinking, if not pragmatically, at least linearly. They'd somehow gotten lost on the way to adulthood and it was getting too late to find their way back now.

"Bohemians have a tradition of what bohemia means," remarks Mike Prichard, a man who would have much to do with what was brewing back in the spring of '65. "It was centuries old, really, and it meant being sensitive, willing to suffer for what you believed in. We were more eclectic. We had no real roots. We attached ourselves to whatever was available, picked up on whatever caught our attention—blues, art nouveau, comic books. We didn't have the same kind of pursuit of consciousness as the Beats did, but it was in the same tradition: search out reality, look for something unique, find yourself and your place in it."

Or create yourself and then find a place for it. In 1965, San Francisco was crawling with people looking for a place to happen. They formed coteries and cliques and confabs of one. They signaled their presence to each other in dress, language and codes of behavior. "We got into dressing up," continues Prichard, "turtlenecks with another shirt on top, real tight pants, Cuban boots or sandals, paisley shirts—nothing was color-coordinated. Nothing matched. We got into 'going out.' We felt cloistered in our own fringe group. We wanted to be the first ones out there that were going to really *be* these particular kind of people. The whole idea was to go out and show everyone what we looked like."

Too Late to Be Beat

"We never had a chance to be straight," insists Luria Castell, another veteran of the big and little bangs going off all over the Bay Area. "And we were caught between huge influxes; too young to be beatniks, too old to be flower children."

All these disparate, lonely outposts of unconventional individuality had begun to coalesce, drawing together for the sake of safety, identity, and the risk of cooperative action. A loose-knit network stretched from North Beach across the city to a sedate, racially mixed neighborhood of ramshackle Victorians known as the Haight Ashbury and from there, south to the sylvan, sprawling campus of San Francisco State.

State was the "street car college", serviced by the electric trolleys rumbling along their tracks past Stonestown to the campus, almost within sight of the quintessential 'little boxes' on the undulating hills of Daly City. It was here that George Hunter had come back in 1962, looking for something, the size, shape and color of which he had no idea.

It was apparent to those trained to discern the subtle but telling traits of breeding and background that George Hunter was cut of a different cloth, woven from the privilege, propriety and the peculiar arrogance fostered only in Southern California. "We were very status conscious," he recalls of his upbringing, "snobs to some degree." One of his mother's best friends was the wife of legendary avante garde composer George Anthile, who'd made his mark with wigged-out performance pieces like "Ballet Mechanique" back in the Twenties. Hunter got to be friends with Anthile's son Peter and together they began hanging around Beat scene watering holes in Venice and Malibu, like the Cafe Positano coffee house, featuring flamenco music and readings by Ray Bradbury. For Hunter the Venice Beat scene "was a big influence on me. I felt an affinity for it and I started leading a little bit of a double life. It wasn't too easy being a beatnik in Canoga Park High School."

Yet even in these formative years George Hunter was already orbiting his own, distinctly 'other' sphere. "He had a tip to toe viewpoint on life," one of his friends remembers. He was absorbed with the way style embodied substance, especially the statements expressed in fashion, trends and life styles.

And a lifestyle was something Hunter was, just then, badly in need of. After kicking around Los Angeles for a few post-high school seasons, he relocated to San Francisco, following a girlfriend who was transferring to S.F. State. "It was as good an excuse as I needed to leave L.A.," he allows.

Strobes and Spaghetti Sculpture

He brought with him a smattering of experience in the burgeoning art form of the Happening. "I'd gotten involved experimenting with electronic music, prepared paino kind of stuff, like John Cage," he continues. At S.F. State he fell in with a group of dancers and began throwing together taped electronic scores for dance concerts. "We used to improvise during the performance," Hunter recalls. "We'd patch into the sound system with throat mikes and provide our own music. I got the idea, I don't exactly know how, of using a strobe light that I found in the Physics department. I decided to incorporate it into the shows also, strobing the audience the whole time."

The Happening was, of course, nothing new. What Hunter and his cavorting friends were groping for with this melange of light, sound and movement, was the same kind of gestalt thrills that prompted Parisian artists/provocateurs at the second annual Festival of Free Expression that same year to attack cars with axes and sculpt a nude model's body with spaghetti in front of their stunned Sorbonne professors. But for Hunter, all this deadly serious statement-making was missing the point. Like Nagle and—with near-simultaneous abandon—dozens of others around the Bay Area, Hunter had eyes on the Beatlesque joys of pop stardom. "I was still into Happenings when I first got the idea of starting a music group," Hunter recounts. "What I wanted to do was build a mixing board with bell gates, ring modulators and other synthesizing devices that could mold and shape the sound of the instruments and have everybody patched into that—a massive sound system for us all to play through. It was really just all concept back then. I hadn't really worked on the direction the music was going to take."

He was hardly, however, short on strange notions. "I was going to call the group The Androids," continues Hunter. "I wanted to put together a group of men and women with identical haircuts and clothes. Sort of a unisex-android approach, early techno-pop, a combination of everything I'd been working on up to that point."

A sign of the times.

Courtesy Ron Nagle

The Plot Thickens

What actually emerged was an even more random result than Hunter's hodgepodge of found elements. In the fall of 1964, while living in a flat on Downey St., which was later to become known as "Upper Downey", he ran across an old high school cohort. "Mike Wilhelm was a close friend," he recounts. "His dad had once been a professional adagio dancer and I used to hang out at his house, listening to Johnny Cash and Nervous Norvus records." Hunter and Wilhelm, in San Francisco pursuing his own convoluted destiny, began hatching plots with the help of a baby-faced Chicagoan named Richard Olsen.

Hunter had met Olsen at S.F. State two years before, when Olsen, majoring in music and studying sax and flute, had been recruited as a dancer for one of Hunter's freeform Happenings.

"I guess we decided to chose up instruments," is how Hunter describes the beginnings of the band. "Mike got guitar, Olsen picked bass." Hunter's roommate at the time, Peter Vandergelder, then a classical music DJ, introduced him to Sam Linde, a friend Vandergelder fetched from out of Madison, Wisconsin. "Sam said he could play drums," Hunter continues, "and we took his word for it."

And Hunter? The fact that he couldn't play anything hardly struck him as a hindrance. He picked up the tambourine and subsequently the autoharp (because it was easy to learn, melodious and unobtrusive), for something to do on stage. It was, characteristically, as simple as that.

The elements were in place, or nearly so. "I got to talking to this guy in line down at the unemployment office and he told me he was a piano player," Hunter relates. "I told him he ought to come over."

Proto-Charlatans. Left to right: Mike Wilhelm; Richie Olsen; Sam Linde; Mike Ferguson; George Hunter

Courtesy George Hunter

Mike Ferguson, lean and eagle-eyed, with a receding hairline and a hustler's hungry looks, did come over and provided, precisely and perfectly, the missing ingredient to Hunter's formula for success. A San Diego boy, middle class, suburban and strange, Ferguson shared more than passing similarities to Hunter, and a more than casual affinity for Hunter's ruling obsessions. "He was into motorcycles," remembers one friend, "hooks, knives and guns." "Mike was an eclectic dresser," recalls Michael Prichard, "always sharp, precise, conscious of how he looked, very mannered." He was, in short, intense and he knew all kinds of people who vibrated with equal intensity. "He lived in a commune, the first I'd ever seen," says Prichard. "That place was the focus of all kinds of energy. They had a great Halloween party there one year with Cassady and Ginsberg and everyone in costumes. Even though we were just kids, we knew we were part of that somehow."

Costumes. Dressing up. Playing a part. It was all a glorious game, everyone feeding off each other's fantasies and the most fantastic receptacle of the collective spirit was the Magic Theater For Madmen Only. Ferguson, with the sporadic help of some of his communal conspirators, had opened the place (with its name taken from Herman Hesse's hip gospel *Siddartha)* in a seedy neighborhood bordering the Haight back in 1964. Ferguson had stocked it with a phantasmagoric collection of antiques, clothes, books, junk and paraphernalia. "It was probably the first head shop in San Francisco," ventures Hunter. "They didn't even know that's what they were doing." "He had poetry readings, musical groups, it was a vehicle for all kinds of products and ideas, a gathering place," sums up Prichard, who lived in an apartment in the rear of the store, rented from Ferguson.

"I really appreciated the fact that Mike had stocked the place with antiques and nostalgia," says Hunter. Indeed he did. It was largely from the inventory of the Magic Theater that the fledgling band would construct its all-important image, sprung full-blown from Hunter and Ferguson's abiding love of the city's gas-lit past. "I'd been collecting bits of old time stuff since coming to San Francisco," Hunter explains. "You'd go into these little thrift shops and find all kinds of things from the turn of the century; ladies' silver handbags, sequined dresses, frocked

Courtesy George Hunter

The Charlatans, dressed for success, circa 1965

coats, waistcoats, shirts without collars, collar buttons, cufflinks, straw boaters . . ."

It was the spring of '64. "A style emerged," continues Hunter. "A musical and visual concept. It had to do with simply seeing what style was already there and picking all the good pieces of it, bringing them together. It was the blues guitar of Wilhelm; baby-faced Olsen, the kid from Chicago; an old time piano player who looked like he'd just stepped out of a saloon. Together it had a certain connotation. It was set against what was going on in society at the time, with everyone getting tired of a 'plastic world.' It seemed like a good assemblage and people were ready for it."

Well, almost. Hunter had started the group with the name George and the Mainliners, a name conjured from his abiding affinity for the drug-addled novels of William Burroughs. After a series of rehearsals, it became apparent that the hapless Sam Linde was not the drummer he claimed to be. Still another S.F. State student, a radio-TV major named Dan Hicks, was recruited, in December of '64, to fill his place. "When I joined, they hadn't really formulated the musical style they were to adopt later," Hicks told one writer. "At that time it was mostly Chuck Berry stuff, tunes that John Hammond had done . . . and all sorts of R&B standards like 'My Babe,' and 'Got My Mojo Working.' "

As the group continued rehearsing through the early months of '65, Hunter schemed to sharpen their look, if not their sound. The others gradually took the band out of blues and Fifties rock and into music more suited to the flights of stylistic fancy being fashioned around them. "Johnny B. Goode" gave way to rock & roll versions of "Wabash Cannonball" and "Alabama Bound." It was folk-rock, but hardly the seamless, harmonic hybrid being practiced by the Byrds and others. "It was 1920's country-folk music with something done to it," Hunter remarks. That something owed a great deal more to the haunting, honky-tonk roots of the material, than the prevailing pop ethic of the moment. It was, in some puzzling but undeniable way, authentic.

A name change was in order. "We tried to figure out what to do for a name," explains Hunter. I guess I'd always had some vision of these guys in black coats and hats, on their way through the countryside to the next little town. I was thinking 'Here we are, I'm not a musician at all, yet here we are, putting this thing together.' So I figured I was really a charlatan." That same day, Hunter designed the logo for the Charlatans.

There was no question about it: Hunter had found the perfect outlet. There was no stopping him. "George came in with a copy of *Vogue* Magazine," recounts Mike Prichard, "the one with Dylan in it along with a lot of other pop figures who'd not only made it, but were now being identified as significant figures within the social fabric. He was pissed off. 'Look at this!' he said, 'How come we're not in here?' I just looked at him and said, 'George, why should you be in there?' He knew, he was sure, that he was doing something significant. He and Mike had been able to take this rough thing and hone it, clean off the edges and make it palatable. They were really onto something."

Could George Hunter's fantasy really crack the big time? "George was totally caught up in marketing the group as a complete entity," affirms Prichard. "I remember him putting up the first Rolling Stones album cover on his wall, the one with them all lined up. I knew it impressed George, that whole 'we're together, we're a group' phenomenon."

"We had great aspirations," Hunter reveals. "We wanted to be a pop hit." As big, say, as the Lovin' Spoonful or the Byrds, the biggest American finds since the British Invasion? "We certainly thought we'd do better than that," says Hunter.

Screaming teens who Believed In Magic and *Vogue* editors looking for the next big thing would have to wait. For all Hunter's careful plotting, the Charlatans weren't exactly ready to lay siege to the pop world. "We thought we were the Beatles," Richard Olsen told one reporter, " 'cause we were like the only group in the whole area. And we didn't hardly even play. We'd just walk around dressed up; we were the only cats with long hair. Everybody'd see us and they'd scream from two blocks away. They'd think we were some far-out British group.' "

A Tiny, Teeming Scene

It wasn't as if, by the summer of '65, the quartet was out there all alone; the city and its suburbs were, in fact, teeming with tiny scenes ready to break out at a moment's notice. Nagle's Terrazzo Bros. had become The Mystery Trend—named after a misreading of Dylan's "mystery tramp" line in "Like A Rolling Stone"—and were getting ready to cut a demo. Some acoustic strummers, Paul Kantner and Marty Balin, were thinking electrically, while a reformed jugband featuring banjo player Jerry Garcia and a blues shouter known as Pigpen was switching to amplified blues and R&B. Everyone was poised, ready for the signal that would take it all aboveground, announcing to the world-at-large that the wait was over.

When the time did come, it was in a place as completely unexpected as the Charlatans themselves. Virginia City, stuck fourteen miles south of Reno in the scrub and mesquite ratlands of Nevada, was, prior to June '65, primarily known for its location smack atop the fabled Comstock Lode, a silver vein mined in the mid-1800's for over a billion dollars' worth of metal. Mark Twain had made his name there as a reporter for the *Territorial Enterprise,* and after most of the old

Virginia City

Photo: Larry Tanner

© 1964 London Records

town had burned to the ground around the turn of the century, the place had been slowly transformed into a forlorn tourist attraction too far from the ghastly gambling meccas to make much difference to anyone.

Anyone, that is, except for the owner of a rough and tumble Virginia City bar called the Red Dog Saloon and his entrepenuerial-spirited bartender, Chandler Laughlin. Laughlin, looking for an attraction to bring business to the place, ventured down to San Francisco in early June with the unlikely notion of booking the Byrds, still riding high on "Mr. Tambourine Man." The fact that the group was based in Los Angeles and would be as likely to play the Red Dog as they would a convention of morticians, didn't deter Laughlin in the least. Cruising North Beach, he spotted Olsen and Wilhelm on the street. "Are you the Byrds?" he asked. No, they allowed, but they were a rock band and took him to talk with Hunter. The encounter was enough for the amateur talent scout; the band was invited to spend their summer in beautiful Virginia City.

Right Time and Space

"We were still piecing our image and sound together at the time," explains Hunter. "Everyone kept bringing in new elements. Wilhelm was doing country & western and blues, stuff like 'Folsom Prison Blues.' Ferguson was into Mose Allison—we did 'Seventh Son,' and the Coasters' 'Searchin' ". Olsen came in with The Big Bopper and we added 'Chantilly Lace.' We had some very heavy Edwardian

Courtesy George Hunter

leanings, high collared shirts and frilled cuffs with just a taste of Old West, cowboy hats, vests and boots. We were in exactly the right time and space to go to someplace like Virginia City."

Of course! Why not? "When we first got there," Olsen recounted, "all the local people really flashed on us . . . we were on a sort of old timey trip and they thought we were furthering the authenticity of the place and would attract more tourist trade." "We found a pretty hip little scene there when we arrived," agrees Hicks. "Everybody seemed to know how to enjoy themselves and have a good time."

Oddballs on Acid

And no one was having a better time than the Charlatans. Upon arrival, they discovered that they hadn't actually been hired at all, but were required to audition. An audience of 25 were corralled and the Charlatans stepped out on stage for their very first public appearance. "We'd only just got there and we were all a bit paranoid," Olsen told *Zig Zag* magazine. "Wilhelm didn't even have a guitar and had to borrow a Japanese electric one from some guy. George was very uptight on account of never having sung in public before . . ."

To soothe their first-night jitters the group—along with a goodly number of the audience—downed stiff doses of LSD, the still-legal reality-enhancer that had been making the rounds of the 'Frisco oddball corps. "By the time we'd finished dinner everyone was like in outer space," Wilhelm recalled for *Rolling Stone.* "It was the first time Richie'd ever taken acid, the second time George had . . ."

"We were all so zonked that we weren't even playing together," Olsen barely remembers. "Wilhelm had taken it first and was the first to feel the effects—he just sat down on the stage and started looking around him; then I started to come on and we were just sprawling about and playing each others instruments, just collapsing with laughter." The audition was a smashing success. "That's the funniest thing I ever saw in my life," opined the Red Dog's owner.

The boys wasted no time making themselves right at home. Hunter and Ferguson got carpenters to build a raised stage, eventually knocking out three walls to accommodate the crush of the curious. The front of the saloon was festooned with an orange and black rendering of a red dog, courtesy Mike Ferguson, while inside, above the stage, hung a light sculpture flashing in time to the music and built by two friends of the band, Bill Ham and Bob Cohen. "We completely decorated the place," says Hunter. "We brought rugs and Victorian tapestries from the city. We were recreating the Wild West, pretending it had never gone away."

They were doing one terrific job of it, too. To announce their arrival, their short-lived manager—one Phil Hammond—took out an ad in the *Reno Orbit.* "LANDING LIKE 5 RADIANT SPARKS IN A FLASH . . . THE CHARLATANS HAVE ARRIVED," it read. "Superior musical craftsmen and rhythm technicians, The Charlatans excel all others as performers of classic rock 'n' roll for all time."

Courtesy George Hunter

George Hunter, virtuoso

Musical Bat Mastersons

By the time the Charlatans had a few shows under their belt, they were beginning to take their fantasy personas a little *too* seriously. If it had been anywhere else but Virginia City at any other time than that wide-open summer, the whole crazed trip would certainly have come to a screeching halt. But there was something up there in the blistering, rarified Nevada highlands that seemed to actually encourage taking it to the limit and beyond. The line that separated playing the dandified cowboy and actually becoming some kind of latter-day musical Bat Masterson was getting distinctly blurry. "The owner of the Red Dog was a real gun nut," Hunter offers, by way of explanation. "He had a big collection, broom-handled Mausers, the whole thing. A lot of stores in town sold collectible guns. Well, Ferguson had sort of underworld leanings anyway, so the first thing he did was to go out and buy a Baretta. He had to watch it when he was playing the piano. He kept the pistol tucked in his belt and he never went too far down on the keyboards because he didnt want to expose the gun on stage."

There was, according to Olsen, a rivalry, ostensibly friendly, between the Red Dog and another Virginia City watering hole called the Bucket of Blood. "It could have gotten a little weird," Olsen admits, "because everybody had guns. We used to pile into the car and take rifles and 45's a mile or so up the road and have a bit of target practice."

"We bought Winchesters and a lever-action repeater called a Marlin," Hunter confirms. "It wasn't stage regalia. The fact was, no one would walk around town without being armed. There were some elements that didn't cotton to what was going on down at the saloon; had to be careful."

And, no doubt, know who your friends were. Every Sunday night, like clockwork, the whole bizarre assembly that had collected around the Red Dog goings-on would close up shop and drop cubes of acid. The following 24 hours were then spent enforcing the mutual weirdness that was mushrooming everywhere in the sleepy little tourist trap. "I never could figure out who the clientele was," admits Hunter. "They'd come to dance, or just watch, from Reno and Frisco. Alternative types." The fact was, people started showing up from as far away as Los Angeles, Portland and Seattle—pot heads, college students; anyone with hair below their collar seemed to coagulate at the Red Dog during those roaring summer nights. Even the Governor of Nevada caught wind of the action and spent a night in town.

Guns, LSD and an increasingly tight repertoire of rollicking rock & roll. The Charlatans managed, just barely, to keep on top of it all. "We did four sets a night, five nights a week for a hundred dollars a week apiece along with bed and board, and we were getting really good," asserts Hunter. "I wasn't doing much singing. I felt like a guy with some kind of cameo role; the music wasn't that crucial to me. I'd dance, play the tambourine and a little autoharp. I was more important visually." Hunter was, however, beginning to write songs; quirky numbers such as "I Always Wanted A Girl Like You," "Walking" and "(Never Thought I'd Know You) Like I Know You Now."

The Red Dog was packing them in and the whole mad merry-go-round seemed like it might go on forever. "It was a real carnival," recalls Prichard, who showed up from San Francisco at Hunter's invitatition. "The band was on the brink of some kind of success and were playing it to the hilt, looking good, doing the minimum, buffaloing people. It was all part of the act."

The local authorities, for their part, were initially delighted, playing out their own Wild West fantasies as regular customers of the Red Dog. "One of the bartenders we'd nicknamed Comstock Mcloaded asked the sheriff if he could check his rifle at the bar," Hunter relates. "The sheriff agreed and handed it over. Comstock blew off a few rounds behind the bar. 'It works,' he said. When things got really rowdy, people would start shooting moths off the ceiling. Once somebody was cleaning his gun when it went off. The bullet went through the ceiling, through a chest of drawers upstairs above the stage and shattered the glasstop just as some guy was emptying his pockets onto it."

As the season reeled on, events around the Red Dog took on a dangerous kind of lunacy that no one was willing to claim responsibility for. The townsfolk's initial, bemused but tolerant attitude turned to sullen hostility as Virginia City was beseiged by long-haired, pot-puffing fun seekers. Paranoia was rife. "We heard some detectives were coming up from Reno to investigate the hippie influx," recalled Olsen. "The sheriff, who was on our side, just told us to shoot them in the leg if they tried to hassle us. So we had these two guys, barmen, totally zonked out, guarding the door in case they showed up."

When it all came to an end it seemed as sudden and inevitable as the day those five sparks landed in a flash. Wilhelm and Chandler Laughlin, the bartender who would later change his name to Travis T. Hipp, made a run down to San Francisco to stock up on marijuana. It was just after Labor Day and on their way back, loaded with acid caps, a pound of grass and the obligatory inventory of handguns, they stopped in the tiny burg of Rodeo, 25 miles north of Frisco to check a leaky radiator. They were rousted by the local constabulary and hustled off to the hoosegow. "The word came over the teletype that these guys had been busted for pot," Hunter recounts. "That threw everybody at the saloon into incredible paranoia. It blew the lid off the whole thing. We figured, "Oh God, now they know!' The whole thing was shut down real quick; there was a massive clean-up."

"After that," confirms Hicks, "the residents had an excuse to hassle us all the time; food inspectors would keep showing up in the kitchen and police would come down and search people . . . It got to the point where it was plainly obvious that it was all over. All we could do was to pile into our cars and head back to San Francisco—which is what we did."

Not before, however, another band of dedicated freaks made a last minute appearance. "On the night we were leaving," recalled Olsen, "who should show up but Ken Kesey and his busload of followers . . . they'd come to take a look at what was going on. Some of those cats had been on acid for sixteen days. Neil Cassady was there, driving the bus . . . it was just so very bizarre."

It was indeed. The whole time-warp, gun-toting, cube-dropping, rock & roll summer was the first real hint of the fine and special madness to come. "After Virginia City it was all kind of downhill for us," admits Hunter. "We maintained a following, but no time was as exciting as that initial breaking of ground."

"The Charlatans," says Mike Prichard, "if they were anything, were a real amalgamation of prima donnas, ego-bound people who had their own talents but no ability to synthesize those talents into something cohesive. They wouldn't take the time to learn anything; either they had it or they didn't. It was part of the Charlatans' approach; could you get away with it?"

The Charlatans had and, returning to San Francisco just as fall began to nip the air, they discovered a whole lot of other people picking up their cues.

Lawrence G. Chambers
822 west Washington St.
Carson City, Nevada 89701
April 13, 1966

Courtesy George Hunter

The Charlatans
2125 Pine Street
San Francisco, California

Mr. Hunter;

I seem to have noticed a lapse in your payments on the Ampeg amplifier purchased in August of 1965. You will send, within two weeks, the amount of two-hundred dollars, or the amplifier itself, to the address indicated above. If you fail to act in the prescribed period, legal steps will be immediately taken through our family lawyer and the Storey County Police Department, who, as you probably realize, have no use for you. I have a check from the First National Bank of Nevada stamped for insufficient funds. This alone will get you arrested. I also have the papers from Greco's House of Music, Redisco Inc., and Ampeg Inc., which prove that I am the owner. (you have no written contract) This entails being prosecuted for passing a bad check, grand theft, and transportation of stolen goods across state lines. It would be accurate to say you're in serious trouble unless you send the full amount within two weeks.

Sincerely,
Lawrence Gilbert Chambers

"By all the hoary hosts of Hoggoth! I have finally reached my goal, but what inconceivable wonder awaits me here?"
—Dr. Strange

Back in San Francisco, the sound of music was growing louder.

The commercial folk-music boom of the late Fifties and early Sixties had also generated a surge of interest in more traditional, "ethnic" repertoires. In the Bay Area, followers of these two schools were virtually at war, at least ideologically. On one side were the chummy collegians in pastel candy-stripes who emulated the Limeliters and Kingston Trio. Pitted against these "sell-outs" were the self-proclaimed "purists", the denimed, work-shirted faction for whom Pete Seeger, Joan Baez and the acoustic Dylan carried the flag.

Paul Kantner knew which side he was on. A blond, square-jawed Catholic kid who had gone to Santa Clara University and then San Jose State, he played banjo and guitar on the ethnic circuit where a solid version of "Greenland Whale Fisheries" and no clowning around really counted. He'd sung with a small trio and by himself, played for pennies on L.A.'s Venice beach, even started his own club, the Offstage, in San Jose. One summer night in '65 he was working the Drinking Gourd in San Francisco.

"They had a 'hoot' or audition night where anybody who came in could perform. I was playing to an audience of juicers. After three songs, I just got up and left. When I got offstage, this guy comes up to me and says, 'You want to start a group? I'll call you tomorrow.' I said sure."

Quest for the Best

Unlike Kantner, Marty Balin was dark, Jewish, and came from the enemy camp, having just exited the Town Criers, a robust Christy Minstrels-ish ensemble that had pursued commerciality to the point of having played Las Vegas. Singing, along with painting, was the one thing Balin had done all his life.

"My mother told me I whistled when I was a baby," Balin remembers. "I didn't talk for three years, because I was an autistic child. Then I began to sing. And then I talked. As I grew up, I was always singing." Growing up meant living in San Francisco and the East Bay, learning music from a local black pianist named Shaker, and dancing in a production of "West Side Story". In 1962 he'd even cut a pair of pop singles produced by Dave Burgess of the Champs (famous for "Tequila"); "I Specialize" and "Nobody But You", both on Burgess' Challenge Records label.

He'd also scored himself an acting scholarship to S.F. State, which he dropped out of after two weeks. "They required 18 units of drama arts, but I really wanted to take archaeology and anthropology. I thought, 'You know, this is really boring. I think I'll just go out and do it—something.' " The something turned out to be founding a nightclub. In the spring of 1965 he got together with some friends, came up with $10,000 and bought a small bar on Fillmore St. in the Marina called the Honeybucket. He almost singlehandedly rebuilt it, redecorated it and finally renamed it the Matrix. He also talked the place up to anyone who'd listen, always making a point of touting its nonexistent house band as "the best in town." From the dozens of curious musicians who dropped in over the summer, he recruited the members of his house band.

"When Marty first approached me," Kantner recalls, "we didn't even think in terms of forming a 'rock group', just a group." Indeed, Balin's next finds were a soft-spoken folk-blues guitarist named Jorma Kaukonen, and Signe Toly Anderson, a full-throttle folk thrush who sounded like a sweeter version of Judy Henske. Balin's pliant tenor rounded the group out. Weeks went by before they added standup bassist Bob Harvey, and a permanent drummer, Skip Spence—

Marty Balin, 1965

Courtesy Victoria Aguirre

whom Balin grabbed one day at the Matrix when the guitarist was rehearsing with another band. As he'd done with Kantner, Balin was working on instinct; if Spence was a guitarist and not a drummer, no matter. "You look like you should be a drummer", he told the affable Spence who thereafter picked up a pair of sticks and followed. The band's lineup was virtually identical to that of the We Five, a semi-amplified folk-rock group-with-a-girl-singer, also from the Bay Area, who were riding a Top Ten hit called "You Were On My Mind."

The band debuted Aug. 13 at the Matrix, under a hastily assumed name. Per Kantner, "A friend of Jorma's had a dog named Blind Thomas Jefferson Airplane. Jorma, being into the blues, had thought up the name as a sarcastic comment on white California people trying to adopt funky names. It was like a take-off on blues singers like Blindboy Willie McTell or something. We hadn't found a name we liked, so we said 'We'll call ourselves Jefferson Airplane until we think of something good . . .' "

If the naming of the band seemed merely expedient, by this time their musical direction was deliberate and clearly discernible—as first-generation American folk-rock, from the tip of their chiming vocal harmonies down to the pickups on their Martin hollow-bodies. They covered the Byrds' 'I'll Feel A Whole Lot Better" and raided their own pre-electric repertoires; Billy Ed Wheeler's "High Flyin' Bird", Fred Neil's "Other Side of This Life", "Let's Get Together" by Bay Area folkie Dino Valenti (aka Chester Powers). From publishers' demos they picked up Dylan's "Lay Down Your Weary Tune" which Jim McGuinn heard from them and subsequently incorporated into the Byrds' songbook.

In short order, the Airplane began

An early Airplane flight. Left to right: Paul Kantner; Signe Toly Anderson; Marty Balin; Jack Casady; Jorma Kaukonen.

Courtesy Victoria Aguirre

The Great Society. Left to right: Jerry Slick; David Minor; Grace Slick; Peter Vandergelder; Darby Slick
Photo: Herb Greene

writing their own songs (Balin's "It's No Secret", their first single; "Let Me In" and other Balin-Kantner tunes that show up on the *Jefferson Airplane Takes Off* album) and found themselves a manager. Matthew Katz was from Boston, drove a sleek white Jag, wore wide Spanish hats and tossed a cape over his shoulders. He had left a successful career as an industrial design executive to get involved in the music business in California. Though a novice, he was a savvy entrepreneur whose skills, like those of Big Daddy or Bill Graham, would serve the Airplane and the San Francisco scene remarkably well in the months to come.

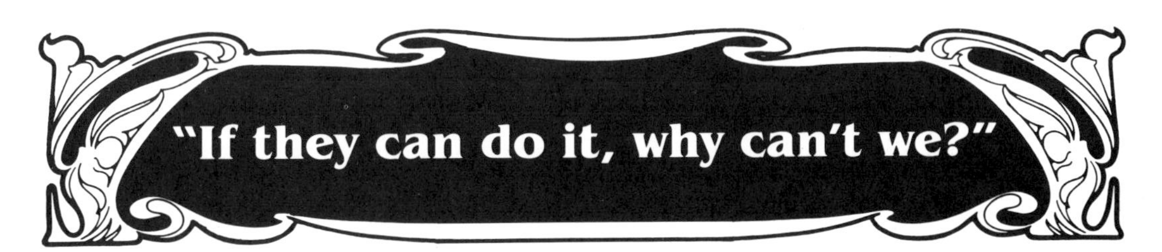

"If they can do it, why can't we?"

One of the people who came to catch the Airplane's maiden flight was Grace Slick, Ivan and Ginny Wing's rambunctious daughter, just out of college and just married to Jerry Slick, a nice, trust-funded neighbor boy from Palo Alto. Having felt uncomfortable with the deb-ball status pageant that came with growing up affluent, Grace was enjoying something of a mild revenge. She and her husband were living up in the city now, delicately skirting the boho edge; he was finishing up a film major at S.F. State, shooting *statements* like "Everybody Hits Their Brother Once", and she was scoring them—on piano, guitar, recorder. There was dope, the Beatles' liberating message, then Gleason's enticing reports on the goings-on at the Matrix. Real escape seemed possible. Grace might postpone indefinitely her surrender to the whole two-car, cocktails-at-seven trip—with the right key to this fascinating otherworld.

Seeing the Airplane pressed the key into Grace's palm. Soon Jerry ditched his hand-held Bolex and disappeared behind a drum kit. Grace took to her piano, writing songs, working her voice, while Jerry's brother Darby stepped in on lead guitar. As a band the trio had more zeal than chops ("At first, all we could play was free-form jams," says Darby), but the zeal was enough to attract Bard DuPont. "He wasn't a musician," Darby continues, "but he was into the whole mystique of being one. We were green enough to say 'You can play bass in *this* band.' "

DuPont's chief contributions were to bring the Slicks a rhythm guitarist, David Minor, and to give the fledgling band its name—the Great Society, courtesy of a friend, David Freiberg, who suggested President Johnson's slogan as a suitably ironic moniker. The Slicks acknowledged the irony but did not wear the name without some difficulty. "We thought it was a good joke," says Darby, "but we always felt other people would think it made us sound stuck up." Within weeks, DuPont was replaced by Peter Vandergelder, a bassist who doubled on sax. A former roommate of George Hunter's, he was also studying sarod and sitar at Ali Akbar's College of Indian Music in Marin, with Darby.

They were a curious collection, this Great Society—a melting-pot of amateurs and exotics dedicated to the propostion that they could, and would, make a significant musical mark. "If guys like McCartney and Lennon could compose a bunch of gold records," Grace told biographer Barbara Rowes, "we could probably put together one." To that end, they worked diligently, rehearsing at Grace and Jerry's Tiburon cottage, then moving to a house on Twin Peaks and a Castro area garage down the block from the Mystery Trend.

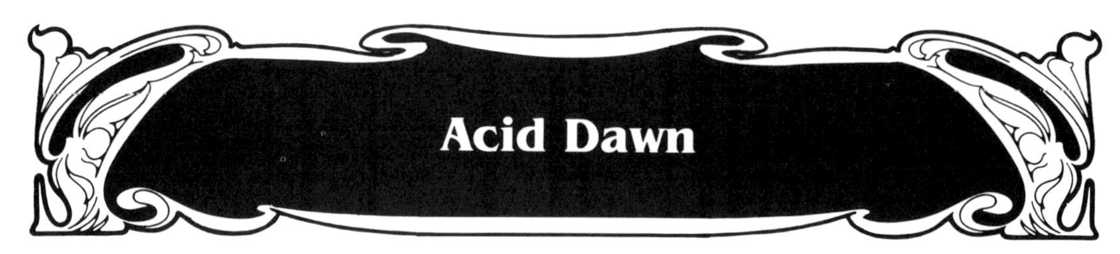

Acid Dawn

Unlike most young bands, the Great Society relied little on cover material, outside of Dylan's "Outlaw Blues" and "Its All Over Now, Baby Blue" and the Jaynetts' 1963 hit "Sally, Go 'Round the Roses." Darby: "We figured if we did only our own material, audiences wouldn't know when we were screwing up." Grace penned a paean to Lenny Bruce ("Father Bruce", performances of which often ended with the group yelling an unsubtle "Fuck!"), Minor contributed a saw-toothed rocker "You Can't Cry". Then Darby came in one day with a "sad song" he'd written, "Somebody To Love."

"I'd just been dumped by this girl, and I was coming down from LSD, in my house on Liberty St. in the Mission. I wrote it at dawn. It came quickly, and I had the feeling instantly that it would be a hit song." The rest of the band felt the same way once they heard it. A similar reception met "White Rabbit", Grace's meld of Lewis Carroll and Ravel's "Bolero". Darby credits the song's appeal to its literary allusions, the way the melody modulates midway through, and the song's thinly veiled theme: "I keep reading Grace saying it had nothing to do with drugs, but I don't agree; they were everywhere, the whole world was opening up to them. It turned out not to be the case, but at that time we all thought they were going to save the world."

Armed with their original repertoire, the Society officially charged onto the scene Sept. 22, with a gig at the Coffee Gallery on Grant Ave., a former Beat watering-hole that had once specialized in local poets and hip comics like Lord Buckley. The band survived its debut and the members braced themselves for the enjoyable trek to the stardom they were certain lay ahead.

Mother's: Big Daddy's Folly

Apart from the fun it foreclosed on, the shutdown of the Red Dog Saloon hinted at a far more serious problem facing San Francisco's would-be rock community. Namely, it was all dressed up with no place to go. Loft parties and rent bashes were all well and good, but if this spontaneously generated scene with all its bands and fans was going to survive, it needed something a bit more permanent. It needed a home.

There had been no shortage of attempts to start just such a venue. Marty Balin had opened his Matrix club in August and it was moving along nicely, showcasing the Mystery Trend, Great Society, Charlatans and others. But Balin's time was increasingly being consumed by his band, which was starting its ascent to the big-time in rather rapid fashion. Mere weeks after forming, the Airplane was getting phone calls from record company talent scouts, thanks largely to Matthew Katz' efforts. And besides, Balin's modest wine-bar-with-a-stage barely seated 150.

Far more promising was Mother's, the "world's first psychedelic nightclub", conceived and grandly executed by Big Daddy Tom Donahue. Having just left KYA, Donahue's interests had drifted from Top 40 to LSD-25, and in Mother's he envisioned a cool, womb-like environment where local heads could congregate to dig live music, groove and hang out. "The idea behind Tom's partnership with Bob Mitchell," recalls Raechel Donahue, "was that everybody got to take a flyer. Meaning, if one of the partners wants to take some of the money and try something out, so can the other. Bob's flyer was buying race horses. Tom bought a nightclub."

Around the time Balin opened the Matrix, Donahue bought and renovated DJ's, a Broadway bar located between Carol Doda's topless joint and the Swiss Hotel where Lenny Bruce was busted a year later. He then hired a clutch of Big Sur artists to drench the club in long, undulating, three-dimensional murals in

Courtesy Raechel Donahue

Big Daddy lights up.

varying shades of purple; lava lamps built into the wall gave the room an eerie glow. But, outside of a well-attended two week engagement by the Lovin' Spoonful, Mother's failed to catch on; by fall it was history.

A variety of explanations have been offered for the club's demise. Its booking policies were inconsistent; subsequent weeks presented exotic instrumentalist Sandy Bull then soft-pop hitmaker Chris ("Call Me") Montez then the Great Society and then an early incarnation of the Grateful Dead (the Emergency Crew). Or it may have been the side effects of the club's gaping violet dawn decor, which, to Carl Scott, looked "like you were inside someone's digestive track". Raechel partly blames the chilly wind blowing across Broadway ("Every time you'd open the front door, it would blow the strings out of tune on every guitar in the house"), but the truth may be that the well-heeled hip clientele Donahue anticipated had simply not yet materialized. "You're never going to make a go off those cats," Mitchell had told Big Daddy. "Man, they don't have enough money to park!"

Do-It-Yourself Dance-concerts

Ironically, the people who finally gave the scene its first home were neither professional promoters nor moonlighting musicians. They were instead four rank amateurs, two men and two women who spent their days mostly listening to rock & roll records, junking in thrift shops and crashing together in a pre-communal pad on Pine St. And they took in stray dogs, specifically a forlorn shepherd-mixed-with-Mexican street-dog named Sancho who became their mascot.

Which is where the "Family Dog" troupe got its name. (Or was it? One later associate claims the name referred to a proposed pet cemetery the group dreamed up as a get-rich-quick scheme. Ralph Gleason maintained they adopted the name after their pup was run over in Pine St.) The original Family Dog was Jack Towle, a wired-up New Englander heavily into motorcycles; Alton Kelley, a commercial-design dropout who'd relocated in San Francisco after stints in Mexico, Los Angeles and Connecticut; Ellen Harmon, Kelley's girlfriend who was from Detroit and liked to lay on her American flag bedspread reading Marvel comics; and Luria Castell.

For someone barely out of her teens, Luria Castell had had some wild times. In junior high, she'd followed the Beats around her Grant Avenue neighborhood. Later she marched and sat in for civil rights, joined an all-night vigil outside the gates of San Quentin prison protesting the execution of Caryl Chessman. She went to Cuba twice, met Castro and Guevara. At the 1960 HUAC hearings, firemen washed her down the stairs and cops carted her off to a paddywagon.

She had also attended several Cow Palace shows, seen the Stones at the Civic, been to Mother's. And she had just returned from the Sunset Strip where, along with Dylan and Zappa and Barry McGuire, Little Richard, Sonny & Cher and Derek Taylor, she'd watched the Byrds usher in the silvery, elliptical era known as folk-rock at Ciro's. Which is maybe where and when she started wearing those Ben Frank glasses and thinking that, compared to the ecstasy of hearing and moving to the sound of jangling electric guitars, little else in life really mattered.

Still, two things bothered Luria. "At the Cow Palace, there was all this pent-up energy; the music was great but the audience had to stay seated. You couldn't dance. For that, we had to go to places like the Peppermint Tree or Mother's and after a while you get real tired of going to bars." If part of her attitude was just generational bias starting to show ("Most of the weed people were very anti-alcohol"), much of it was simply common sense. If your interest was music, why should you be forced to enjoy it only in the company of old lushes and fox-hunting junior execs from Montgomery Street?

The solution presented itself as a scene out of "Babes In Arms". Like Mickey Rooney to Judy Garland, Luria Castell turned to her cohorts and said, "Hey, I know—let's put on a show!" "We all borrowed money from our parents," Luria recalls, "then Jack set up a checking account." Ellen took the phone calls and "kept everything together"; eventually, Kelley would design the posters and

Courtesy Luria Castell

A picnic with Luria (second from left)

handbills. The show would be a "Tribute to Dr. Strange", a "dance-concert" to be presented Oct. 16, 1965 by the Family Dog.

Though her radical phase was behind her ("ever since the guy I lived with took off with my best politico girlfriend"), Luria had not lost her skill for social organizing. First, she rented Longshoremen's auditorium, a newly built union hall on the edge of Fishermen's Wharf. One of the best arguments against modern architecture, the half-sunken dome resembled a sliced golfball fitted with insect legs. It looked like a wayward spider from Mars. Having already hosted a Count Basie concert and an official visit by Nikita Krushchev, it would now be the site of the semi-official coming-out of San Francisco's latest claim to fame: the "hippies".

Next, Luria began rounding up talent. Between sets at the Matrix, she got Marty Balin to commit the Airplane; she also coaxed Grace Slick into donating the Great Society. For the evening's master-of-ceremonies, she got Russ "the Moose" Syracuse, KYA's midnight-to-six disc jockey, an unseen but much heard presence among insomniacs and young heads. Greg Shaw, who would soon found the scene's first music paper, the "Mojo-Navigator Rock & Roll News", was a typical Moose fan: "I almost flunked out of high school because I couldn't stop listening to him. I'd stay up every night. He sounded like some sort of crazy beatnik, making weird phone calls and 'bombing' records he didn't like with World War II sound effects. You'd hear him and wonder, 'Where could they possibly have gotten this guy?' "

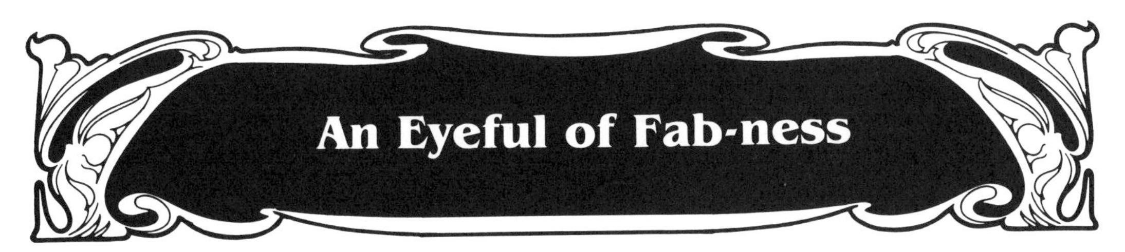

An Eyeful of Fab-ness

After signing up the Moose as their official master-of-ceremonies, the Dog turned their efforts to getting publicity for their show, coloring a thousand 8"x10" handbills (using Magic Marker pens) and distributing them around the S.F. State campus, throughout the Haight and Berkeley. They also made an appointment to meet with the *Chronicle's* Ralph J. Gleason. Gleason's main beat was jazz (he'd been a contributing *downbeat* editor), but lately his "On the Town" entertainment columns had been filled with praise for the Beatles and Stones, and, among Bay Area music critics, he'd been waging something of a one-man war on behalf of Bob Dylan. Gleason generously met with Luria, Ellen Harmon and Al Kelley then touted the Dr. Strange dance to his readers as a weekend must-see.

Soon enough the world would be watching, but that night, Oct. 16, 1965, amounted to something of a sneak preview for the City that Knows How. It got an eyeful. First, there were the crowds, bigger and stranger than those at the Red Dog or Primalon dances; clogging the space-age golfball hall, spilling out onto the street. Where, indeed, *could* they have gotten these people? Gleason's subsequent review tried to get a handle on the dress code, describing it as "ranging from velvet Lottie Crabtree to Mining Camp Desperado, Jean la Fitte leotards, I. Magnin Beatnik, Riverboat Gambler, India Imports Exotic to Modified Motorcycle Rider Black Leather-and-Zippers." Obviously, some of what made Gleason's eyes pop were the Charlatans' fans, whose fetish for frontier drag now matched their heroes', stroke for pearl-handled stroke. But there were dozens of other fresh, personalized, often inexplicable expressions—one of Robin Hood's Merry Men in green cape, felt cap and feather; Victorian widows in button-top shoes; a fat man in a sash covered with buttons advertising everything from SNCC's efforts to end racism to the fabness of the Dave Clark Five. All this and it wasn't even Halloween yet.

Many of the revelers had been to the huge Vietnam Day peace march in Berkeley earlier that day, where Allen Ginsberg had chanted and Kesey had done harmonica pranks. Others had heard the Moose's latenight radio plugs or acted on Gleason's tip. But here they

Ralph J. Gleason

Courtesy Jean Gleason   Photo: Ross Russell

were, frugging and jerking, freaking freely at a booze-less, hassle-free costume ball. LSD was still six months away from being declared illegal.

Chet Helms, a young longhair who'd hitch-hiked from Texas a few years earlier, remembers the Dr. Strange show for its "exhilarating sense of safety, sanctuary. The feeling was 'Well, they can't bust us all.' There was freedom and a moment of pure recognition. These were my people, my peers, all of a sudden together."

To Jack Casady, the Airplane's new electric bassist, Helms and his peers were a bit "different" from the audiences to which he'd been accustomed. "My background was playing bars and military bases around Washington—like Quantico Marine base. The only longhairs I'd seen at that time were at motorcycle races. I'd only been in California a few weeks when we played Longshoremen's."

To some, like George Hunter, the lost tribe's reunion came as less of a surprise. "It really didn't happen overnight. There were so many of these little indicators showing up. You'd drive around the Haight and gradually you saw more and more of these people. Besides, at that time there was such a clear division between the norm and anyone outside the norm. Everybody who was the least bit different felt a kind of change in the air, almost some sort of manifest destiny."

To Luria Castell, it was "a scene just waiting to happen. You'd have to be blind not to have seen it coming." The exact form of what was coming was as yet a bit unclear, but for the time being that was quite all right. The Airplane's Paul Kantner dug the formlessness and "general insanity. It was like a party. The audience often far overshadowed any of the bands, and the distance between the two was not that great. Grace used to say that the stage was just the least crowded place to stand."

Those who weren't standing onstage were chain-dancing, wandering the floor, soaking up the buzz and soar of the Airplane, getting lost in the drone of the Society's raga-rock version of "Sally, Go 'Round the Roses". It hardly mattered that the sound system was mickey-mouse or that Longshoremen's Hall's acoustics resembled those of a blimp hangar. Finally, after so much sweet inspiration and so many false starts, it was all really going down.

Mike Daly was there, begging Russ the Moose to put the Mystery Trend on the Dog's next dance bill, if there was going to be one. Big Daddy was there, gassed by the beautiful chicks and goofing on the fact that these Pine St. kids had gone and pulled it off, got it right the first time. And Peter Albin was there, along with Chet Helms.

Scoping Out Baghdad

Helms was another one of those whose experiences classified them as "outside the norm." A child evangelist at age 15, he'd been raised in a strict fundamentalist family which forbade dancing, listening to pop music, watching movies. In his late teens he became an ardent civil rights activist, eventually join-

1090 Page St.

ing the Young Peoples Socialist League. Caught up in the *On The Road* romance and eager for escape, he split for San Francisco in 1962. He was 20 years old, a long, tall Texas "poet savant in a beret, little pegged Italian pants, a goatee and moustache." He spent his first night in a sleeping bag on an anti-nuke picket line at the old Post Office near Seventh and Market, across from the Greyhound Station where he arrived. Subsequently, he found a pad, crashed, woke up and went looking for the big Beat scene. When he found it, it wanted nothing to do with him.

It might as well have been an assembly of the Duck River Baptists or the Hutterite Brethren, so tightly did the scene heavies clutch the reins of power. "The local poetry establishment was then more or less dominated by Ferlinghetti and City Lights Publishers," Helms remembers, "and his people generally determined who got to read where." Locked out, Helms made an end run around the church elders. Under their upturned noses, he convinced the owners of the Blue Unicorn coffeehouse to let him hold open poetry readings. "It was very democratic. Anyone could come and read their stuff, good, bad or indifferent." The Unicorn management gave Helms free rein—up to a point. Before long, they were chastising him for his rather "open" experimenting with hallucinogens, a brand new no-no to the now graying bohos.

Undismayed, Helms kept at it, scoping out Baghdad for something new. Noticing the "very polished, Kingston Trio-type" folk music scene flourishing in the Bay Area and figuring funky is better, he flashed on a girl he'd met in Austin who belted the blues raw and ragged. "I just thought Janis would knock these people on their ass." He went back to Texas, found Joplin and convinced her to join him on a breakneck 50-hour thumb trip to San Francisco to start her career in earnest.

Janis made a modest dent on the Bay Area folk scene, singing solo and as half of a duo with Airplane guitarist Jorma Kaukonen, at places like Coffee & Confusion. By 1963 she'd even moaned the blues over radio, on one of KPFA's hoary hootenannies that also featured a scuffy young harmonica man, Rod "Pigpen" McKiernan. She was impressive, undisciplined, and near deafening. "Chet had me come and hear her once at the Coffee Gallery," Luria Castell remembers. "She was backed by one electric guitar, and she was so loud I had to stand out on the sidewalk." Eventually Joplin, like scores of others, got hooked on the self-destruction myth of the Beat ethos and fell into a methedrine habit. Fearful for her life, Helms and a bunch of friends took up a collection, threw a farewell party then put her on a Greyhound back to Texas.

By '65, Helms' restless evangelical spirit had found a new mission: pop music. After trying to form his own band, he fell into organizing jam sessions in the basement of 1090 Page, a full-gabled, bay-windowed 25-room Victorian mansion a block north of Haight. Ten-ninety was being sub-let to State students, hipsters and hangers-on by Rodney Albin, who was managing it for his uncle—who was waiting out legal red tape for permission to tear it down and let him build the senior citizens project he'd planned. The mansion's transient population (and the neighborhood's rapidly de-escalating demographic) assured a constant supply of performers and audience for Helms' 50-cent Wednesday jams.

Tom Swift and His Electric Grandmother

Many of those who sang and played were non-musicians like Helms, and quickly proved it after a turn or two on the plywood stage. Others were proficient ax-men who hung around long enough to figure they deserved better, then split for paying gigs. But the most interesting ones were those who "could play a little." Like Helms, they were getting their feet wet here, trying on this new, amplified shake-and-shimmy trip. Many were folkniks, toward busting out of stalled careers as junior New Lost City Ramblers or Carolina Tarheels or whatever.

Once the game of musical chairs settled down, these were largely the musicians who comprised the 1090 "house band" in late '65: guitarist Dave Eskerson and drummer Chuck Jones (both of whom were shortly replaced), guitarist Sam Andrew and Rod Albin's younger brother Peter, an amiable folk 'n' bluegrass picker who'd worked the same San Jose Peninsula folk circuit as Paul Kantner and Jorma Kaukonen. Now Peter was learning electric bass, and turning into something of a rubber-faced madman—throwing his Prince Valiant locks all over the place, shouting out "Satisfaction" and "Spider And the Fly" down there in his uncle's basement. And he was writing songs, songs that, if they weren't as well-crafted as the Stones', were certainly weirder. There was "Caterpillar" ("I'm a caterpillar, crawling for your love/I'm a pterodactyl, dying for your love") and one called "Banana" whose sole lyric was the title repeated endlessly over a thunderous bass riff. Great googly-moogly!

The band coalesced when Dave Getz, a student at the S.F. Art Institute, came in on drums and a Detroit pal of the Family Dog's, Jim Gurley, was recruited as lead guitarist. "Jim said that his first job was being a human hood ornament on his father's car in the Thrill Show," Getz recounts. "They toured around with auto races and demolition derbies. Gurley would be mounted horizontally on the hood with his head out front; the car was then driven at high speed through a wooden wall that had been set on fire. The first time, he was a little scared and moved ever so slightly just before impact and almost broke his neck. Later he learned to keep his head perfectly straight and didn't feel a thing." A part-time traveler on the folk circuit, Gurley listed his musical influences as "a combination of Spike Jones and 'Goodnight Irene'."

The band was ready for action. Helms had signed on as their manager and had publicity photos taken, inside the cable car barn above Chinatown. All they needed was a name. "At first we called ourselves Blue Yard Hill," laughs Peter Albin, referring to a name suggested by Paul Ferez, a 1090 regular who wrote bad Dylanesque poems and served briefly as the band's lead singer. "Then we thought about Tom Swift and His Electric Grandmother, but that didn't really do it either." It was Helms who took matters in hand, sitting everyone down and inviting them to toss out potential names while his wife, Lorraine, wrote them all down on a notepad. "When we'd run out of names, there was this big long list," recalls Helms. "Lori read them back to us, and when she got down to the last two, she accidentally read them together, as one name: Big Brother and the Holding Company. I yelled, 'That's it: Big Brother & the Holding Company.' The band fought with me over it. They argued that it was too long a name to fit on a 45 label. They thought there were too many letters for the space."

Big Brother & The Holding Company, 1965. Left to right: Chet Helms (manager); Sam Andrew; Peter Albin; Chuck Jones; Jim Gurley.

Photo: Michael Rachoff

Dick Tracy and the Day-glo Dadaists

Encouraged by the success of the Dr. Strange show, the Family Dog promptly rented Longshoremen's Hall for two more dates. In contrast to the weekly scheduled dance-concerts that would soon evolve, the Dog pegged their presentations to specific themes. Luria Castell: "We were trying to make each one an event, something special, not just 'put on a dance and run 'em through.' " Dick Tracy's curly-

Courtesy Mike Daly

locked waif Sparkle Plenty was the subject of October 24's "tribute", a gala that paired the Charlatans with the Lovin' Spoonful, then riding the crest of "Do You Believe In Magic." Russ the Moose's co-emcee was Larry Hankin, from the local satire group The Committee.

November 6 celebrated Flash Gordon's arch-foe Ming the Merciless and featured the Charlatans plus L.A.'s big new noise, a furry pack of Day-glo dadaists who called themselves the Mothers and wrote such songs as "Help, I'm A Rock" and "Who Are the Brain Police?" No less inspired than the do-it-yourselfers who were constructing the Frisco scene, the Angeleno band even brought its own audience—a troupe of wildly overdressed dervishes and freeform dancers led by 60-year-old male sculptor Vito Paulekas. The *eminence grise* of the Sunset Strip freakworld, Vito had loaned the Byrds his basement for their first rehearsals; now, with Carl Franzoni, Suzy Creamcheese and Judy Yum Yum, he followed Hollywood acid bands on the road as a kind of good-trips ambassador. The Ming bash was hosted by Howard Hesseman, another Committeeman who was then going by the handle of "Don Sturdy" (after the camp hero of a series of kids books from the Thirties).

By now, a new feature had been added to the dances: lightshows. After the first Dog show, Luria Castell had contacted Bill Ham, a wigged-out apartment manager, martial arts expert and painter who'd been experimenting with liquid light projections. Using overhead slide projectors and colored oils, Ham was able to throw blown-up images of moving liquids onto flat surfaces; at the Red Dog, his blob-like creations bubbled and pulsed with the music, making walls and ceiling swim to the Charlatans' rust-tinged folk-rock. Now Ham was working his magic at Longshoremen's. And George Hunter started bringing his strobelight with him. Set up at the side of the stage, its intense red, white and blue flashing shattered and reassembled the Charlatans' image several dozen times a second, while the band—and the great waving-gravy spectacle—played on into the night.

The Mime Troupe Benefits: "Socially Orgasmic"

Meanwhile, as Ming's minions cavorted under the jellied lights, across town another strange dance was taking place, the first of several benefits thrown on behalf of the San Francisco Mime Troupe. The Troupe, Ronnie Davis' Brecht-inspired guerrilla theatre, staged hit-and-run agitprop and various kinds of political confrontations throughout the Bay Area, and was in the habit of getting busted (often, it was rumored, deliberately)—usually for obscenity. Hence, the endless round of benefits, to pay legal fees and keep the Troupe afloat between culture clashes.

"It was held in this industrial loft, the Calliope warehouse on Howard St., behind the *Chronicle* building," recalls Ron Nagle whose Mystery Trend opened the show. "We pulled up in our '51 Chevy sedan delivery-truck and saw people lined up for two blocks. You *couldn't get in.* I don't know how they all found out, whether it was word of mouth or what.

Courtesy Mike Daly

We were stoked, that there were all these people willing to pay to see *us,* and two or three other bands nobody'd ever heard of." In addition to the Airplane, Sandy Bull and Lawrence Ferlinghetti, the dance featured jazzman John Handy and the Fugs. (As the Mothers were to L.A.'s fledgling freak scene, the Fugs were to New York's: aggressively unconventional, anti-social, self-decribed "dirty old men" singing subversive songs like "Amphetamine Shriek" and "Kill For Peace.") The Committee's Gary Goodrow, who hosted many Frisco shows, was surprised to learn that the hairy East Villagers had played college dances across the country en route to San Francisco. "I said, 'How'd you manage to not get killed, looking like that and playing those songs on college campuses?' Tuli Kupferberg said, 'Easy, we just told the people booking us that we'd be performing our big hit single, "Coca Cola Douche" and we had no problem.' "

The first Mime Troupe benefit proved that the new San Francisco rock, having escaped from the Red Dog lab, was starting to attract a sizeable audience, and one with a voracious appetite at that—Ron Nagle recalls groups of revelers shuttling from the Calliope warehouse to

Longshoremen's Hall to catch bits of both shows. The benefit also marked the public emergence of the Troupe's treasurer/business manager, a transplanted New Yorker who bombed around town in a beat-up VW bug, Bill Graham.

"I left my job as an office manager for Alice Chalmers Manufacturing on Market Street, to work for the Mime Troupe," Graham chuckles. "I did their books, ran the office, set up lights, loaded trucks. I was their only full-time employee, at $125 a month. When they got busted, I suggested 'Let's get some money together through a benefit.' I used their connections to round up the talent. We announced the benefit, and let the city know we intended to fight this obscenity charge stuff. I got a call from someone in the Family Dog, asking if he could help in any way. It was Chet Helms. I told him to show up, he was very nice. On the poster, I had listed the Family Dog as one of the performing acts. When they came in, I asked them where the dogs were. That's how little I knew."

Graham recalls the first Mime benefit as "socially orgasmic. We raised $4800 and everyone was there for the right reasons. People brought fruit, banana stalks and pate. We had steel drums full of vodka and apple juice. I'd never seen anything like it; it was the greatest show of my life. I used a piece of sheetrock to write the admission prices on; if you had a full-time job and earned $100,000 a year, admission was $48. If you had a part-time job and made less than $20 a week, come on in."

Graham staged two more such benefits throughout the winter of '65-'66, generally offering the same bill of fare—respectable portions of jazz and poetry, garnished with much of the city's new rock. The dances also revealed Graham's quick thinking and his gift for promotion. At the Calliope, when the cops came in and tried to break it up, on the grounds that there were too many people out in the street trying to get in, he "told the cops that Frank Sinatra and Rudy Vallee were coming to perform. The cops told me half the people inside would have to leave. So I got onstage and asked everyone who had been there a long time (it had started at six in the evening) if they would please leave. People went out the front door, then they went around to the back of the building and took the freight elevator back in."

On the eve of Dylan's first electric concerts in the Bay Area (Dec. 10), Graham crashed the singer's television press conference, and thrust a Mime benefit poster in the face of the great generational voice. When Dylan obligingly held the poster up to the cameras, examined it then read it aloud and said he wished he could attend, Graham scored a true coup: endorsement of the building local scene by the supreme arbiter of all that was hip and happening in America.

The Jugband Gets A Jolt

By the third Mime Troupe benefit, Graham had begun using the Warlocks, five hairy wonders from Palo Alto who might well have laid claim to being the world's ugliest rock band. If other San Francisco groups had been *inspired* by the Rolling Stones, here was a group that modeled both its image and sound after Britain's baddest boys. The Warlocks looked like they'd just gotten out of bed—long hair all shook up, clothes rumpled, Beatle-style "fruit boots" scuffed and worn; their organist, a sullen-looking, heavyset cat who dressed in soiled Hell's Angeles togs, was the same "Pigpen" who'd jammed with Janis on the radio.

The Warlocks' music was a well-handled R&B roadmap; they covered the salacious "King Bee" by Slim Harpo out of Baton Rouge, Jimmy Reed's "Big Boss Man" (Mississippi), Tommy Tucker's Chicago classic "High-Heeled Sneakers" and the garage-rock grope anthem "Gloria" by Van Morrison's Them from Belfast.

Never mind that six months before, the core of the Warlocks were diddly-diddling their way through coffee houses and folkfests as Mother Macree's Uptown Jug Champions. To a man, they came from uncommon stock and together they were to make unique music. A self-proclaimed "music junkie" and teenage pothead, Jerry Garcia had enlisted in the Army at 17, been court-martialed for going AWOL at 18, and never once stopped playing guitar. Until the Beatles and Stones' arrival, ethnic folk had been his bag. He'd even made his own Lomax Bros.-type research trip, piloting his little Corvair through the Deep South in search of old pickers and new licks. He'd banjo'ed behind his wife Sarah, bluegrassed with the Hart Valley Drifters and with Mother Macree, who played Kantner's Offstage in San Jose.

Photo: Herb Greene

Making their point: the Warlocks, 1965

Bassist Phil Lesh came out of modern classical composing, precisely the West Coast wing that flourished under Luciano Berio during his residence at Mills College in Oakland. Trained as a Kenton-ish jazz trumpeter, Lesh composed stark atonal pieces and ambitious orchestral works; the Mime Troupe had climaxed one of their presentations with a pair of experimental performances by Lesh and acclaimed electronic composer Steve Reich.

Ron "Pigpen" McKernan showed up with a briefcase of funky folk-blues and styled himself as a hard-travelin', juice-fueled moaner in the Lightin' Hopkins mold. Rhythm guitarist Bob Weir was the Warlocks' heartthrob, a young, fresh-faced kid with great straight hair who came from the same Peninsula upper-class as the Great Society's Grace Slick. Drummer Bill Kreutzmann was recruited from the music store where Garcia gave guitar lessons.

While he had first learned to play guitar by listening to Chuck Berry records, Garcia admits the Warlocks "didn't have any real background in playing loud rock & roll. But the Beatles were a big impetus. For one thing, I was kind of froze up in bluegrass; there wasn't enough good bluegrass in the area I lived in to let me play and feel good about playing it. I sort of copped out, and got involved in the jugband as a way of saying 'Let's just have fun.' It was one level of release and going into electric music was another, a step into something that was about just having fun, playing with your friends, not worrying about it being absolutely perfect."

Phil Lesh told Dead biographer Hank Harrison that "we couldn't emphasize the word ELECTRIC enough. When I first played an electric instrument, I played it for seven hours straight, and I couldn't sleep that night. It got me so high that I knew something had to be happening."

Pizza Pubs and Acid Tests

By late 1965, the Warlocks had found an additional means of getting high—LSD, which they'd been introduced to by Ken Kesey at his Perry Lane pad over on the nearby Stanford University campus. Things were getting curiouser. There was acid, and there were paying gigs, five-nights-a-week gigs at places like the Fireside, the In-Room and McGoo's Pizza pub. Garcia remembers these for the "overwhelming crowd of high-school kids who came to see us. Our very first appearance was a total knock-out. McGoo's in Menlo Park. We talked the guy into letting us play, we set up and there was pandemonium. None of us expected that kind of reception. We caught fire right away. It really blew our minds."

After a relatively short apprenticeship in the bars, the Warlocks ventured into the arena of real mind-blowing; they became the official accompanists for Kesey and the Merry Pranksters' Acid Tests. Which was a kind of dubious distinction at best, since music was hardly the focus of the Pranksters' crazed happenings. If the line between performers and audience blurred at the Family Dog dances, it was erased altogether at the Acid Tests, which began with a free-for-all near Soquel in the Santa Cruz mountains then tripped into San Jose, Marin County's Muir Beach and later Watts. No more than a few hundred people participated, but both the new and old-line in-crowds were well represented; Pranksters Ken Babbs and Hugh Romney (before he became "Wavy Gravy"), Kerouac pard and mentor Neal Cassady, legendary kitchen-chemist Augustus Owsley Stanley III—"the Henry Ford of acid", and writer Marshall Efron, carrying a head full of ideas and a doctor's bag bearing the ID "L. Bloom, Dublin."

"Those people were part of our social

Courtesy Editors' Archives

Kesey's Acid Test *record album*

network," claims Garcia. "We all preferred the anarchy of the Tests in a lot of ways. Every person was a participant and everywhere was the stage. We didn't have to entertain anybody. We were no more famous than anyone else."

But even the sympatico cast couldn't prevent the Tests from developing, as it were, dead spots, acute lapses when the euphoria subsided and nothing happened. Somehow,, it all came with the package: spontaneity, formlessness, that old ebb and flow that, well, just went with anarchy. Kesey's rare *Acid Test* LP preserves much of this ambience. Cut by the stoned Pranksters in an S.F. recording studio, the album features such hits as "Trip X", "Bells & Fairies" and "Levitation". Most are spacey ruminations on life, spiced by primitive special effects and lots of giggling. But in the eight-minute interview that starts Side One, Kesey lays down the bottom line: "As navigator of this venture, I try as much as possible to set out in a direction that, in the first place, is practically impossible to achieve, and then along the way mess up the minds of the crew with as many chemicals as we can lay our hands on . . ."

As for musical content, the Warlocks, just as fully zonked as the Pranksters, are reduced to supplying tuneless plunks and tweeking behind the cosmic raps and Ken Babbs' harmonica solos.

The Maddest Tea Party

"There were more dances running here last weekend than any time since the Swing Era. Could it be we are on the verge of another dancing craze? I think so."
—Ralph Gleason, *S.F. Chronicle,* Dec. 1965

By the start of 1966, the new music seemed to be busting out all over. Moreover, this thing was gathering speed, heading toward something definite and inevitable, maybe some grand-scale event which would establish and, as it were, legitimize the whole scene for once and for all.

The Trips Festival was an idea hatched by a conclave of local hipsters. The Merry Pranksters and their friends the Grateful Dead (nee Warlocks) were involved, as were Big Brother & the Holding Co., Allen Ginsberg, photographer Gene Anthony, composer Ramon Sender from the avant-ish Tape Music Center, and a local advertising exec, Stewart Brand, who had two obsessions he wanted the rest of America to get excited about: Indians, and the idea of taking a photograph of the whole earth. After a series of meetings, Bill Graham was hired to produce a three-day gala at Longshoremen's, January 21–23.

The idea was to gather up all the separate but equally groovy elements of the local scene, toss 'em into one big pot and invite the whole town to supper. It would be a mammoth Mad Hatter's ball; no one would be left out.

Advance ticket sales were strong, but it surely didn't hurt when Ken Kesey, out on bail after being charged with grass possession, assaulting a police oficer and trespassing, showed up in Union Square January 20 to do some p.r. of his own. Climbing out of the Pranksters' "Further" bus, with the words "Hot" and "Cold" inscribed on his pants—and "TIBET" stencilled across his buttocks—he regaled the lunchtime crowd of businessmen, old ladies and invited press with details on the weekend "happening". Then, to the accompaniment of Stewart Brand and a comely Prankster ms. in a can-can costume, Kesey released three big, black weather balloons; behind them trailed a banner reading "NOW". It made the next morning's *Chronicle* with little difficulty.

In most respects, the Trips Festival

Poster: Courtesy Peter Albin

At the Trips Festival

was little more than a glorified version of the Family Dog dances and the Acid Tests which preceded it; more lights, strobes and old movies, more people (some 10,000 attended over the three days) and, if it were possible, more highs. By the third night, somebody dosed the rent-a-cops and they were seen playing with toy airplanes and shuffling Slinkies palm-over-palm. A guy stood on an aluminum ladder and broke eggs into the hair of a woman writhing on the stage below. It was, to quote Graham, "a completely insane set-up."

"Chaotic" is what it looked like to Big Brother's Peter Albin. "It was crazy, but a lot of fun. Graham was going bananas, trying to keep track of the gate while Kesey was letting people in for free through the back doors." Grateful Dead historian Hank Harrison alludes to other conflicts, "demagogic power games." One such game involved stage manager Ken Babbs and Big Brother manager Chet Helms, who recalls:

"A bunch of black drummers were up there beating on congas, and Babbs is yelling over the microphone for them to stop: 'All right, you jungle bunnies, we've been hearing that stuff for 3000 years

Photo: Gene Anthony

now.' Then our band gets up, they play one song and Babbs says, 'O.K., that was Big Brother and the Holding Company.' So I went onstage, grabbed the mike and said, 'Goddamnit, these guys were paid to play for 30 minutes and they're going to *play* for 30 minutes.' Kesey and his people were trying to run the show over everyone else's dead body."

What it boiled down to was a clear case of too many acts under one tent. As Gleason's review of the festival put it, "It should be noted that (the show's) success was in direct relationship to the quality and the presence of the music . . . When the dull projections took over, it was nowhere. When the good rock music wailed, it was great."

Gleason had nailed it beautifully. Later for the high-minded, oh-so-Euro "Happening" stuff and Stewart Brand's interminable solemn slides of the noble Apache. Later for the whole Acid Testy-idea of *waiting around for the next act.* Hadn't these stiffs heard? A new power was now loose, and it gratified instantly, consistently, in the jolt of Big Brother's great dark chords, in the Dead's rushing sonic blues. Move over, boys, and give it a wide berth . . .

"The most historical point," ruminated Jerry Garcia, years later, to Charles Reich, "I suppose, was the Trips Festival, when another form was starting to evolve. It was turned into the most obvious kind—you take a light show, you take a rock & roll band and that's your psychedelic experience. And that's not it. That wasn't it at the Trips Festival . . .

"But in order to keep on playing, we had to go with whatever form was there. Because for one thing, the form that we liked always scared everybody. It scared the people that owned the building that we'd rent, so they'd never rent twice to us. It scared the people who came, a lot of times. It scared the cops. It scared everybody. Because it represented total and utter anarchy. Indoor anarchy. That's something that people haven't learned to get off with. But our experiences with those scenes is that that's where you get the highest . . ."

High on anarchy. That was one way of looking at it, back in the spring of 1966. Talking about it was like nothing so much as the proverbial crew of blind men, groping at the elephant, describing the whole based on the part they'd grabbed hold of. Kesey'd done his best to put it in a box, but regardless of how many bugles his package could accommodate, the whole scene didn't seem to quite fit. The Pranksters wandered off in search of new paisley-hued pastures, leaving San Francisco to figure itself out. With no lack of audience, energy or increasingly confident bands ready to push on to the next frontier of ogling sensory overload, all that was lacking was some consistent, coherent look and feel—a scene with rituals, rites and revelatory touchpoints that everyone could see, smell and taste and say "That's it. That's what it's about."

Anarchistic Buzz

It wasn't as easy as it sounded. Quite aside from the problems of renting, insuring and filling halls for their nascent dance/concert/happenings, the pioneering promoters were faced with the job of fashioning an evening of entertainment that was stable enough to be self-supporting while still retaining the anarchistic buzz everyone craved. The Red Dog, not to mention the Acid Tests and the Trips Fest, were not exactly paragons of organizational virtue. Firing off sidearms for an encore wouldn't impress the city fathers and dropping eggs on dancers' heads was a novelty certain to quickly wear thin. For a concert model, the Longshoremen's gigs seemed more like it. Nothwithstanding Luria Castell's assertion that each one was an attempt at "an event, something special," the Family Dog dances, like Graham's Mime Troupe benefits, seemed to assemble the best of the burgeoning subculture's creative handiwork while keeping the distracting, destructive or plain silly elements at least marginally in check.

It was a question, ultimately, of simplifying. Avantish 'happenings,' droning poetry mantras and non-scheduled free-form freaks were becoming less daring and shocking than plain boring. 'Serious' bohemian pretenses were fading, quickly being replaced by what was fun, flashy and workable from week to week.

Distilling and synthesizing was the next order of business, but for the foursome over at the Family Dog house, just trying to keep things from splintering entirely was a full time job.

"We'd put on four shows," Luria Castell recounts, "everyone loved them, but we were starving. We just weren't making any money." Counting on the all-for-one spirit of the moment, the Dog paid a visit to their only competition, Bill Graham. Chet Helms, a close friend of the Family Dog contingent at the time, picks up the story.

"They approached him about not doing shows at the same time. Graham was doing very well with the Mime Troupe benefits—there was a lot of community energy behind them—and he took a very cavalier attitude. He just went ahead and did another benefit on top of a Longshoremen's show. The audience then wasn't really large enough to split, so the Family Dog approached him again and offered to do all the legwork for the next benefit, just for the credit." It's a story Graham denies. "I never talked with them about coordinating shows."

Finding the Fillmore

"He told us he had absolutely no interest in doing rock & roll shows," insists Luria. Interested or not, Graham, according to Helms, asked them where they would hold the benefit if he agreed to let them on to the Mime Troupe bandwagon; they told him about a faded glory auditorium down in the heart of the ghetto called the Fillmore. The hall, which could hold 1,500 people, had long been a venue for visiting black artists, as Ron Nagle recalls. "I saw Ray Charles there around 1955 and I was the only white kid in the audience. This was way before civil rights and it was pretty scary. People were doing the dirty bop and lying on the floor twitching. One night a fight broke out and they turned off all the lights. All you could see was cigarette embers. Charles kept playing; he didn't know what was happening."

The Family Dog had been able to land the place, recalls Helms, "at something like $65 a night, $500 a month." Graham told the Dog he'd think about it and hightailed over to Fillmore and Geary to secure the lease on the place from its black owner, Charles Sullivan, just in time for the second Mime Troupe Benefit.

"Ralph Gleason, who was a big supporter of the benefit, suggested that I look at the Fillmore as a venue for the second benefit after I'd run all over town trying to find a place," recalls Graham.

Considering the subsequent rivalry between Helms and Graham—a fierce competition that would enrich San Francisco's psychedelic music scene—it's hardly surprising that accounts of their earliest efforts would vary. What's more intriguing, however, is the cooperative effort that marked the first shows at the Fillmore. It was a bit of early detente coming quickly on the heels of the original Family Dog demise. Earlier that year, disenchanted with the lack of income and the clock-punching hard work that went with producing the Longshoremen's shows, Alton Kelley and Ellen Harmon had pulled up stakes and headed for balmier climes—specifically Mexico in a yellow school bus. Jack Towle hung on for a few more weeks until he too lit out for points unknown, leaving the willing, but barely experienced Luria Castell holding the bag. Determined to keep the Dog on its paws, she had booked California Hall, adjoining the city's Civic Center, to hold what were going to be the biggest gigs yet—featuring all local line-ups, including the Charlatans and Jefferson Airplane.

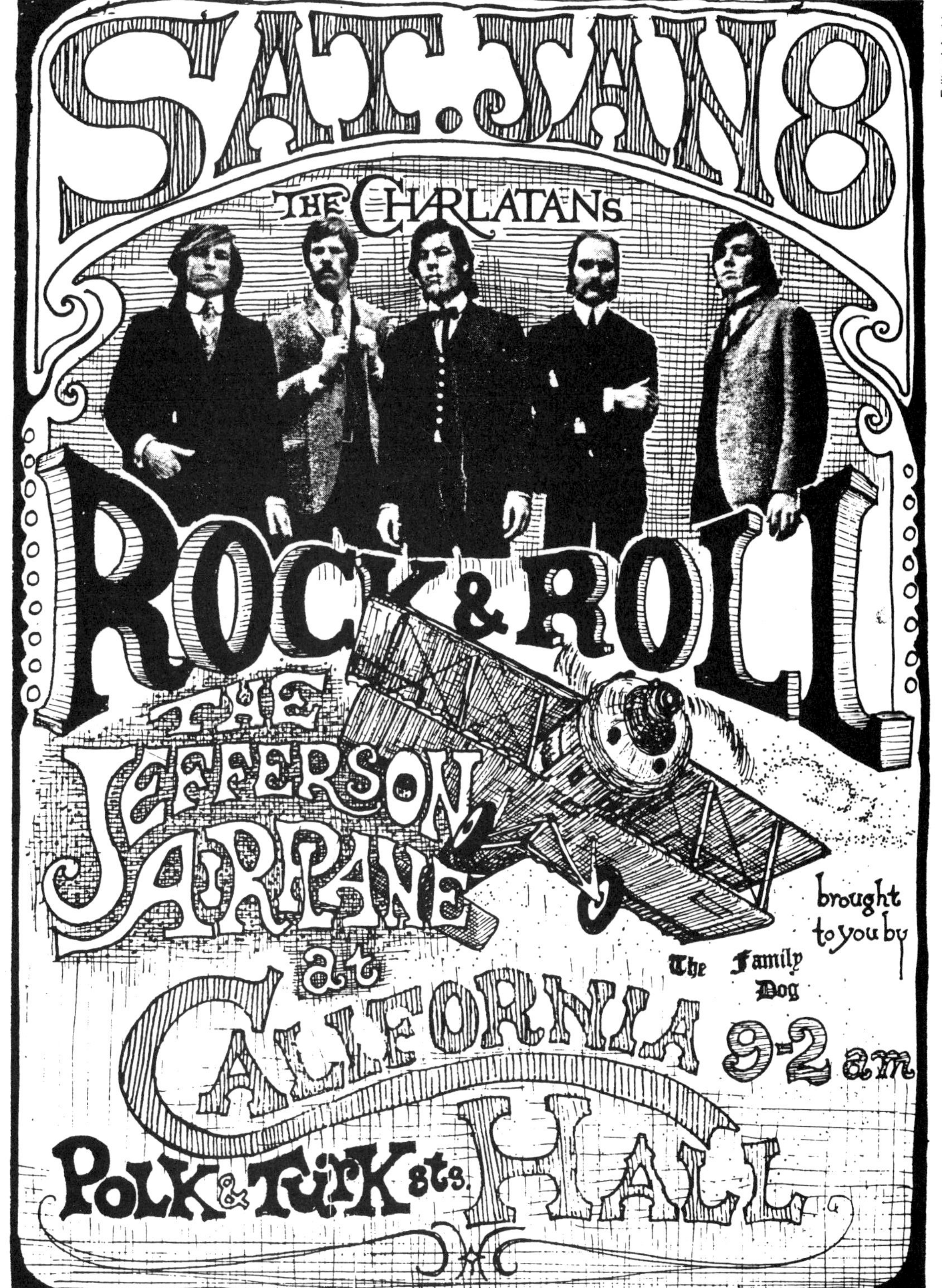

Editors' Archives

Man Buys Dog

But by now even Luria's visionary fervor was beginning to flag. Enter Chet Helms. "Chet had wanted to get into the original Family Dog, but we didn't think he had the force or energy to stage shows," Luria confides. Force or energy notwithstanding, Chet—who'd worked as a volunteer on the first Dog shows—had once thing Luria was desperately in need of. "She'd already booked the hall," Helms recounts, "and the show was in trouble. I loaned her all the money I had at the time,$250. Some of those early shows had budgets like that. At the last minute she split with the money. I don't blame her, she was under a lot of pressure, being left in the lurch and all." The date—which was to feature the Airplane, Los Angeles' Sons of Adam and a Chicago harpsman named Paul Butterfield—was aborted as Luria took up the trail of her cohorts south of the border. "I met a guy over at George Hunter's," she shrugs. "I fell in love and he said he wanted to take me to Mexico."

It was, after all, the tenor of the times. The financing and finagling of actual, ongoing concert promotion had the suspicious aura of real time employment about it. Something was changing. The Charlatans might still be dazzling the faithful with a full-blown fantasy crated complete from the Red Dog Saloon, but there was, in March of '66, already a certain . . . edge to the proceedings. There was money here, somewhere, a chance at the big time. "We had real freedom," Luria recalls. "We experimented with great stuff but we never followed through. I wish we'd been more committed."

Environmental Protection

Commitment, along with a talent for cold, calculating creativity, was something Bill Graham had in plentiful supply. "The Family Dog and I had a very different approach about who the public was and how they should be treated," he remarks. "It was a question of conducting business. I wanted to start on time. The attempt I made at the Fillmore was to turn people on, to give them a good time, but to work at it from the sidelines. There was no blueprint, no set of rules. You just had to work hard to create the right kind of environment. I remember at the end of concerts, I wanted to provide an atmosphere that would help people ease back into reality. We played taped classical music and showed slides of birds and trees. I always tried to put myself in the position of the ticket holder."

If Chet Helms lacked the same hardheaded opportunism as his rival, it seemed for a time that he'd made up for it with sheer visionary elan. His on-going management of 1090 Page Street's former basement band, Big Brother & the Holding Company, had set him on to a continuing quest to get the band

Editors' Archives

Editors' Archives

booked—somewhere, anywhere. "We played a lot of rent parties," he recalls, "and a couple of shows at a place called the Open Theater in Berkeley. It was the odd mix of bashes, benefits and theater events." Helms' partner at the time was the hard drinking manager of the Great Society, John Carpenter. "We made a deal to produce our own shows featuring our bands," remembers Helms. "We'd made our arrangement with Luria, but she had just split, and the holds on the dates at California Hall had been relinquished by default." The question was, where? "We went to the second Mime Troupe benefit at the Fillmore. John was a friend of Graham's and we got to talking to him, standing around the Coke bar. We told him about our bands and the trouble we were having booking them and he offered to let us use the Fillmore on alternate weekends. He asked us what name we would use and we kind of looked at each other and said, 'Family Dog, I guess.' "

Phonebooks and Thumbtacks

Helms and company set about staging shows back-to-back with Graham through February, March and early April; shows that headlined, among others, Big Brother, Jefferson Airplane, the Charlatans and the Great Society. It was a communal effort that would not be matched again in the ballroom annals. "We'd bring bands for Graham to hear," Helms continues. "Both John and I had phone books with a couple of hundred names in them. If we called every name in our books we could fill the hall. Posters were really not as important a factor in getting the word out as the fact that John and I actually phoned the audience."

Helms, in fact, emcee'd Graham's dance/concerts as well as his own, while John Carpenter sold tickets. It was not a partnership destined to flourish. Eventually, Helms asserts, Graham threw the duo out of the Fillmore on the pretext that they had not provided their own tape and thumbtacks to put up posters in the hall. "We had some dialogue about the way I ran things and the way they ran things," is Graham's account of the falling out.

The Family Dog was on the street again, but not for long. Helms heard about another available auditorium on Sutter Street, just around the corner from the auto showrooms along Van Ness Ave.

Family Dog at the Fillmore

Editors' Archives

Editors' Archives

The Avalon, with a capacity for 1,600 revelers, was perched atop a steep flight of stairs and when Helms first laid eyes on it, the place seemed like one more extension of the Charlatans' Barbary Coast daydreams. The red-flocked wall paper, crenellated balconies and gilt trim gave it the look of a Victorian vintage whorehouse or some kind of vaguely naughty can-can parlor. "The Avalon had a lot of nooks and crannies in it," recounts Helms, "a place for puppet shows, a lounge with fireplace, and lots of places to just hide away and smoke dope and ball, and there was this strange pit under the stage that could only be entered by a trap-door. The place had been built around 1913 and was originally the Puckett Academy of Dance—a name we had all sorts of fun with. The guy we rented it from agreed to a lease of $800 a month, but nothing was in writing. Actually the rent varied between $800 and $1800, depending on how we were getting along." The Avalon opened its doors April 22nd and 23rd with a double bill featuring the Great Society and visiting New Yorkers the Blues Project. That same weekend, Graham hosted L.A.'s Grass Roots, the Family Tree from Stockton and another up and coming Frisco band, Quicksilver Messenger Service, at the Fillmore.

Cooking Down the Chaos

By early summer 1966, the accidental, anarchistic thrill of finding good music when and where you could had boiled down to a choice betwen two competing halls, with barely a mile between them. If the thrill of the search was gone—the exhilarating rush of stumbling into some seedy loft or dim-lit warehouse and hearing the real stuff come rushing up to swallow you—the advent of the Fillmore Auditorium and the Avalon Ballroom marked a new era for San Francisco's blossoming home-grown sound. Suburban kids, savvy tourists, old-timers and upstarts—anyone, in fact, with a yen to be where it was at, now knew where to look.

They also knew what it looked like. Both Graham and Helms had cooked down the chaos of the Acid Tests to a single and simple formula for success. "I

Courtesy Raechel Donahue

Truce: Chet Helms and Bill Graham at Tom Donahue's wedding, 1969

evolved a lot of theories," says Helms. "Graham was always very into the giving apples away at the door type of thing and to me that set up a particular kind of psychology—it felt like if you didn't get your apple you didn't get your money's worth . . . the Green Stamp psychology. I didn't like that, so although we gave away favors and souvenirs and various things, I'd always have a crew of four or five people who would circulate through the audience and they would never be in any obvious way connected with the establishment. We always tried to create the atmosphere that this was the type of place where you went and people spontaneously gave you things."

"At the benefits," Grahams recalls, "the audience was mostly artists and others who were already on the scene. At the Fillmore they were all searchers and explorers. They left where they were and came in to exchange their identities. People just left the straight world and put on other clothes—like Clark Kent getting into a phone booth."

Whether or not the light shows, free apples and dress code would remain an indispensable part of the 'experience' or go the way of all flash remained to be seen. On those weekends, however, within the reverberating confines of those halls, all the acoutrements were unmistakably a part of 'groking' the flow, Being Here Now to codify the Aquarian credo for future generations. Somewhere along the line, *raisons* had gotten a little fuzzy. This was no longer entertainment—this was a grand goose up the evolutionary ladder.

By the time the summer of '66 roared up, the sound of San Francisco was a furious rush of creativity, naive pretense, and a hodge-podge of influence and innovation. San Francisco's long-percolating music scene was being championed by a handful of groups whose growth and development was, by any measure, extraordinary.

And the exemplar of all that extraordinariness was the Grateful Dead. Something strange and wonderful had taken hold of the band since their first tentative forays into electric music as the Warlocks. "It was Pigpen's idea," Garcia asserts. "He'd been pestering me for awhile. He wanted to start an electric blues band . . . theoretically it was a blues band, but the minute we got electric instruments it was a rock and roll band." The sudden switch in identity was accompanied by a quantum musical leap. Their fortuitous fellow-traveling with Kesey, Oswley and the Prankster circus had undoubtedly etched some intriguing new notions of the Possible into their collective synapses. The mix of styles brought to the band—Garcia's rootsy folk diet, Pigpen's degree in bluesology and Lesh's electronic orbits—was another contributing factor in the quintet's rapid musical growth. But the resulting sound, that dense, "scary", inexorable *wash,* was a galloping imponderable, as ominous and omnipresent as "rolling thunder," to use Ralph Gleason's words.

Chalk it up to the zeitgeist. After all, what the Dead were up to that summer had little in common with the hormone-activating ploys of traditional rock & roll and even less with lockstep pop formulas. In the hands of the Grateful Dead, rock was the soundtrack for a scene agog at the unfolding spectacle of psychedelia. Mystical eastern arcana, Indian headtrips, sci-fi fantasy flights, the secret teachings of the delta blues fathers, motorcycle fetishism, the Beat cosmos, the Wild West and the next frontier—somehow the Dead personified it all.

The Yardbirds Meet Bunny Berigan

"I really love the music scene," Garcia's long time girlfriend Mountain Girl, was quoted as saying, "but I still want to do something while I"m listening. I have this urge to be doing something." For Ms. Girl, like almost everyone else clogging the Fillmore and Avalon boards, that "something" was dancing. The Dead, along with all the other successful psychedelic aggragates in the city, was first, foremost and finally a dance band. Plugged into the surging communal high, audiences wanted nothing more than to sway, jiggle and stomp the night away.

Shades of Swing! Back in the late Thirties and early Forties a whole other youthful generation had danced their cares away to the sounds of the Big Bands. And whether it was Count Basie's "One O'Clock Jump," Bunny Berigan's "I Can't Get Started" or any number of Benny Goodman classics with the Let's Dance Band, each ensemble had a signature tune—a chance for the band to stretch out, showcase their soloists and improvise.

Things weren't so very different with the cream of San Francisco's ballroom bands, except for, maybe, a lack of highly polished musical chops. Songs had to be as long, rhythmic and sinuous as the lines of snake-dancers sliding across the floor. "We played long songs because people wanted to dance," Jerry Garcia concurs. "That's what it was all about. We always had a tendency to play a little long anyway, even when we were back in the pizza parlors and a lot of stuff we did was just open-ended. We had a piece later called 'Caution,' that was really just a long breakdown. It went from uptempo to ridiculous."

The notion of rock improvisation was not exactly dreamed up in the communes and rehearsal halls of Frisco. It had, in fact, taken root a few years earlier back in England with yet another band of art school dropouts called the Yardbirds. Evidence of the British quintet's extended approach to both blues and rock was in ample evidence on *Having A Rave Up With The Yardbirds,* featuring a five minute-plus harp and feedback transfiguration of "Smokestack Lightnin';" the LP was released in America in January of '66.

The approach was right up the Dead's blues cluttered alley, with a single, significant difference. In five minutes, Fillmore and Avalon terpsichoreans were barely

Up from the jugband: Jerry Garcia, 1966

Courtesy Victoria Aguirre

"Don't look for premiums or coupons as the cost of the tobacco blended in CAMEL cigarettes prohibits the use of them." TICKET OUTLETS: San Francisco—Discount Records, 262 Sutter; Bally Shoes; Music 5, 5th & Market; City Lights Book Store; Psychedelic Shop; Cedar Alley Coffee House. Oakland—Cal Records, 1320 Broadway; Stairway. Berkeley—Cal Records, 2350 Telegraph; Record City, 234 Telegraph. San Mateo—Record Specialist, Hillsdale Mall. San Carlos—Kramer's, 765 Laurel.

The Jordan Collection

Photo: Gene Anthony

The Dead rehearse downtown, 1966

getting warmed up. The energized audiences, consuming huge blocks of dance time, was ready for whatever the bands could dish up. For as long as they could dish it up.

And the Dead were more than equal to the challenge, pushing the limits of the most fundamental urban blues and folk riffs up and out beyond the realms of time and space, erecting huge spiral edifices of sound that seemed, after fifteen minutes, twenty minutes, a half an hour and beyond, to be fueling themselves, hurtling around the room in a perpetual motion centrifuge.

It was not, like most things that summer, a conventional approach. Traditional improvisational 'technique' had been, up to then, the exclusive turf of the jazzbos. No one on the scene then had the practiced skills of Parker or Coltrane or Monk. "None of us could really jam," admits the Mystery Trend's Ron Nagle. "That was something jazz musicians did. They were articulate on their instruments. We were incapable of doing that."

"Most of our songs we'd do in different tempos from show to show," recounts the Great Society's Darby Slick. "We thought of ourselves as jazz-influenced and were always looking for vehicles for improvisation. On 'Somebody To Love,' for example, I'd do a ten minute guitar solo before Grace would start singing. At different times Peter Vandergelder and Grace would trade off playing bass. It was fun, even though we didn't know a lot about music. I'd gotten a reputation for playing far-out solos and since I never really knew what I was going to do before a gig, the only thing I worried about was, you know, was it going to work this time?"

In fact, most of San Francisco's improv innovation (and excesses) was pretty elementary stuff, a simple game of hide and seek with the beat. Which was fine with the dancers. The Yardbirds formula with "Smokestack Lightin' " and later live with "Train Kept A Rollin'," "Good Morning Little School," and others was to play fast and loose with the tempo, building to a go-for-broke climax and then walking away from the smoldering wreck. The Dead and their brethren simply did the same thing three or four times in each song, leaning on the tempo, taking their time, slowly accumulating enough to drive the song into a solid wall of sound, then picking up the pieces and starting all over again.

Editors' Archives

The special, sometimes majestic, strength of The Grateful Dead was in their ability to play subtly but tellingly off each other's cues. The band was like a huge, cumbersome machine that, once cranked and humming, could accomplish all manner of delicate, elegant maneuvers. "We didn't sit around and work it up," explains Garcia. "Some songs were compositions, some were just evolutions."

Their repertoire of blues and R&B standards—the Rascals' "Good Lovin'," Martha and the Vandellas' "Dancin' In The Streets," the Stones' "Empty Heart," Bobby Bland's "Turn On Your Lovelight," and their tour de force—an epic, Pigpen-growled version of Wilson Pickett's "In The Midnight Hour"—was leavened by a smattering of folk-rock. But even their rendering of "Morning Rain," "I Know You Rider" or "Deep Elum" bore little resemblance to brittle, jangling Byrds-music. Pigpen's lumbering organ, Weir's chunky chording and the fat, rolling notes of Lesh's bass gave density and rich coloration to all the group's music. It was topped off by Garcia's patented filigree guitar runs—psychedelic roccoco at its finest.

The Grateful Dead had become the heavyweight champions of the scene, playing longer and rocking harder than any other band. The mantle had passed from the Charlatans with almost no one the wiser. "There was a disparity between us and a lot of the other groups," admits

Courtesy George Hunter

The Charlatans in a nautical mood

George Hunter. "I could see it growing. As a band, we didn't necessarily want to be associated with the hippie movement per se. Bands like the Airplane had some real tight numbers, but a lot of the fringe groups were getting really carried away."

While it remained true that the Charlatans lacked marketable musical skills, they had, by the time the ballrooms were in full bloom, evolved a nifty little folk-rock repertoire. "Their music wasn't taken as seriously as some of the others," recalls Ron Nagle. "They had a lighter approach." The band sported jaunty, ragtime rhythms in a carefully pruned selection of original and cover material. Drummer Dan Hicks had emerged as a genuine songwriting talent and some of the band's most popular numbers—"How Can I Miss You When You Won't Go Away?" and "I Scare Myself"—were from his pen. It was, more or less, a novelty sound, a conscious attempt to match music to their personas, and the group's hurdy gurdy tunes contrasted sharply with the mammoth epiphanies of the Dead.

The Charlatans did, however, have one genuine showstopper, their chance to stretch out and strut their stuff. The band transformed the modal harmonies and melodic hooks of the rural folk song "Alabama Bound" into something completely their own and as close to awesome as they ever got. On the right night they could push the song as fast and as furious as any other group's opus, sparking their minstrel show with a jolt of galvanizing rock & roll.

Nude Speakeasy

But the quintet was, even then, living on borrowed time. Since their return from Virginia City they had played a strange series of gigs, including a stint in a Broadway topless bar, highlighting the city's first totally nude girl, hoisted high above the patrons on a swing. "Dan would get up and sing 'Sweet Sue' to open her act," Hunter laughs. "It was really a speakeasy-type place, and it got kind of tight in there. Ferguson ended up pulling a knife on some guy . . ."

A short year later, the Red Dog seemed very a long way off and a very long time ago.

For Darby Slick's Great Society cohorts, the ballroom bonanza was a perfect opportunity to indulge their eclectic leanings. They were, in fact, star pupils in the earn-while-you-learn school of musicianship. Mike Daly, manager of the Mystery Trend, remembers one incident in particular, a gig on the night of the Trips Festival. "We were playing with the Great Society at the Gate Theater in Sausalito," he recounts, "and our guitarist, Larry West—we used to call him 'Way Out' West—got into this, like, twenty-minute guitar duel with Darby. It ended up with Larry smashing his guitar into the amp and storming off stage, totally freaked out." After the set was done, Darby recalls, he did his best to comfort the fused West. "We took a long walk," he says.

The Great Society had developed, through their devolution to jazz improvisation and eastern music, their own loopy brand of raga-rock, long before the Beatles invited the world to turn off its mind

THE MYSTERY TREND
THE GREAT SOCIETY
IN CONCERT AT THE GATE THEATRE, SAUSALITO
SUNDAY JAN. 23, 2 P.M. & 8 P.M.
DONATION $2.50

Courtesy Hamerschlagg Archives

and float down stream. Their standard approach was to build hypnotic, cyclical drones, then cut loose with freeform solos that lasted exactly as long as they felt like it. Aside from Darby's strange excursions, the mesmerising wail of Peter Vandergelder's saxophone became one of the band's trademarks, along with some high pitched yodeling from Grace, characteristically on the tune "Free Advice."

The band's often indulgent self-expression obscured the fact that they were, in fact, coming up with some real songs. "White Rabbit," and "Somebody To Love," were, in the hands of another band, to prove among the cleverest and most durable of San Francisco's forays into the pop mainstream. Grace, for her part, knew early on the direction she wanted the band to go. Her biography reports an incident at the very first Avalon show, where, after hearing the studied licks of The Blues Project, she railed against the rank unprofessionalism of her own group; a timely omen of changes afoot.

A Moment's Freakery

Yet if any one group personified the sheer, perverse freakery of the moment, it was 1090 Page's erstwhile basement jammers, Big Brother & the Holding Company. If the Grateful Dead were all mythic *strum and drang*—a rock & roll Ride of the Valkeries—Big Brother was an cosmic prank, a gaggle of miscreant savants whose jump-started sound lurched and careened with spastic abandon.

Since their Page St. apprenticeship, Big Brother had wandered off into some directions bizarre even by San Francisco standards. "At first we did a lot of cover material, but it got freaky pretty quick," recounts bassist Peter Albin. "A big influence was what the other bands were into; we fed off each other. After we'd gone through folk-rock and early Stones stuff, we veered off toward a jazz thing."

The improv imperative again; but at the hands of Big Brother, it bore no resemblance to anything even vaguely respectable. Some of the band's early shows highlighted their version of the theme from the Russ Meyer's sleaze flick *Kill, Pussycat, Faster, Faster* and an extended jam based on "Hall of The Mountain King" from Tchaikovsky's Pier Gynt Suite. "We'd do six bars and then go into something different every time. At the end we'd come back to the theme and James would shake his Danelectro amp for a funky reverb effect that sort of sounded like thunder, you know, in the spirit of the piece. We were never really into jazz. We *thought* we were, but we could never play a single jazz lick."

And precious few traditional rock licks, either. The mainstay of the band's early incarnation was the berserk guitar playing of Jim Gurley. "He reflected a lot of the sounds and noises and dissonances that were his childhood and it was wonderful," asserts Chet Helms. "He could make sounds like breaking glass on guitar and it was somehow still rhythmic. There was something fresh and innovative about him that was, in some ways, diminished by the demands that people put on him to become a formal musician."

Hamerschlagg Archives

Maybe. But by mid-'66, there was nothing holding Gurley back—certainly not the niceties of musical etiquette. The sounds he coaxed from the guitar on songs like "Light Is Faster Than Sound" were indeed the aural equivalent of bent wires, broken windshields, overheated metal and screeching rubber; the whole super-charged ambience of his destruction derby youth. "He used to play the national anthem to open up the races," Helms reports of the Gurley's early musical education.

Once on stage, however, while Gurley stood like a golem with blurry fingers, it was bassist Peter Albin who commanded attention. Wearing, more often than not, a black frock coat, he would shout his songs into the microphone like a Romilar-addled frog, leaping and twirling, exhorting the crowd in his alter-ego as 'The LSD Preacher.' "I did a thing tacked onto 'Amazing Grace,' " Albin recalls, "which was an improvised rap about a guy getting psychedelicised . . . he goes into church and this ranting priest gives him 'the sacrament.' "

"Since they had less of a mastered, polished approach, they could sometimes do really interesting stuff and make it work," recalls Jefferson Airplane bassist Jack Casady. "They'd play solos or some combination of notes that, if you've ever played live music, you'd never think of doing, but somehow it worked. "You'd scratch your head and say, 'It works, but what key is that guy in?' "

It's not surprising that the band got more than its share of strange gigs. Until they were replaced by the Dead, Big Brother had been adopted as the house band for the Frisco chapter of Hell's Angels and did a number of party/benefits for the motorcycle gang, along with innumerable one-off event and happenings. "We once did an art show called Blast," recounts Albin. "There were a lot of weird acts, including a black woman who played piano and sang to comic strips, mostly Flash Gordon. She'd use the lines from the balloons as lyrics; you know, like 'Flash, you can't go into that cavel ' and there were dancers behind her, going back and forth on swings."

Janis Arrives

There's no telling to what extremes of strange the group might have gone to if left to its own devices. But with the addition of a final member, in May of '66, Big Brother—along with the rest of the rock & roll world—would never be the same. "We talked about getting a vocalist very early," recounts Chet Helms. "I suggested Janis, but both Peter and Jim said, 'No, we saw her at the Coffee Gallery and she's too weird.' I didn't pursue it. But we couldn't find anyone else that measured up, so I suggested tracking her down again."

Janis Joplin was, in fact, back home in Austin, healthy again after a sustained absence from drugs and the frantic pace of the Frisco underground. "She was very concerned about getting back into drugs again," Helms continues. "I did my best to assure her that everyone had cleaned up from the hard stuff. It was LSD, a very different thing. She came back and the first few times she sang with the band, they weren't sure it was going to work out."

Not so, claims Albin. "We didn't really audition her," he insists. "Jim and I had seen her before and persuaded the others to bring her back. 'She's good, she'll work,' we kept saying. 'We know you're gonna like her.' "

Considering what Janis Joplin was to mean to Big Brother and, very quickly, the whole San Francisco music scene, it's small wonder that both Albin and Helms claim credit for recruiting her. Whatever the actual circumstance, Joplin returned to the city on June 5th and immediately began rehearsing with the band at their Henry St. digs. The group's first performance with their new vocalist was on June 10th at the Avalon Ballroom. She sang only two songs during the whole set, sitting out the lengthy freak-rock interludes atop an amplifier, banging a tambourine.

"I wasn't a strong singer," admits Albin, "and the fact was, girl vocalists were an added attraction to bands at that time. We worked with her a couple of weeks, maybe less before the show." Albin says that after Janis joined, the group began to tighten up considerably. They began a verse-chorus-verse regimen to showcase her considerable vocal skills and turned down the volume, when her throat began giving out from shouting above the din. She also insisted on better equipment, particularly an upgraded P.A.

"She brought a lot of songs with her," Albin continues. " 'Women Is Losers,' and the Chantels' 'Maybe.' We used to do a duet on 'Let The Good Times Roll' and

Janis goes electric, 1966

Courtesy David Getz

The Jordan Collection

'High Heel Sneakers.' " After the first couple of shows with their new front woman, including their first out-of-town gig down to Monterey, the group began getting comments from old-line (and hardcore) fans. " 'You guys are losing the craziness,' " is how Albin remembers the reaction. " 'You're getting more like the other bands in town. Get rid of the girl.' "

But if Janis was changing Big Brother, Big Brother was having a similar effect on Janis. "Vocally she started out with a very acoustic sound," Albin recounts. "It was very full and, in a lot of ways, very folksy, like Bessie Smith on some songs." One of the first times Albin had seen her was during her early trip to the coast, when she'd performed on a radio show called "Midnight Special," on station KPFA. "Everyone sat around a mike, kind of hootenanny style," he continues. "The Chambers Brothers were there, doing acapella gospel and I remember this kind of plumpish broad in a man's button-down shirt, no bra and a pock-marked face. She'd close her eyes when she'd sing and she had a lot of soul."

"She was a very folk-oriented person," concurs Mike Prichard, who spent time with Joplin around the same period. "She knew about her roots and was very serious about her intentions. I remember playing guitar with her. I was very into art music and she wanted to sing the blues. I was trying to play along and she just looked at me and said '*That's* not the blues.' 'It's the right notes,' I said. 'Yeah,' she said, 'but it's not the blues.' "

Three years later she was revved up and ready to match the wailing electric energy of Big Brother. "She had to change her vocal style," Albin continues. "It became much less colored. The range she had when she sang at low volume was fantastic, but she really had to *push* for that range with a rock & roll band. Towards the end of her first year with us, she started getting nodules on her throat. You could hear two or three overtones in each note."

Pieces Of Hearts

You could also hear the consuming passion that scorched the ears of the ballroom denizens. By the end of the summer, the billing, in most people's mind, was already 'Janis Joplin and Big Brother.' Whether she was transfiguring blues and R&B chestnuts or adding her keening moan to Big Brother's skewered originals (numbers such as Dave Getz's "Harry" or a yodel epic called "Gutra's Garden"), Joplin had become the group's larger-than-life focus. Tunes such as "I Know You Rider," Willie Mae Thornton's "Ball and Chain" or Erma Franklin's "Piece of My Heart" (a song suggested by Airplane bassist Jack Casady) were driven to raw emotional extremes by her flayed, ragged voice. Hunched over the microphone, her hands clutched and her hair falling into her face, she seemed, at times, peculiarly out of place in the paisley utopia of the psychedelic scene. The doomed urgency in her voice, shrill and hoarse by the end of every performance, unsettled the nonstop revelry.

"One day we all piled into a car, drove over to Marin, picked up a newspaper and looked up 'Houses For Rent,' Dave Getz

Big Brother & The Holding Company somewhere near Argentina

was to write, years later. "That same day we found a big house in the little town of Lagunitas . . . It was a beautiful day. Everything seemed to work out right. Nothing could go wrong; God had taken care of us perfectly . . . The house was at the end of a road way back in the woods with no other houses around it. On a big butane tank coming up the driveway, someone had scrawled 'God Is Alive And Well.' Later another had added 'In Argentina.' Eventually the house became known as 'Argentina.'

". . . Janis had a lovely, sunlit room like a porch which she decorated with plants. Like the room, she became her most peaceful and beautiful self during that time . . ."

"A lot of the early bands were just a collection of friends," ruminates Jerry Garcia, "some of whom could play instruments, some of whom couldn't. Later on, bands were constructed—put together for every specific purpose. Sometimes it was a manager's concept, sometimes a musician who wanted a certain kind of sound and went out and auditioned until he found the right people."

Which put Marty Balin way out ahead of his time. From the get-go there was very little that was accidental about the Jefferson Airplane. When asked by one of the band's biggest fans, Ralph Gleason, about his earliest ambitions, Balin remarked, "I really decided I wanted to be a singer. First I was going to get a band to back me . . . The musicians couldn't play well enough and I kept dropping guys and getting guys and dropping guys. When I first got the band together I ran it with an iron glove. I'd physically fight somebody to get my way because I knew the way it had to go. I was the navigator. I was the pilot. I knew how to fly it."

By the watershed summer of '66, the line-up was almost complete. Jorma Kaukonen had summoned a D.C. bassist to the coast to try out for the fledgling group late in 1965. The affable Jack Casady: "He told me they needed an electric bassist for a band he'd just joined with a funny name. I really wasn't into folk music at all. I'd played rock & roll in clubs back east for years." It was September of '65 and, as Casady recalls, the group was still stradling the folk fence. "Signe brought a stool onstage and sang something about strawberries. I wasn't real fond of the spruced-up folk approach, but I stuck around anyway."

Casady's rocking bass, replacing the stand-up plunking of Bob Harvey, helped crystallize the group's emerging musical style. "First we put pickups on the guitars," Kantner recounts. "Then Jorma got a Rickenbacher 12-string and I got an electric 6-string. We were very enthusiastic, once it got rolling." "We'd always considered ourselves folk people," Balin adds. "Then Paul and I said 'No, this is rock; that's where it's at.' "

It was indeed. "We'd like to break nationally," Balin told Gleason, "that's one thing we'd like to do." They stood a better chance than most. The band, under the firm creative guidance of Balin and his increasingly collaborative sidekick Paul Kantner, had evolved a distinct, palatable brand of folk-rock. The band's sound was, initially, a bracing contrast to the prevailing ethic of dwarf-star density and rampant freedom of expression. There was a disciplined edge to even the Airplane's highest flights of fancy—an emphasis on vocal finesse that kept the extraneous instrumental highjinks in check.

Echoes In The Stratosphere

If Garcia and Gurley dazzled ballroom audiences with fanciful and fearsome picking, the Airplane held the crowd in thrall with intricate three-part harmonies that highlighted Balin's plaintive and alluring tenor. Kantner and Kaukonen's dual lead guitar work defined a kind of tasty understatement that was to become the band's trademark. At a time when overload was the order of the day, the Airplane championed a less-is-better aesthetic. "We didn't do a lot of extended solos back then," Casady confirms. "The more freeform, stretched-out stuff didn't develop until later," adds Kantner.

"It was Jorma who eventually brought out the improvisational part of the band, or at least pushed it up front," recalls Kantner. Balin's distinctive vocals continued, in the meantime, to be the centerpiece of the group, particularly on numbers such as the turgid I-gotta-be-me ballad "And I Like It," and a soaring rendition of John D. Loudermilk's "Tobacco Road," previously a Top 40 hit for England's cheery Nashville Teens. "It's No Secret,"

Editors' Archives

another Balin showcase, made instantly accessible use of Balin's folk-rock chops with lots of ringing guitars, rich harmonies and diverting wordplay. It quickly became the group's signature tune. Other ballroom favorites included a delicately arranged Balin/Kantner ballad "Come Up The Years," the brooding, evocative original "Blues From An Airplane," and the rocking "Bringing Me Down."

While other groups reveled in relentless experimentation, the Airplane was working hard to hone a sound capitalizing on the sextet's not-inconsiderable skills at writing and playing. The resulting musical mix was among the most distinctive on the scene. The illusion fashioned by the band at its best was that of vast, empty spaces, a kind of sonic stratosphere in which the separate musical elements approached from a long way off, blending briefly before soaring off on their own trajectories, trailing thick, textured echoes.

Yet the Airplane, like the other ballroom heroes, swung wildly from transcendant to terrible on stage. When it wasn't working for Balin and company the whole carefully constructed assemblage flew apart for lack of sturdy structure. All the drama of the arrangements could collapse, at a moment's notice into a confused babble of conflicting musical monologues, revealing that even the most polished of San Francisco band's was subject to the same uncertainties that made each dance/concert an exercise in not-so-calculated risk.

Jefferson Airplane, 1966: Signe cleared for take-up

Hamerschlagg Archives

Blues Madonna

While other bands could make up for gaffes with a shrieking, improvised lead guitar solo, what the Airplane did was too precisely packaged, too interdependent to survive a shoddy performance. It was an ironic fact of the band that the *music* was the main attraction. The Dead had become a cultural event; Big Brother, a freak show starring a tattered blues madonna; the Airplane's focus was a short, shy, singer who seemed more interested in hitting his notes than blowing your mind.

Signe Anderson wasn't much help. Normally the focus of a group, this particular girl singer seemed more like an extra from an American Friends Service fund raiser. With braided hair parted down the middle and tied off in ribbons, she appeared on stage to be exactly what she was: an adjunct to Balin's vocal prowess. By the close of the summer Anderson had, in fact, a distinct conflict of interest. She'd given birth to a daughter and her husband, who served as the group's lighting man, was threatening to withdraw his wife if certain concessions weren't made. The group decided it was time for a change; the departure of Signe Anderson was hardly a crippling blow to their image.

Neither, for that matter, was the loss of drummer Skip Spence. He was replaced quickly by a New York-born, L.A.-raised, jazz-inclined percussionist named Spencer Dryden. Signe's replacement was another matter. "I've always liked a strong woman who can sing," Kantner admits, "so I used to go around to the different clubs to check out the competition."

The Great Society's frontwoman, Grace Slick, could certainly sing. She was also about as strong a woman as Kantner and his cohorts could have bargained for. Iron-willed, independent and ambitious, Grace's tenure with her husband's band was not going particularly smoothly. She had, in fact, been discontent since the Great Society played with the Blues Project back at the Avalon opening. "After I heard the Blues Project," she says, "I knew what I wanted to do, but it wouldn't be possible to cram five years of musical knowledge into two months in order to open up our band with intricate harmonies and improvisations."

Grace's soaring voice and galvanizing stage presence was just what the Airplane was looking for. "The Great Society had played with us on some shows," recounts Jack Casady, "and I remember liking some of their numbers; 'Sally Go 'Round The Roses,' and 'Somebody To Love.' " "The band was okay," adds Kantner, "but it was Grace who made the main impression." She made such an impression, in fact, that Kantner couldn't bring himself to ask her to join the group and recruited Casady instead. Grace was ready.

And the Great Society, in Darby's words, "was crushed." The band had been waiting around all summer for their manager, Howard Wulfe, to land them a long-promised record deal. Darby Slick: "Grace came and told us she was going to join the Airplane. She asked Jerry what he thought and he said 'great.' I felt betrayed. The really ironic thing was that the next day a recording contract came in the mail." It was too late. In October of '66, the Society disbanded, canceling

The Jordan Collection

their deal with Columbia Records. Darby left, shortly thereafter, for India to study music, while Jerry re-established his ties to the advertising industry.

For the Jefferson Airplane, it was apparent almost immediately that Grace Slick was the potent factor that would push them over the top. Although still technically the artistic property of Howard Wulfe, she was 'purchased' for the

Airplane by their manager Bill Graham (taking over from Matthew Katz, who promptly sued) for the sum of $750. "She brought a lot to the group," says Casady. "She had a unique voice, she wrote songs and played the recorder, piano and some guitar. Her stance on stage wasn't that of a standard female singer of the time; she was aggressive, she attracted attention."

On October 14th, Grace showed up backstage at the Fillmore to listen to the band she was shortly to join. Signe Anderson had not yet officially left the group, but with minutes to go before they were to take the stage, it was clear she was not going to make the gig. "I thought Signe was going to still be singing for another couple of weeks," recalls Grace. "And she didn't show up!" Paul asked her if she thought she could fill in. "I really wasn't ready," she continues, "but I guess I figured it was only rock & roll and why not. The first thing that struck me was how loud they were . . . I couldn't hear myself singing. I had no idea what notes I was hitting, but . . . the audience seemed to enjoy the novelty of a new singer."

It was a novelty that was soon to become the catalytic factor, both in the band's music and their popularity. Grace Slick added an element of unpredictability to the sound of the Airplane with her booming, almost operatic vocal style, powering through the carefully arranged tunes and sparking them with crackling energy. The band's repertoire was enriched with the addition of some Great Society showstoppers, particularly "White Rabbit," which became a surreal, spiraling 'trip' and "Somebody To Love," which quickly replaced "It's No Secret" as the group's trademark.

If Balin's subtle vocal colorations were sometimes lost in the wash of Grace's overpowering pipes; if the early odd and endearing juxtaposition of styles and nuances became subordinate to this imposing female's voracious vocal style; if folk-rock had given way to real-rock, well then, so much the better. San Francisco had found its musical ambassadors in the Jefferson Airplane—the band who could take it to the hinterlands and make it stick.

"Psycho-babble In A-minor"

For the Mystery Trend, meanwhile, things were rapidly becoming unstuck. The band that had been around from the beginning was getting precious little recognition and for some very obvious reasons. "It was put to me specifically by Chet Helms," Ron Nagle relates. "He told us we couldn't play the Avalon because we didn't have 'missionary zeal.' Which meant either we didn't take enough acid or the nature of our music didn't fit into whatever the message was."

Or, maybe, that Nagle's group had gotten out of step with the times. By late '66, the San Francisco Sound had, for all practical purposes, been codified. For all the lip servcice paid to experimentation and Doing One's Own Thing, the music was adhering to a specific set of criteria—long, meandering songs with big spaces for jams and improvisation, obscure and/or obtuse lyrics and a sense of self-importance directly proportional to the growing status of musicians as quasi-religious

Grace bestowed on Airplane. From left to right: Kantner; Slick; Balin; Kaukonen; Dryden; Casady.

warrior/heroes. "I was somewhat older than the people who were starting to delve into this thing," continues Nagle. "I was aware of *songwriters* and I knew there was something else beside all this psycho-babble in A-minor. I knew a song had to have structure. It was nothing new; it was the same thing that Ray Davies and John Sebastian knew, and they were having hits . . ."

Having hits. That's where Nagle and company parted ways with the emerging San Francisco establishment. "You can't be in music and not think of the commercial aspect of what you're doing," concedes Jerry Garcia, but in Frisco's glory days, wanting to hear yourself on the radio was the last thing you'd admit to your friends. "Nobody listened to Top 40," confirms Paul Kantner. "We didn't start out wanting to be on the radio or even working in that direction. We didn't want to know anything about that stuff."

Nagle did, but it wasn't doing his group any good. "We got to be known as the most uptight band in the Bay Area," he laughs, "neurotic, nervous, unsure of ourselves on stage unless we got completely bombed. Which was another reason we couldn't get a gig. The whole thing between druggies and drinkers was still going on and we definitely enjoyed cocktails."

The problem, Nagle concludes, was simply a lack of naivete. "How could I be impressed with improvisational rock?" he asks. "I'd been to the Jazz Workshop and the Blackhawk in the Fifties. I'd heard the best. Why would I want to get up there and wank off?"

But in the pulsing wombs of the Fillmore and Avalon, the Fifties seemed light years away; a decade when no one knew the transcendant, mind-altering, social/political/sexual/spiritual power of sacramental rock & roll. San Francisco, the band's and their followers, were sure they'd found the key that unlocked the secrets of rock's ancient tribal heritage. A lot of the pretense—charming and otherwise—that accompanied the flowering of San Francisco's psychedelic music scene was a holdover from socially conscious folk era so many of its musicians grew out of. They'd come of age, after all, singing Woody Guthrie laments, getting their skulls cracked for Civil Rights and earnestly slumming with beatniks in cold water flats. "Significance" came naturally.

Chopped, Channeled Cipollina

"I was raised in Mill Valley a couple of miles from Sausalito. West coast jazz was really big then—Dave Brubeck, George Shearing, Ahmad Jamal, Cal Tjader, it was all part of this Beat thing. We'd drive past the houseboats and my mom would say,'That's where the bohemians live.' Back then there was a real division within the Beats, you know, the serious ones and the ones who were really the same as hippies. They were like beatnik party animals who really had no social comment to make, who were just looking for a good time. That's where I was at, a lightweight beatnik, you know? When I first heard the word 'hippie,' I thought, 'Hey, that sounds pretty bad, like 'beaners' or 'spearchuckers.' It's degrading . . . I can go for it.' "

For John Cipollina, all the deeply serious and socially relevant aspirations of folk-spawned and Beat-nurtured musicians was sort of . . . well, beside the point: the point being the frivolous and transitory joys of rock & roll. Back when Mrs. Cipollina drove her eldest son past the boho houseboat enclave on the mudflats outside Sausalito, there was nothing even remotely respectable, not to mention significant, about playing loud electric instruments.

For Cipollina the real charge came from the glitzy, high-gloss lure of rock. He couldn't, he admits, help himself. "I remember the first time I ever heard an electric guitar. I asked my mom, who was a music teacher, what that sound was. It was like John Glenn seeing a jet airplane for the first time."

He learned the instrument by watching others play. "I was a spacey kid. I'd go to a dance and my Dad would be real happy because I was getting social. He always wanted me to go out and get laid. So when I'd get home he'd ask me if I'd danced with any pretty girls. I'd say, 'Well, there was this guitarist . . .' He was really worried."

Cipollina's unhealthy attraction to the icons and idols of rock & roll put him outside the prevailing work-shirt-and-picket line ethic of the Bay Area music establishment. The difference was evident even before he tried making a living off his guitar. "While most kids were drawing '49 Fords or '50 Mercs on their binders I was drawing chopped and channeled Telecasters. It just wasn't socially acceptable. I mean, I was ostracized from the local folk scene, completely blackballed. Barbara Dane was the only folkie who would let me play with her. All-acoustic Martins were the mainstay; folk music was an attempt to do something 'refined.' Playing electric guitar was really just another way of saying fuck. It was an unwritten law; it's okay to play rock & roll until you were eighteen; after that it was folk."

Or nothing. Cipollina's obligatory, and sometimes hair-raising apprenticeship with a string of teen bands—including the Deacons and the Penetrators—refined his penchant for the rumbling, twanging licks of Link Wray and Duane Eddy, along with sharpening his survival instinct. "In the teen groups we were always being threatened by other musicians. You know, you'd hire a VFW hall or something, provide drinks from the local Coca Cola bottler and at the end of the night, collect the money and divvy up what was left. It was a common practice for guys in other bands to come in and flush a cherry bomb down the toilet. You'd have to pay for the plumbing repair and it would wipe out the profit."

After graduation Cipollina served a brief and unhappy term as a real estate salesman. Anything, it turned out, was better than hawking office space for Trade Center Properties in a suit and tie, and eventually he fell in with another local guitarist and harp player, Jim Murray. The two, in turn, met a transplanted Greenwich Village folkie by the name of Dino Valenti, who had some very grandiose ambitions indeed. "He was the first person I'd met who was a totally professional entity," relates Cipollina, "a really intense little guy. He was being managed by Donahue at the time and had a history of folk stuff along the lines of Chad Mitchell and the Kingston Trio. But Dino wanted to go new wave. He wanted to start a rock & roll group to do his stuff. He'd already attracted a lot of attention with 'Get Together.' "

Dino Valenti, aka Chester Powers, lured Cipollina and Murray with the time honored c'mere-boys I'm-gonna-make-you-a-star ploy. They fell for it eagerly. "Up to that point all I'd ever done was Top 40 covers," confesses Cipollina. "Here was a guy with original material and a real manager. I jumped at the chance. He had all kinds of ideas; he talked about getting a chick in a low cut deerskin dress to play a tambourine with real coins for clappers. He talked about wireless guitars, he talked about all kinds of things. He used to have a valet who drove him around. It looked like the real thing."

Waiting For Dino

It was late '64 and Cipollina had moved right in with the beatniks on Sausilito's floating houseboat ghetto, living in an old ferryboat with a flamenco troupe and an assortment of sodden n'ere-do-wells. Valenti hired him as a lead guitarist, along with Murray, and lined up some dates at Big Daddy's North Beach club, Mother's. It looked like Cipollina was finally going to turn a buck from his childhood obsession.

Until, that is, Dino got busted for possession of killer weed. " 'We'd start rehearsals tomorrow', Dino told us, but the next day, before we had a chance to play a note together, he was busted in Sausalito and hauled off to jail. Jim and I sat around thinking he'd be out real soon—they told us he'd be sprung on Tuesday, then Thursday, then the following Tuesday and meanwhile we were sleeping up on Mount Tamalpais in my '54 Plymouth."

While they waited, they met another recently incarcerated musician who happened also be a friend of Valenti's. David Freiberg was a died-in-the-wool folknik, a twelve-string guitar player who had once been in a duo with the jocular name of Folk Singers For Peace. FSFP had toured South America, celebrating the joys of pacifism, and on their way back home had been arrested in Mexico for fomenting revolution and promptly deported. All that was past him now, however; when he hooked up with Cipollina and Murray, Freiberg had just gotten out of the slammer where he'd served time for the same herbal offense as Valenti. "He wanted to play bass," Cipollina recounts, "so I loaned him one I had in the trunk of my car and he started hanging around."

Shortly thereafter, they recruited a drummer named Casey Sonoban and another guitarist named Skip Spence—the same Skip Spence that was soon to be pounding skins in Marty Balin's Airplane. Balin was letting the fledgling group practice at the Matrix and it was there that he stole Spence away. It was not long after that Sonoban also left the band, leaving Cipollina, Freiberg and Murray to fend for themselves.

Enter Gary Duncan and Greg Emore, a guitarist and drummer respectively who had planted the same kind of rock roots as Cipollina. The two had served a lengthy apprenticeship in a string of San Joaquin Valley garage bands, culminating in an outfit called the Brogues which had disbanded when its bassist enlisted and its keyboardist, according to Cipollina, "went gay or something." Duncan and Elmore were living in North Beach at the time, in the basement of 52 Water St. "It was a crazy little alley," Cipollina recounts. "My Plymouth happened to break down in front of their house. We were just gonna stay the night, but ended up there for four months. It was a wild place; a bunch of neighbors had gotten together and painted a long, Chinese dragon down the street. There was lots of LSD, no money and lots of living off the streets, which, coming from a good family was very strange for me. It was Fat City . . ."

Editors' Archives

Quicksilver on their ranch. From left to right: John Cipollina; David Freiberg; Jim Murray; Greg Elmore; Gary Duncan.

Courtesy Evelyn Cipollina

I'll Start My Own Charlatans . . .

In more ways than one. With the addition of Elmore and Duncan, the group finally began to jell. "They weren't folkies," asserts Cipollina. "I mean, folk musicians at that point were trying to get naughty, playing folk structured music on electric guitars. But Gary, Greg and myself. . . we were already deep into it. . ."

And getting deeper. The band had, in fact, a distinct leg up on the rest of the psychedelic elite, laboring gamely to transmute folk and jazz influences into the electric idiom. For Cipollina and company, rock was already the common coin; even when they dabbled in jazz and blues, it was filtered through a collective appreciation of backbeat fundamentals. The band's early repertoire included songs that would serve them well throughout their career—"Mona," "Who Do You Love," "Smokestack Lightning" and later, Del Shannon's "Runaway." The quintet's penchant for syncopated rhythms and cyclical arrangements would become perfectly suited to the demands of ballroom audiences. But the contrast to the eclectic extensions championed by other groups was marked; this was music that owed less to riffing and strumming than unadorned rock & roll licks. The folk contingent in the group, specifically Freiberg and Murray, knew a good thing when they heard it—the result was the first Frisco aggregate with rock & roll in its blood.

John Cipollina, guitarist

Courtesy Evelyn Cipollina

Cipollina was, however, still keeping his options open. That summer he went on a pilgrimage to Virginia City to see the Charlatans. "They were outrageous," he recalls, "they had long hair and were playing weird rock & roll. They were way ahead of their time and I was totally in awe of them. I heard rumors that they had copped a Thompson submachine gun and I thought, 'How do I get in this band?' Then I heard Wilhelm had been busted and I saw my chance. I went up to them and said, 'Hey look, I'm letting my hair grow, I've got my own gun and everything. Just give me a chance.' They kind of patted me on the head and told me to go out and practice, you know, shoot some bottles or something. So I

Courtesy Evelyn Cipollina

went back to Frisco, thinking, 'If they won't let me into the band I'll start my own Charlatans.' "

Back home, Cipollina discovered that Dino Valenti had at long last been sprung from jail. The band at last had a full cast assembled, but for reasons known only to the inscrutable Valenti, he took a strong dislike to Elmore and Duncan and refused to join the band that he'd brought into being. It was just as well. Two days later, he was popped again and promptly returned to jail without passing 'Go.'

Who needed him? The Valenti-less gang went on to play their first live shows at the Matrix in the fall of '65. They had remained, up to that point, nameless. "Finally we were given an ultimatum," Cipollina recounts. "We couldn't work there anymore unless we had a name. We came up with a few ideas; the Cosmic Crystal Set was one, and we played a gig as Vulcan. It came down to 'Find a name by Wednesday, or else.' They needed something to put on the marquee. Jim and David kind of pieced Quicksilver Messenger Service together. It sounded funny enough to use."

The newly christened band played its first official show as Quicksilver Messenger Service at a Christmas party hosted by the Committee. "Howand Hesseman offered us two ounces of grass if we would record a rock & roll version of the 'Star Spangled Banner.' The Charlatans had been hired first, but that fell through and we agreed to fill in. The only problem was, we didn't know the words and had to go out and buy the sheet music."

The band was paid, aside from the weed, $200 for their pre-Hendrix rock rendering of the National Anthem and with the money made a move to Marin Country, to another houseboat enclave near Larkspur. "We lived that winter on the water," Cipollina continues. "We didn't have much work and it was really cold. We burned everything we could in the house to keep warm and when we used everything up, we'd sneak out in the middle of the night and rip up the neighbor's boardwalks."

Vibrato and Timberwolves

The group's next stop was a brief one: the redwood bedroom community of Mill Valley where they met their manager Ron Polte. "He was a gangster," Cipollina says flatly, "a hardcore stick-up man and a four time loser. Basically, he was a lock artist who could break into anything, which came in handy for getting into clubs sometimes." Polte, it turned out, arrived just in time to pull the band from yet another run-in with the law. "Our place in Mill Valley was three blocks from the bus station and we had all these 13-year-old runaways hanging around. The cops didn't like it at all. We told Polte we needed space to 'be artists,' that we'd be a great band if we could get out in the country and not be bothered. What we *really* wanted to do was go out in the woods to shoot off guns and raise hell. So he got us a ranch."

Quicksilver was now prepared to take the Charlatans' fantasy one preposterous step further. In the meantime, however, their music was beginning to take shape. Rehearsals at their 88-acre ranch near Point Reyes Station, 25 miles northwest of Frisco, were resulting in a sharp, stinging instrumental attack centered around Cipollina's guitar playing. It was a trebly, staccato, vibrato-ladened sound, bolstered by Duncan's lean, mean rhythms. Even in the heat of extended improvisation there was a cool economy to Cipollina's work, and as the group began landing more and more ballroom shows, the gaunt guitarist with shoulder-length hair became the center of attention. Around this razor's-edge pivot, the rest of the group had begun to mold a driving, uncluttered ensemble sound, highlighting slickly arranged tunes that were turned inside out and stood on their head during the course of lengthy, labyrinth-like jams.

Throughout the spring and early summer, Quicksilver shared the stage with the city's best bands and the cream of the visiting musical statesmen, including Bo Diddley, Paul Butterfield, Young Rascals and even, on one bizarre Fillmore billing, frat crooners The Association.

But it wasn't all hard work. "Gary Duncan and I went right out and bought cowboy's hats," Cipollina recounts. "If we were going to live on a ranch we'd do it in style." Cipollina also bought a genuine Northern McKenzie timberwolf as a pet. "The only bands living out there in the San Geronimo Valley were us and the Grateful Dead . . . They really got into archery and went into this big red Indian trip as a result. So there we were, acting out our cowboy fantasies while the Dead were whooping it up with bows and arrows."

It was Virginia City with a vengeance. One evening, when Quicksilver and their extended family were gathered in the bunkhouse for an after dinner smoke, the entire Dead clan burst in, decked out in their finest Apache regalia and toasted on LSD. "They were all over us before we knew what happened," Cipollina admitted to *Zig Zag's* Pete Frame, "carrying tomahawks and firing arrows into the walls." The cowboys wasted no time in plotting their revenge. "Two weeks later," Cipollina continues, "the Dead were due to play the Fillmore with the Airplane . . . Our plan was to wear all our cowboy gear, masks and guns, and take over the stage. We practiced a 15-minute version of 'Kaw-liga Was A Wooden Indian' which we were going to play on their instruments to humiliate them."

Reality, however, has a way of intruding. On the night of the raid, the black community in the Fillmore ghetto was up in arms over a recent police shooting incident. As Quicksilver arrived at the ballroom, guns and masks in place, cops swarmed out of the woodwork. "They were all over us," Cipollina laughs. "We tried to explain, but they wouldn't believe we were anything less than hippie revolutionaries bent on exploiting the indignation of the blacks." Murray and Freiberg were hauled off to the cooler and the Dead's massacre went unrevenged.

The music of Quicksilver Messenger Service, however, continued to define much of what was exciting about San Francisco rock & roll. The band's repertoire eventually sported as wide a range of influences as any other group's, but even folk numbers like Hamilton Camp's "Pride Of Man," or "Babe, I'm Gonna Leave You (St. John's River)," both brought to the band by Freiberg, were subject to the wicked domination of Duncan and Cipollina's slashing style. The band's reworking "Co'dine", stretched taut as a bow string and punctured by dramatic pauses, consistently cut other bands' versions of the same song to ribbons. Quicksilver could creep, cat-like, around the edges of Mose Allison's "If You Live (Your Time Will Come)," then pounce on the beat and explode in an intense interplay. Their "Walkin' Blues" became a steely, metallic march and "Backdoor Man" a menacing walk through a bad neighborhood—in comparison, the Doors' rendering sounds flaccid.

It was a sound designed to flay away the superfluous and, late in '67, founding member Jim Murray himself proved expendable. With his departure, the group reached its creative apex, reworking its sound as a lean quartet and playing an astonishing set on New Year's Eve at the Winterland Ballroom with Jefferson Airplane and the Grateful Dead. A few days before they had signed a recording contract with Capitol Records for one of the healthiest advances of the time.

Quicksilver Messenger Service completed the pantheon of San Francisco's premier psychedelic groups. Along with Grace Slick and the Airplane, Big Brother and Janis and the good ol' Grateful Dead, they were attracting international media attention as musical spokesmen for the entire, baffling sub-cultural circus. Whatever was going on down in that hunk of genteel Frisco ghetto called the Haight Ashbury; whatever it was that was drawing the youth of America's middle class like lemmings; wherever it was all going, it was the music of the Bay that was fueling it. A single, feedback-drenched note could tell you more than all the pontifications of social scientists put together.

The World Is Watching

Which didn't keep the newsmen from trying to put their finger on it. By 1967, no self-respecting newspaper or magazine had neglected its own expose on the Frisco explosion and more often than not, the focus was on the music. It was no longer up the *Berkeley Barb,* or indigenous fanzines like *Mojo Navigator*

Courtesy Gary Goodrow

to spread the word. *Time* and *Newsweek* prose-masters worked overtime to bring the sights and sounds to the heartland, encouraging, in the process, the mass exodus. "Until recently it was an underground sound," intoned *Newsweek* in December of '66, "the personal and private expression of the hippies, the new Bohemians who have flocked to permissive San Fransicisco. Today, aboveboard, the San Francisco Sound is the newest adventure in rock 'n' roll. It's a raw, unpolished, freewheeling, vital and compelling sound. And it's loud."

But not so loud as the sound of journalists' thundering hooves as they beat a path to the temple of Now. "In its permutations," declared *Time* in June, '67, "the San Francisco Sound encompasses everything from bluegrass to Indian ragas, from Bach to jug-band music—often with the framework of a single song. It's a raw, raucous, rough-hewn sound that has the spark and spontaneity of a free-for-all jam session . . . The sound is also the scene. With its roots in the LSDisneyland of the Haight Asbury district, the music is a reflection of the defiant new bohemians . . ."

Do tell. Or rather, do see. In March of '66, *Life* ran a lurid spread on the "Exploding Threat Of The Mind Drug That Got Out Of Control," featuring blurred and time-lapse snaps of wildly frugging dancers at an Acid Test. Not to be outdone, *Look* sent its correspondent on a journey to the heart of weirdness. "An explorer of the worldwide Underground," the tag read, ". . . finds, behind its orgiastic Happenings and pot-seed pancakes, a wild Utopian dream." In fact, most of the wild new world had already passed into history. Ken Kesey and his Pranksters had planned one last Acid Test—a graduation—for Halloween night, 1966, at the Winterland Ballroom. When Bill Graham got wind of Kesey's plan to dose the crowd, he quickly called off the whole thing.

Once they got started, there was no stopping the newshounds. January '68 gave middle America its first good look at Frisco freaks in a special issue of *Look*. Under the heading "The Incredibles", an Irving Penn photo spread featured group shots of Big Brother and the Dead, along with assorted Family Doggers and a portrait of Mike Ferguson, his wife and kid. "People reading *Look* Magazine in Montezuma, Iowa, might see our clothes and say, Wow," read the unattributed captaion next to the Big Brother shot. "To us, it's just a life style, a total thing."

The opinions of Montezumians notwithstanding, it looked, by late '67, as if psychedelic music was here to stay. And there was no better indication of the sudden commercial viability of all things Frisco than the appearance on pop charts of tunes celebrating the good vibes of the Flower People. When a painfully sincere Scott McKenzie reminded the world to "be sure and wear some flowers in your hair" when visiting "San Francisco", it was not to the drone of an electric guitar—the tune reached the Top Five in July of '67. Two months later the Animals' Top Ten hit "San Francisco Nights" did a better job of talking about what was happening than giving listeners a taste of the real thing. Across the Atlantic, the Flower Pot Men's "Let's Go To San Francisco (Parts I & II)" clued English fans to the transcendant joys of psychedelic togetherness.

But the scene's flirtation with its own commercial potential was by no means limited to outsiders looking in. The San Francisco Sound was beginning to spring up all over the place.

Photo Chuck Kroll

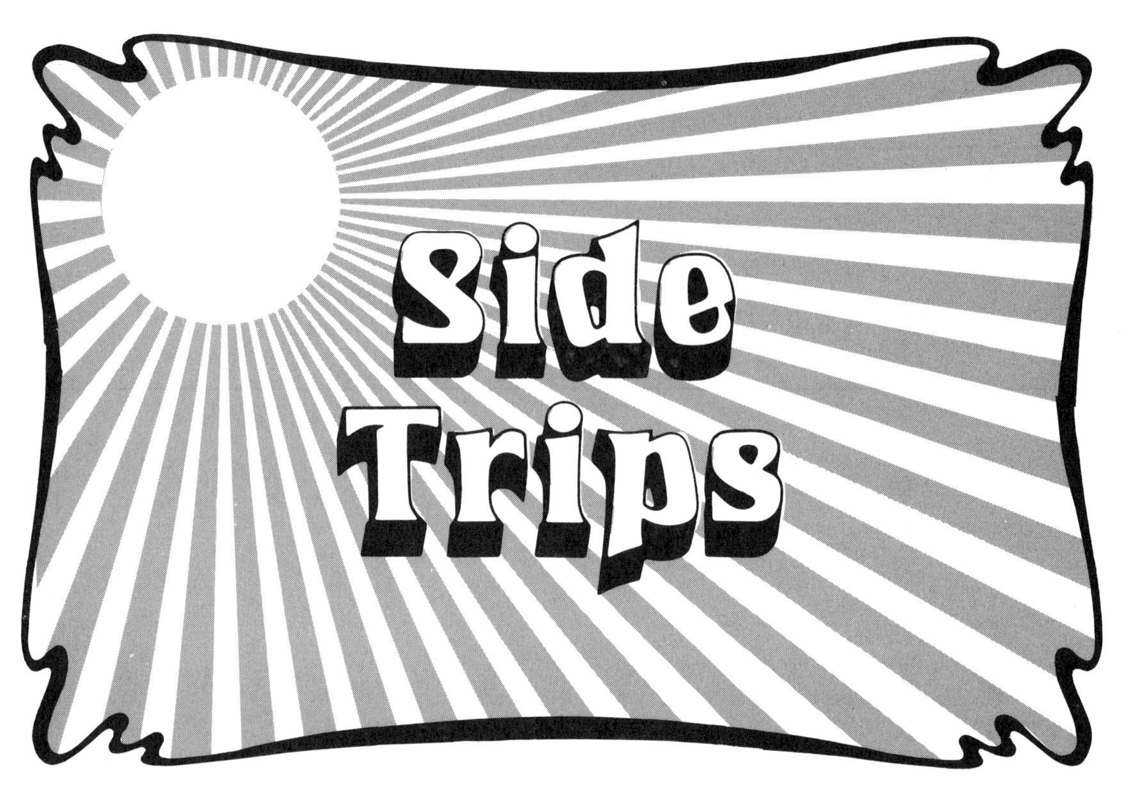

"Here's the group that started the surf-dancing craze all over the country, even in places where the nearest thing to surf is maybe the froth on a chocolate shake!"
—Liner notes, Beach Boys' *Surfin' USA* lp, 1963

For all the national attention it was starting to attract, it's ironic that until 1967, very little San Francisco music was being heard outside San Francisco. Unless you'd bought *Jefferson Airplane Takes Off* (released Sept. 1966) or caught the Airplane's Midwestern promo tour (Fargo, North Dakota, and other stops), Big Brother's ill-fated Chicago stand or the Dead's acid-tasting in Watts, you had to travel to the source to hear those much discussed new sounds. Fortunately, however, the scene was rich in visual as well as audial stimulation, which hastened the pre-selling of the music even in places where the closest thing to acid-rock was maybe a Top 40 band high on Pabst Blue Ribbon.

Most stories filed on the Liverpool of the West included mention of "light-shows," the dazzling variable-speed dance of images that played over the dancehall walls in time to the music. While this blend of art and craft surely soared to some unique heights inside the Avalon or Fillmore, its "mind-blowing" capabilities were not exactly new. There were plenty of antecedents in the world of academic art and experimental cinema.

The most prominent dabbling in the

area of combining music with multiple-projection was the Vortex concerts, held in San Francisco's Morrison Planetarium in Golden Gate Park from 1957 to 1960. Henry Jacobs, a poet and electronic music composer, and his collaborator Jordan Belson surrounded the planetarium's 60-foot dome with 36 loudspeakers and hundreds of projection machines. Seated under the dome, spectators were bathed in a mystifying sea of Stockhausen, peppery Afro-Cuban rhythms and more cosmic images than the average eye could process; blink once and the world sped gaily past. Synchronicity between light and sound was all-important, and delicately handled, as Jacobs told Gene Youngblood in *Expanded Cinema:* "We could tint the space any color we wanted to. We could get it down to jet black, and then take it down 25 degrees lower so you really got that sinking feeling. At one point, the entire dome was bathed in a deep kind of red. As the color began to fade away, there was a point when it overlapped with this beautiful starry sky, it was a breathtaking moment."

Jacobs and Belson did over a hundred Vortex shows, even taking them to the 1958 Brussels World's Fair. Then in 1960, planetarium support dried up and the series was cancelled. Which did not keep its breathtaking moments out of the memory of the planners of the Trips Festival who, six years later, advertised the Vortex lightshow as part of the three-day bash. Like lots of other Festival attractions, most notably Marshall McLuhan and Allen Ginsberg, it did not materialize; but other light-related spectacles did—Stewart Brand's "American Needs Indians" slideshow, the Stroboscopic Trampoline and an assortment of experimental or otherwise unclassifiable films.

Experimental filmmakers, in fact, had been having a field day with assemblage and montage techniques. Gerd Stern and the USCO group had used multiple projections in *Yield We Are All One,*

Inside the Fillmore Photo: Gene Anthony

Stan Brakhage's *Dogstar Man* (1964) worked with complex overlays and Bruce Conner's silent short features had been celebrated for their "parallel editing" and escalating "crescendo of accidents." Conner had even run some of his collaged footage at Chet Helms' jam sessions in the basement of 1090 Page.

Moving Murals, Cultural Debris

By the time the Summer of Love approached, lightshows had become an essential part of the ballroom adventure—whether that adventure was presented as a "drugless psychedelic experience" (the Trips Festival) or as the diverting rock & roll "event" Luria Castell had envisioned. The intent was to create an environment, one that differed substantially from that which patrons had left outside when they paid their two-fifty and ascended the stairs to the Fillmore or Avalon's second story dancefloors. There, enclosed by four walls, the runaway freight intensity of the Dead or Quicksilver was turned loose. A good lightshow company suppporting a good band could complement all that energy and heighten its effect—by filling and emptying and refilling all available eyespace with mile-a-minute impressions.

To accomplish this, outfits like Bill Ham's or Tony Martin's, Jerry Abrams' Headlights or the Holy See or the North American Ibis Alchemical Co. utilized both overhead slide projectors (for the pulsing liquid effects) and standard film projectors—to screen everything from cartoons and "camp" classics to old newsreels, dated commercials, even industrial training films (often run backwards or otherwise modified). The result was a sort of moving mural, a rhythmic panorama of pop-art images and assorted cultural debris. In addition to all that kinetic activity, most psychedelic emporiums also utilized fixed light sources—chiefly a variable-speed strobe (usually located some distance from the stage) and blacklight fixtures. Handbills for Graham's earliest dance-concerts advised those attending to "wear your best fluorescent clothes and makeup"; upon paying admission and plucking a red apple from the tub in the lobby, few could resist the temptation to linger a moment under the lilac tubing at the rear of the hall.

San Francisco lightshows were exported or imitated around the world (Glenn McKay's enjoyed the honor of being top-billed over the rock groups for a few weeks at the Fillmore East), and flourished until 1969. That July, most of the Bay Area light companies organized themselves into the Light Artists Guild and struck both Graham's newly relocated Fillmore West (Carousel Ballroom) and Helms' Family Dog on the Great Highway. The demands: a minimum pay scale which would double their standard $150-$200-a-night fee plus more publicity for their unique "art-form."

The strike effectively destroyed the already ailing Family Dog. "They broke us in one night," explains Helms. "Part of their demand was billing. That just flew in the face of the reality of the music business; there was no way the bands were going to give lightshows equal billing." Graham concurred, telling the *Chronicle* that the lights were "not responsible for mass attendance. They help make the place look better and feel better, but the big draw is on the stage." A year later, it was all a moot point. With the Dog only infrequently presenting shows and Graham declaring his intention to give up the Fillmore, the lights would soon go out for good.

The Poster Trip: Hip Hieroglyphics

For many people, their first exposure to the San Francisco sound came in the form of a 14-by-20 inch sheet of heavy paper vibrating with color, hieroglyphic calligraphy and mysterious symbols. While lightshows rarely saw duty outside the ballroom (except for a brief vogue when they were used by the Joffrey Ballet and such stage companies as *Hair* and *Dionysius 69*), so-called "psychedelic posters" enjoyed a wide and lasting impact. Throughout the late Sixties, the work of such Frisco poster pioneers as Stanley Mouse, Al Kelley, Wes Wilson and Rick Griffin was displayed in museums, studied in schools and copied, lock, stock and filigree, by commercial design firms eager to tap the lucrative youth market.

San Francisco poster artists outside the Avalon. Front row, left to right: Rick Griffin, Bob Fried, Bob Simon, George Hunter, Mouse. Back row, left to right: Satty, Avalon guard, Victor Moscoso, Wes Wilson, Alton Kelley.

Photo: Gene Anthony

Editors' archives

"I remember that the first poster which bore the Family Dog logo was done for us when we were still at the Fillmore by Wes Wilson," Chet Helms recalls. "It was the first instance of psychedelic lettering and I remember Graham hitting the ceiling because you couldn't read it. That poster was unique in terms of what had previously been done in posters, and from that time on people began to steal them. It took me three weeks to get beyond anger and frustration with that and to realize that that was the signal of our success, that the most we could hope for was to create posters that people *would* rip off the walls. That was the magic. When we had that going, we were really moving."

Of course, the notion of such highly stylized, slightly surreal posters was not at all unique. Their principal predecessors had been the works of two turn-of-the-century illustrators, American Maxfield Parrish and France's Alphonse Mucha; Parrish's neo-classic scenes, brimming with pale golds and rich blues, had advertised everything from soda water to the Woolworth's chain. Mucha's elegant art nouveau illustrations sold perfume, tobacco and accessories.

The new posters' more immediate roots were the Charalatans' Red Dog Saloon handbills done by Mike Ferguson and George Hunter, tidy pen-and-ink drawings which trumpeted the band as "The Limit of the Marvelous." "That first one was inspired by an old Karmi Troupe poster," Hunter explains. "You know, Indian sword-swallowers and all. We borrowed the 'Marvelous' term from that poster also. We did two prints; after we did the first, we decided we needed more detail, so we redid it." If only a few of the subsequent Frisco posters relied on the *graphic* style of Hunter's old-timey sketches, most owed a great deal to their tone—whimsical, highly crafted low-tech with a heavy dose of camp. And there was a subtlety about them, something supremely "cool" in the McLuhanesque sense, that demanded the viewer take a second or third look.

"We always tried to incorporate things that would hold the interest on just a glance," said Helms, "so that as you began to look at the poster you would notice there were other things in there, and that tended to make people *expect* that there was going to be something like that there week after week. Rather than just glancing at the poster and seeing what band was playing, they would stop to see what was going on in the poster itself." A main feature of all Avalon posters was the Family Dog logo, a cameo depicting a world-weary Indian in a top hat. "It was a photo we got out of the *American Heritage Book of Indians,*" recounts Helms. "He was described as a fur-trading Indian of North America. Wes Wilson and I collaborated on the shield that went around the picture."

Bump in the Night

The April 22, 1966, poster for the Blues Project-Great Society dance marked the first appearance of the Dog's legendary slogan; across the Indian's chest a small banner read "May the baby Jesus shut your Mouth and Open your Mind." The slogan was given to Helms by Big Brother guitarist Jim Gurley who had seen it written on a bathroom wall at 1090 Page.

Aside from this sage admonition, Dog posters offered other prayers and advice; "From Beasties and Grumplies and Things that go Bump in the Night, Dear Lord Protect Us", and "What you don't know about copying and duplicating won't hurt you" (a possible warning to bootleggers). Another source of bemusement was themed dances. One of Graham's earliest Fillmore shows was a

The Jordan Collection

A Moscoso Poster

three-day "Batman Dance" whose poster promised prizes, old serials and a free mynah bird. Helms' theme shows ran intermittently through August of '66. In addition to the two Tribal Stomps, there was "Wonderland," "Euphoria (An Air Conditioned Dance-Concert)" and the intriguing "Hupmobile-8 (A Free-Wheeling Vehicle)."

The first Fillmore posters were drawn in spring of 1966 by a 29-year-old psychology dropout from S.F. State who was working as a printer. A self-taught designer, Wes Wilson was passingly influenced by Aubrey Beardsley—he also developed a style of calligraphy which bent and distorted the alphabet in unusual rhythmic sweeps. While the lettering on some of Wilson's 1967-68 posters edged toward the indecipherable, he defended his sensual embrace of type and art as "a reaction against 50 years of dull, bland posters." When Helms' Family Dog left the Fillmore for the Avalon Ballroom (April '66), Wilson stayed, designing the majority of Graham's posters, for the next two years.

Wilson's work

Editors' archives

While there was no shortage of acclaim for Wilson's Fillmore work (it was profiled in *Time* and *Newsweek* and seems to have heavily influenced such interlopers as Peter Max), it was the Avalon posters which launched the careers of the bulk of the era's prominent designers. Unlike Wilson, Alton Kelley, Stanley Mouse, Victor Moscoso and Rick Griffin had taken formal art-school training (Moscoso had studied at Yale and the San Francisco Art Institute). Just as importantly, each one tempered this formal background with an undisguised love of the popular—since they'd all come, like Ed "Big Daddy" Roth before them, from what Tom Wolfe once described as "the teenage netherworld." For Mouse and Kelley, this meant the work they'd done pin-striping motorcycles and custom cars. For Moscoso, it meant a self-described "contemporary eclectic" approach that utilized styles gleaned from postcards, comics and other pop-ish arts. Griffin, already popular for his "Murphy" cartoon strip done for *Surfer* magazine in 1963 and '64, was influenced by comic books of the Forties and by artists like *Mad's* Jack Davis.

According to Griffin, ballroom operators would "call you up toward the end of the week with all the copy information. They'd generally give you five or six days to come up with your design. Then we'd go together down to Cal Litho and they'd run them off." For their efforts, the artists were usually paid a flat $100 per poster.

Blazing Mementos

Initially, the brightly colored, offset posters were purely promotional. Graham, Helms and their help routinely passed out hundreds of free posters to the next week's dance as the bands blasted away onstage. Once the posters' collectability became apparent and a sizable backlog of old posters developed, they began turning up in retail outlets like the Print Mint on Haight St. Before long,

Editors' Archives

Groovy Griffin

the ballrooms were upping their press runs to accommodate the number of fans willing to pay $2-3 for a blazing five-color memento of last month's big gig. Purchased by out-of-towners, the posters often traveled thousands of miles to wind up on bedroom or dorm walls in Oshkosh or Ottawa—a point that was not lost on Quicksilver's John Cipollina. "Since we were one of the last bands to sign a recording contract [1968], we played in town a lot and were featured on a lot more posters than some of the other bands who were already out on the road, promoting their records. Consequently, when we *did* go out, there were lots of people who'd never heard us but knew about Quicksilver strictly through the posters."

Eventually, San Francisco's psychedelic art inspired a general poster boom that encompassed political broadsides ("War is not healthy for children or other living things"), personality portraits, op artifacts, even flower-power wallpaper. By then, the ballrooms had gone from merely retailing their surpluses to wholesaling posters to headshops and record stores—the Family Dog through an arrangement with Capitol records, Graham through his own Winterland Productions. During the 1967 peak, Wes Wilson Fillmore posters were selling at the rate of 60,000 a month.

When the ballroom activity finally wound down, the reduced demand for psychedelic dance posters sent most designers diversifying—most often into album covers and, later, group logos, t-shirts and promotional merchandise. Kelley and Mouse's collaborations are probably the best known; *American Beauty, Terrapin Station* and other Dead albums, Journey's scarab logo and the *More American Graffiti* soundtrack. Wes Wilson's work has been less prominent in recent years, though his lettering was widely (and most often crudely) imitated by lp designers in the late Sixties and early Seventies. Moscoso contributed the landmark psyche-out sleeve for Steve Miller's debut *Children of the Future,* while Griffin has done covers as varied as the Dead's *Aoxomoxoa* and Man's *Slow Motion;* both Griffin and Moscoso gigged in *Zap* and other early underground comics as well.

By the end of 1966, San Francisco's pioneer bands had been joined by a host of hopeful new arrivals. In contrast to the original groups—who, along with their small audience, had stumbled into each other in the dark and discovered they made a scene—the new bands had the benefit of becoming members of an existing community. Like ships following the sound of a foghorn, they knew where to go—to play, to find management and publicity and otherwise take advantage of the standard music biz apparatus that was being erected in the city. Despite all the social and political significance that the newsmagazines extrapolated from the scene, most Frisco bands actively shunned any association with politics per se. Dancing, it seemed, beat marching any day. For everyone, that is, but Country Joe & the Fish. Raised in El Monte, Southern California, by Communist parents (who are said to have named him for Stalin), Joe McDonald had been in the

Navy, been to college and to Japan when he moved to San Francisco in the early Sixties to "become a beatnik and give up structured lives." Falling in with Berkeley's loud new leftists, the young guitarist labored simultaneously as a singer of social protest songs and as part of the 13-member Instant Action Jug Band, a sort of East Bay version of Mother Macree's Palo Alto bunch. Instant Action put him in touch with two other Southern California transplants, guitarists Barry Melton and Bruce Barthol; Melton was also a socially concerned folkie, with enviable roots—as a kid in Brooklyn, he'd lived in the same apartment house as Woody Guthrie and actually watched the master strum first-hand. It was McDonald's solo protest singing, though, which put him on record—long before most of San Francisco's other young rock ers.

Country Joe's Poli-Psyche

"I was putting out a magazine called Rag Baby at the time," recalls Fish manager Ed Denson. "Mainly we published music and lyrics to topical songs, sort of like *Broadside*. At one point we decided to do an issue of the magazine that came as a disc, and we recorded the writers whose songs we'd been printing. Joe sang a couple of his original tunes on that little Rag Baby e.p., calling himself, I think for the first time, 'Country Joe.' "

As the only member with a record out, McDonald naturally assumed front-and-center position when the jugband amplified itself in 1965. In addition to Barry Melton and fellow Instant Actionist Bruce Barthol (who became the new band's bassist), McDonald recruited David Cohen, a relocated Greenwich Village guitarist who agreed to take on electric organ. Drummer John Francis Gunning joined (only to be shortly replaced by Chicken Hirsch) and Country Joe & the Fish were born. While they were omnipresent at peace rallies and marches, they didn't make their official ballroom debut until August 1966, opening for the Quick and the Dead at the Fillmore. Shortly thereafter, they became something of an Avalon mainstay, and played most of the Family Dog's New Year's Eve shows. "We signed with Vanguard in late '66," Denson explains. "I think the advance was $5000. Not that much, compared to what the Airplane got, but then Vanguard wasn't RCA Records either." The debut album, *Country Joe & The Fish: Electric Music for the Mind and Body,* was cut, like the Rag Baby e.p.'s, at Sierra Sound in Berkeley.

Photo Chuck Kroll

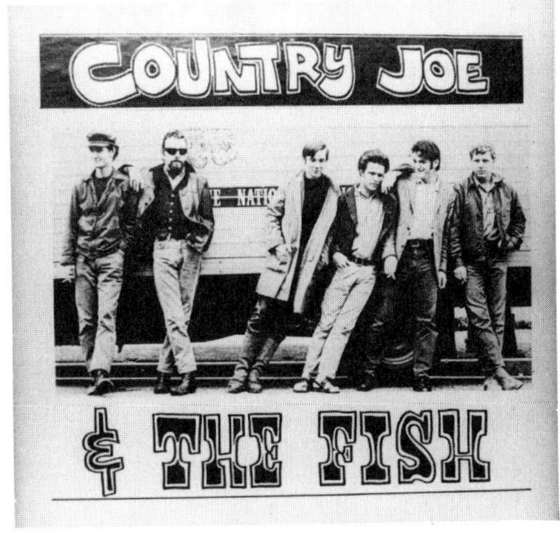

Country Joe McDonald

Sam Charters, a long-time friend of Denson's produced. "Charters' background was blues, which he'd written about quite a bit, and he'd even done field recordings. He came out here to sign Quicksilver to Vanguard, 'cause they were doing a lot of Chicago blues. While he was here, though, he stayed with us at the Fish place and eventually he changed his mind and signed us instead."

The album was released in March of 1967 and became one of the new underground's first hits, eventually stopping just short of the 500,000 sales figure required for a gold record. It established Country Joe & the Fish as one of the counter-culture's first national draws. Between 1966 and 1970, Country Joe & the Fish broke up and reformed half a dozen times, drove Woodstock wild with their infamous Fish cheer ("Gimme an F, gimme a U," etc.), and gave the anti-war movement the closest thing it had to a themesong: "Feel Like I'm Fixin' To Die Rag", an early McDonald solo tune the group updated. In addition to *Woodstock* and *Monterey Pop,* they also appeared in two others movies—1970's *Gas!,* a Roger Corman film that one critic described as "*Beach Party* meets Berthold Brecht" (Country Joe plays a character named "A.M. Radio"), and 1971's *Zachariah,* billed as "the world's first electric western."

Despite their reputation as San Francisco's most overtly political band, CJ&F had a flip side that was at times far freakier than many of the hardcore acid-bands. That is, cuts like "Section 43" and "Bass Strings"—different versions of which are heard on the '66 Rag Baby e.p. and the band's debut album, are among the few recordings of the era that might legitimately be termed "psychedelic." These are highly charged atmospheric pieces, eerie and ever-changing in tone. At times, they sound vaguely Mideastern or Japanese. At others, when Cohen's swirling organ lines curl around the guitar chords like pipesmoke, altogether otherworldly. Not surprisingly, these twin temperaments made for some inconsistent performances both onstage and on record. Rarely did the politics and druggy wonder meet and mesh without friction; instead, the band's five Vanguard albums reveal separate but equal portions of both, and an even number of highs and lows. Among the former: Barthol's euphoric instrumental "Cetacean" off *Together,* McDonald's psyche-Dylanized "Not So Sweet Martha Lorraine," and Melton's blistering "Death Sound" blues and the revved-up Lyndon Johnson putdown "Superbird" (all from *Electric Music).* Among the lows: Melton's noxious blackface vocals on "Love" *(Electric Music)* and "Rock And Soul Music" *(Together).*

"I was producing the Sparrow (who became Steppenwolf) at the time. They were headlining at this place called The Ark in Sausalito, and I watched them get totally blown offstage by the opening band who, I found out, had only been together six weeks. This group was staggering, unbelievable, the closest thing to an American Rolling Stones I'd seen. I said, "Who *are* these guys?' 'Moby Grape.' '*Moby Grape'?* "
—David Rubinson

It's not surprising that David Rubinson was impressed. Record producers are supposed to be able to recognize professionalism, image, material, presentation, all of which Moby Grape had in abundance, even after only six weeks together. It also wasn't merely coincidental or accidental that Rubinson was in the right Ark on the right night.

Fate had nothing to do with the formation of Moby Grape, unless fate was a caped managerial expert doing business as Matthew Katz. Like the roving gambler in Dylan's "Highway 61," Katz was very bored by the fall of 1966. A year earlier he'd knocked the locals for a loop, signing the Airplane to RCA for an unheard of $25,000 advance and thereby suggesting the potential size of this new pot at the end of the day-glo rainbow.

For his next trick, Katz would build his own band from the ground up, a talented, good-looking bunch who could write hits and were in every way record-ready. For starters, he had Skip Spence; the Airplane drummer had already proved he could write ("My Best Friend," a day-dreamy near-hit that had preceded "Somebody To Love" as the first single from *Surrealistic Pillow)* and was itching to return to the guitar. Through Los Angeles friends, Katz next connected with Peter Lewis and Bob Mosley. Lewis was a showbiz kid, a guitarist with an uncanny melodic knack who'd led his own group Peter & the Wolves; Mosley was a blond Dennis Wilson type, an athletic white-bluesologist from San Diego who'd played bass in a band called the Misfits.

Summoning Mosley and Lewis to San Francisco, Katz teamed them with Spence, then found drummer Don Stevenson and lead guitarist Jerry Miller, both of whom had ditched the Frantics, a Northwest Wailers-type combo that specialized in surfish instrumentals with titles like "Fog Cutter" and "Straight Flush."

While the group would disband over personality clashes and a hair-raising drug incident less than two years later, things went swimmingly for the Grape at first. Spence proved a peppy front-man, the three-guitar lineup packed an undeniable wallop and audiences—particularly the younger ones who were rapidly changing the composition of Fillmore and Avalon audiences by 1967—made the band an instant hit. "Omaha" and "Hey Grandma" were guaranteed crowd-pleasers, popping with firecracker intensity, while "Dark Magic" was the Grape's version of the Dead doing "Midnight Hour" or Quicksilver's "Who Do You Love"; an extended, largely instrumental spacewalk that allowed lots of room for Jerry Miller's genuinely articulate soloing.

Unfortunately, Moby Grape was to become a victim of the too-much-too-fast syndrome. They began rehearsing at the Ark in September of 1966, broke onto the ballroom circuit in November and by Christmas were in serious negotiations with Columbia Records and David Rubinson—who was then making a name for himself as the label's exclusive producer for "underground" product, having cut Tim Rose's "Hey Joe" and "Creators Of Rain" by Smokey and His Sister. An ill-fated recording career and subsequent bizarre travails were to follow.

The Sopwith Camel: Too Pop to Pass

"We were like the second San Francisco band to be signed to a record deal," Peter Kraemer told rock historian Pete Frame, "and this caused some resentment from groups who had been 'paying their dues'. It was a known fact that we were not hardened musicians; we had not played all the bars down the Peninsula, we didn't do a very convincing job on Chicago blues or do extended versions of 'In the Midnight Hour' . . ."

On the other hand, the Sopwith Camel had a pedigree as impressive as that of any San Francisco band. After all, guitarist Terry MacNeill had come out of the Art Institute, drummer Norman Mayell had hung tight with the Pranksters, and Peter Kraemer, the mustachioed singer who looked like Ernie Kovacs with a pituary problem—Peter was born in Nevada City, had gone to S.F. State and was living at 1090 Page with Rod Albin and John McIntyre (later manager of the Grateful Dead) way before Chet Helms

The Sopwith Camel (Peter Kraemer, center)

Courtesy Erik Jacobsen

jumped off the Greyhound from Texas. Boho roots? Erik Jacobsen, who produced the Camel (as well as the Lovin' Spoonful and the Charlatans), recalls that Kraemer's mother had been the center of an artists circle in Nevada: "They lived in a 15-room brewery, and Dali visited them once and chased a bird through Peter's house."

What, then, was the rap against the group? Plainly and simply, that they'd gone and got themselves a hit single—a bonafide, AM radio ditty-smash called "Hello Hello." It was lightweight, clever, camp as all hell and it nudged itself into *Billboard*'s Top 30 right next to "Pretty Ballerina" and "Too Much To Dream" and all those records by the Monkees, the Buckinghams and the Bob Crewe Generation.

"I'd been out to California when the Spoonful played Mother's and Longshoremen's Hall," Jacobsen explains. "And I'd already started working with the Charlatans. On one of my trips, somebody gave me a tape of these guys doing 'Hello Hello.' I flipped and knew I had to have it. I just knew it was a hit song. So I make arrangements to go meet the group. They're living in Corte Madera in Marin County, in a little house built on stilts over this swamp. To get there, you had to walk a quarter of a mile on this rickety old one-board walkway that went out over the mud. I meet them half way out there, high tide, and here are these five guys coming through the fog on this walkway, wearing tuxes and tophats and white gloves. They'd just come from playing some deb ball at a fancy girls' school. I mean, they looked pretty weird."

The meeting led to a Kama Sutra contract, as well as the Camel's signing with Spoonful manager Bob Cavallo for representation. Then came the trip to New York to record the album. There, between the San Franciscans' first exposure to the big city (especially the seedy confines of the Albert Hotel) and Peter Kraemer's debilitating go-round with the flu, things fell apart. Rhythm guitarist Willie Sievers decided to quit, and was followed by Terry MacNeil; the cumulative effect was to postpone completion of the album that might have provided the Camel the momentum to get over the hump.

While it owes much of its inspiration to the good-timey Spoonful sound, the Camel's first and only album reveals an engaging, idiosyncratic band clearly enjoying itself. "Cellophane Woman" struts Sixties punk moves, while "The Great Morpheum" and the feedback-strewn "Frantic Desolation" suggest more ambitious ideas at work. "Postcard From Jamaica", the group's second single, continues the sunny approach of "Hello Hello." But *Sopwith Camel* arrived too late to save the drowning band; released almost a year after its only hit single had peaked, the album's cover sticker read "Remember 'Hello, Hello'?" Fifteen years later, the band recorded a comeback album, *The Miraculous Camel Returns From the Hump* (Reprise), but by then there was little magic left to believe in.

Blues for Steve Miller

If the Camel's sins found disfavor with the city's hip community in the Sixties, Steve Miller's were simply not evident at the time. The singer-guitarist who would reap multi-platinum a decade later with such out-and-out bubblegum sticks as "Rock'n Me" and "Jet Airliner" was merely a blues technician who arrived in town in mid-'67 leading a capable, if routine, Chicago blues band.

While blues were the Miller band's musical roots, the Michigan-Wisconsin college circuit provided its social background. As the Marksmen and later the Ardells, Miller, rhythm guitarist Boz Scaggs and various sidemen served up Fifties rock and R&B for frat gigs, mixers and campus one-offs. By '65 Miller had split for Chicago, to take the ethnic route down home with Butterfield, Bloomfield, Charlie Musselwhite and Dylan sideman/organist Barry Goldberg. The two formed the short-lived Miller-Goldberg Blues Band which cut the superbly punkish "Mother Song" (Epic) single in '66 then disbanded.

Ever the careerist, Miller sensed a scene out West and developed a case of California blues. He made for Frisco with a new unit, the Steve Miller Blues Band. If the SMBB's repertoire was stock (Muddy Waters, B.B. King, K.C. Douglas' "Mercury Blues"), his players were top-notch. They consistently delivered sharp, professional shows (with the requisite amount of guitar grandstanding by the coolly expressive Miller) at the ballrooms, toured and took their time scoring a record deal. After backing Chuck Berry on his *Live at the Fillmore* LP (Mercury) and a cameo appearance on the *Revolution* movie soundtrack (United Artists), the band lost its Blues qualifier, replaced rhythm guitarist Curly Cooke with Scaggs, and signed with Capitol in December 1967. The deal called for a $50,000 advance plus a $10,000 bonus and, as reported in *Rolling Stone*, "four year options with a cumulative total of $750,000."

Children of the Future, produced in England by Stones engineer Glyn Johns, comfortably mixed the band's B.B./Broonzy blues with a tasteful smattering of studio psychedelia (the "Day In The Life"-inspired "In My First Mind"). Plans to record the followup album with the Oakland Symphony Orchestra failed to materialize and Miller's blues gradually devolved to R&B-ish pop, robust at first (*Brave New World, Your Saving Grace*), then later pale (*Fly Like An Eagle*). In the late Seventies, Miller cut an entire lp of disco music but had second thoughts about releasing it.

Visiting Statesmen: Butter and the Project

As early as spring of 1966, San Francisco was becoming a magnet for "underground" bands from other cities. If they didn't put down roots like Steve Miller or Texas' Thirteenth Floor Elevators, many made repeated trips through town—since the city was part of a limited hip-rock circuit that included few stops outside New York City, Boston and L.A.'s Sunset Strip. If you weren't playing commercial Top 40, you had few places to play; planning an itinerary was easy work.

The most distinguished early visitors were Paul Butterfield's Blues Band, whose first appearance, a full-house Family Dog stomp (with Quicksilver Messenger Service) at the Fillmore the weekend of March 25, was a pivotal gig. Simply put, Mike Bloomfield's incendiary guitar and the six-man band's swinging ensemble approach were inspirational to San Francisco's new musicians. The tight, compact songs from the group's year-old first album were now stretched open, retaining their shape but brimming with solos by Bloomfield, second guitarist Elvin Bishop and organist Mark Naftalin. There were real jazz licks, Oriental riffs and wailing Mideastern desert winds—all compatibly placed in the instrumental travelogue "East West," as yet unrecorded. After the second set, local boys like John Cipollina and Jerry Garcia went home with their ears buzzing and their fingers twitching, eager to put as much into—and get such sustained highs out of—their own music.

The Blues Project blew into town not long after Butterfield, preceded by a similarly heavy rep and their Verve album, *Live at the Cafe Au Go Go.* The Project's dexterity and precision impressed, but their appeal was different than Butter's; hyperkinetic rock-blues that rushed from climax to climax, crescendo to crescendo ("I Can't Keep From Crying Sometimes").

Photo Chuck Kroll

In the hands of Danny Kalb (lead guitar), Steve Katz (rhythm), Al Kooper (organ), drummer Roy Blumenfled and bassist Andy Kulberg, "Spoonful" or "Got My Mojo Working" sped by in a blur, informational bits tossed about in a firestorm. Onstage, Kooper and Kalb frequently seemed to be engaged in a friendly battle for the honor of playing loudest or pushing the tempo hardest, usually with crowd-pleasing results.

Buffalo Springfield: Brawls & Beauty

In the Buffalo Springfield, the brawls weren't always friendly. If the match-up of twin lead guitarists Neil Young and Steve Stills produced a captivating kind of second-generation folk-rock ("Pay the Price", "Go And Say Goodbye"), it just as often produced spiteful dueling onstage—Stills bellowing above the din of Young's airstrip solos for him to turn down, Young ignoring him, Stills upping his own dials past deafening, Young going for the sound barrier, on and on until one or the other unstrapped his axe and stomped offstage. San Francisco's reaction? For lots of ballroom regulars, there was always something a bit too sprightly about Buffalo Springfield; Richie Furay mugged and bopped around the stage almost as much as Skip Spence of Moby Grape, a band with whom the Springfield shared an emotional as well as musical affinity. Or maybe it was the obvious AM radio potential of the songs, or the full complement of Southern California beauties who seemed to gather whenever the band appeared. While they sold tickets, the Springfield always had to fight the age-old Frisco taunt: "too L.A."

Kaleidoscope and the Captain

Because of its proximity, Los Angeles supplied the majority of out-of-town acts to San Francisco. The most consistently popular SoCal export (until the Doors showed up to claim a vast audience of boppers and freaks alike) was Kaleidoscope, David Lindley's eclecto-bizarre group that mixed Howlin' Wolf, Doug Kershaw, Cab Calloway, Balkan, Turkish and Irish trad elements. As with the Dead and others, bluegrass 'n' banjo roots, under the influence of LSD and amplification, bore strange fruit. "Beacon From Mars," a sort of extraterrestrial vamp on "Smokestack Lightnin' ", and a skewered reading of the folksong "Cuckoo" were

Kaleidoscope publicity photo

The Jordan Collection

Captain Beefheart & His Magic Band (Don Van Vliet, center)

but two lengthy excursions by one of the few bands of the day qualified to carry out such ambitious improv. Solomon Feldthouse, whom Lindley once described as resembling a cross between Rasputin and Lazarus, played oud, bouzouki, dobro and caz.

While some fans prefer to think Captain Beefheart burst onto the world as the wildly original free-versifier they've come to know and love, the facts argue against it. A San Fran regular by fall 1966, the early Beefheart & His Magic Band were in fact a highly derivative blues band who'd got their start playing a Teenager Fair at the Hollywood Palladium in 1965. Beefheart himself (Don Van Vliet) is probably best recalled from this period for his uncannily accurate renderings of the great masters. Seated on an orange crate on the Avalon's low stage, hawonking into his harmonica, he could sound exactly like Waters, Wolf, Elmore James. Only a few weeks earlier, he'd enjoyed northern California Top 40 airplay with his A&M single, "Diddy Wah Diddy." The record had failed to click, as it was locked in battle on most stations with the Remains' version of the same song. (The *KYA Beat* newspaper even ran a think piece in June: "Too Many 'Diddy Wahs'?")

While the Magic Band had always gone over well there, San Francisco was in no way prepared for the later 1966 model, which Beefheart unveiled at the Avalon well in advance of his debut Buddah album, *Safe As Milk.* Gone was the Rich Little-of-the-blues; in his place the real Captain Beefheart stood up, in pre-New Wave plastic wraparound sunglasses, tassle-topped Shriner's fez and a braided bandleader's corset straight out of *The Music Man.* Like some Kool Aid-spiked Robert Preston, Beefheart barked out an entire new repertoire whose only link to his earlier blues were the dissembled chords, shuddering and clashing in a brilliant, thoroughly original cacophony. The Captain Beefheart the world would know arrived in San Francisco then, nursery rhyming "Abba Zaba" and premiering "Kandy Korn" by pelting the audience with handful after handful of the yellow and orange candy.

The Texas Factor

"In the Sixties," explains Chet Helms, "the repression in Texas was so severe that to escape it you had to create these vivid mental spaces, so I think you find in Texas some really strong characters with really vivid imaginations, really creative people who've found a way out of that repression to make a place for themselves, for their own sanity. I will always feel a very strong kinship for all the people who've escaped Texas."

Helms should know. Under his administration, the Family Dog virtually functioned as an underground railway for California-bound Texans. In addition to Janis Joplin, the Avalon booked the laconic Doug Sahm and his Sir Douglas Quintet, Tracy Nelson's Mother Earth and all its offshoots, and a curious quartet from Houston which featured the sounds of an amplified jug and a self-admitted alien (Martian variety) at the mike (Roky Erikson). After stints in high school bands, Erikson joined lyricist—jug-blower Tommy Hall in forming the Thirteenth Floor Elevators; the band cut "You're Gonna Miss Me," a primitive "Gloria"-type garage-rocker, scoring a regional hit and national bookings. In San Francisco, where many mistook the shrill vocalist on "You're Gonna Miss Me" for Janis Joplin, the band found its home away from home. In concert, they alternated exotic originals like "Reverberation," "Monkey Island" and the banshee-esque "Fire Engine" with unorthodox interpretations of material by Buddy Holly ("I'm Gonna Love You Too"), Solomon Burke ("Everybody Needs Somebody to Love") and the Beatles ("The Word").

Hargis, Saabs & Hysky: The Birth of Rock FM

San Francisco was being inundated by music, its own and that of all the fringed fellow-travelers making the psychedelic pilgrimage west. Acid-rock was everywhere—in the dance-halls and parks, in the hip record stores and head-shops, in Gleason's glowing *Chronicle* columns and the mimeographed pages of the *Mojo-Navigator*. Everywhere, it seemed, but the one place where rock & roll had traditionally been found: on the radio.

"Tom and I were living on Telegraph Hill, not doing much of anything," Raechel Donahue explains. "One night we were playing pinochle, stoned to the tits on acid, because Abe Kesh came over and *he* wanted to play cards. We couldn't tell jacks from aces. Abe was a promotion man for Elektra at the time and he'd brought over the Doors' first album, which was brand new. We're playing pinochle and the record's on and suddenly Tom looks up and says, 'Did he just say "Father, I want to kill you"?' Who knew what he said? We went on with the game.

"The next morning I get up and find that Tom's been up for hours. He's rifling through the telephone book, calling FM stations. He kept calling till he got one that had a disconnected phone. That's what he was looking for. He said, "Look, ever since I quit [KYA], what've we been doing for 18 months? Sitting around taking acid and playing records for our friends, right?' "

San Francisco's hardest blow against the old empire may have been landed that morning. Big Daddy got on the horn to Leon Crosby, who ran KMPX-FM. It was April 1967, and Crosby's station, which programmed a crazy-quilt of foreign language shows, was literally in the basement—of an ancient warehouse on Green St. down near the Ferry Building. KMPX was considerably lower in the areas of cash-on-hand and audience, both of which were nonexistent. Which is probably why Crosby let Tom Donahue buy himself an eight-to-midnight slot, for all intents and purposes founding what came to be known as the country's first "underground" radio station.

Donahue's achievement has been

Raechel and Tom Donahue

Courtesy Raechel Donahue

Couresy Raechel Donahue

The original KMPX staff, 1967

questioned over the years by dozens of other programmers who claim to have thought up the idea before him; in fact, a month previous to Donahue's arrival at KMPX, a jock named Larry Miller had hosted a folk, blues and rock show there from midnight to six. While it may have been the psychedelic pinochle game and Morrison's oedipal redress that prompted him to action, Donahue himself once credited right-wing evangelist Reverend Billy James Hargis with being the first to come up with the idea of programming selected LP cuts on radio. He told an interviewer of a trip to L.A.: "It was the middle of the night and we were fishing around the dial, trying to get something. We picked up Hargis coming out of Denver. He'd play a Phil Ochs record and say 'Listen to that commie.' Then he'd play Joan Baez and then Dylan, and after each one he'd give a little rap about 'Did you hear what that commie said?' But in the process he was putting together the best radio show I'd heard in a long time."

At the time, Big Daddy and company weren't entirely confident their new venture would succeed. "We got all our records together," Raechel recalls, "Tom and I, Kesh and Bob McClay, and we took them down to the station and color-coded them, identifying each one's records by a separate color. In case the whole thing failed, we knew we'd at least get our records back." It didn't. By June, Donahue, Raechel, McClay, Howard Hesseman—a full roster of air talent and an all-female engineering staff—were on regularly, displacing the last of the Irish and Portuguese Hours.

However, their only sponsors were a downtown ski shop and the Berkeley Saab dealer. There was no promotion and a weak signal. Joe Smith, a longtime Donahue friend and the man through whom Donahue helped sign the Grateful Dead to Warner Bros. Records, recalls KMPX as "one of those old type FM stations. They were usually so far off to the right end of the dial that they fell in your glove compartment."

Worst of all, the people at KMPX had few new records to play when they went on. "Our staples," Raechel remembers, "were Hendrix's first British single, 'Hey Joe' backed with 'Purple Haze,' an import copy of *Fresh Cream*, plus the Doors album. We played a lot of Aretha Franklin, but no Motown. Tom's reasoning was you had to let people distinguish us from the AM stations in town and they were playing lots of pop Motown. So we didn't. But we played blues: T-Bone Walker, Albert and B.B. King. We played about 60% familiar rock like the Beatles, Stones and Dylan, and maybe 20-30% R&B, and probably 10% jazz."

Ultimately, KMPX became hugely popular in the Bay Area, selling lots of ski masks, Saabs and records. In fact, the station was such a hit that in February 1968 its air staff went on strike against Leon Crosby—for a raise from their average weekly salary of $125, and for such demands of the day as paid holidays for Halloween and the Summer Solstice. They didn't get any of it, but eventually Tom and Raechel and cohorts took their Cream, Dead and Quicksilver records and set up shop at KSAN-FM, the local outlet of the Metromedia chain.

In January of 1968, Donahue had begun making trips to Los Angeles in hopes of opening a similar operation for Southern California. In Pasadena, he found a willing Presbyterian church with an unused basement and soon had KPPC shooting the Beatles, Cream, 13th Floor Elevators, John Cage and Canned Heat into hip households across the Southland.

Underground rock FM was clearly an idea whose time had come. By May 1968, the front page of *Billboard* gushed: "Hip Rock Radio Busting Out Across U.S.; Invades Canada." In New York, Murray the "K" had already debuted a "progressive rock" format on WOR-FM and been fired for his trouble; but, he told *Billboard,* he was ready to bow a successor new show, "Radio Free Toronto", over Canada's CHUM-FM. In Los Angeles, KPPC had given way to KMET with Donahue flying down from San Francisco to handle weekends and ex-Top 40 screamer B. Mitchell Reed handling weekdays. At Boston's WBZ, Dick Summer was hosting "Summer Subway," *that* city's underground show, spicing up the rotation of Airplane-Beatles-Stones with his own psychedelic poems, often read to the accompaniment of instrumental tracks from Country Joe & the Fish's first two LPs.

Irony was the rule of the day, it seemed. Only weeks before, most Top 40 programmers had sneered at the idea of the new music, let alone its place on their airwaves. Rick Sklar of New York's WABC to the *Wall St. Journal:* "Often this kind of music runs on and on, with no melody line built in. It's designed to simulate an LSD trip." Often the turnaround was dramatic, if not incredible; when superspieler Hy Lit left Philadelphia's Top 40 WIBG-AM and showed up across town at WDAS-FM, talking 33-rpm mellowspeak between Doors cuts and hawking it all as "Hysky's Underground," it was pretty hard not to laugh. The revolution rolled on.

"Every town must have a place where phony hippies meet psychedelic dungeons popping up on every street."
—The Mothers, "Go To San Francisco"

In 1968 and '69, almost every hamlet worth its zipcode boasted its own headshop, hippie hangout or imitation Fillmore. By then, San Francisco had become a very public image, a highly desirable experience that was being duplicated or approximated the world over. Just a year or two earlier, however, San Francisco was the westernmost outpost of a small, hip underground. Butterfield, Beefheart, the Elevators—all were, one way or another, emissaries from fledgling freak scenes along the underground network.

By far, the oldest, most established scene was New York's, with a tradition dating back to the birth of American bohemianism. In the Fifties, Greenwich Village had served as a sort of sister city to North Beach, with Kerouac, Ginsberg and the rest shuttling bi-coastal in their frantic kicks-search. In 1965, the Lovin' Spoonful launched their career out of Joe Marra's Night Owl Cafe (followed by the Magicians and New York's proto-psychedelic band the Blues Magoos). By this time Howard Solomon's Cafe Au Go Go was transforming itself from a folk club to a rock-house with the Blues Project serving as house band. As the premier "new music" club, the Cafe would later host Cream, Procol Harum, Arlo Guthrie and Richie Havens, even the reclusive writer of "Eve of Destruction," P.F. Sloan, who staged a memorable set there in '67.

Clubland

Despite the presence of Roseland and dozens of dime-a-dance halls, the Big Apple never had its own bonafide psychedelic ballroom as such. Until Bill Graham opened the 3000 capacity Fillmore East March 8, 1963, the only outlets for the new rock were small sit-down theatres and smaller clubs. The Fillmore itself had been the Village Theatre, which hosted the first East Coast appearance of Big Brother, Quicksilver, the Yardbirds, Cream and others. The Village also gave locals a chance, most notably the Rich Kids and Leslie West's Rascals-ish pre-Mountain band the Vagrants, famous for their workout on Otis Redding's "Respect". There was also the Anderson Theatre where the Fugs played, and the Garrick which in 1966 presented the New York debut of the Mothers, whose first LP had not yet come out. In typical Zappa fashion, posters touted the show as "hateful, repugnant and a waste of $3." The N.Y. *Times* reviewer described the band as "Hell's Angels without their bikes."

As late as 1968, deejay Murray the "K" was still running top-heavy revue type shows at RKO's 58th St. theatre, presenting the Who, Cream, Rascals, Buffalo Springfield and others. Around the same time, Murray opened his own multi-roomed psychedelic club, Murray the "K" 's World on Long Island, which proved short-lived and unsuccessful.

New York's most notorious venue was the Dom, a converted Polish social hall

New York's Fugs

The Jordan Collection

on St. Mark's Place. Upon entering, patrons were given food chits; later, seated at wobbly formica tables in the dark hall, they'd be served bowls of soup or goulash by dumpy Polish waitresses as Tim Buckley, Jackson Browne, Nico or Zappa wailed onstage. The Dom's downstairs room also hosted early hell-raising performances of Andy Warhol's Exploding Plastic Inevitable—the Velvet Underground opening with furious versions of "Waiting For My Man" as lights splashed the wall behind them, and Mary Woronov did a whip dance with Gerard Malanga, Malanga careening around the room shining flashlights in faces.

The Dom eventually became the more conventionally psychedelic, strobe-struck Electric Circus, run by promoter Jerry Brandt and featuring out-of-town attractions like the Dead and Airplane. There were also such clubs as the Balloon Farm and Salvation, a semi-plush, 200-capacity sensorium which boasted a floorful of cushions instead of chairs. Manager Brad Pierce, ex of the once-fashionable Ondine discotheque, brought the Doors and Springfield to town.

Less classifiable was the Group Image, which at various times was a band, a nightclub and a commune. As a venue, the GI moved around a lot, for a while lighting at the Palm Gardens on Wednesdays, later taking over the Cheetah disco on the West Side. The band is recalled as an inept copy of the worst of San Francisco: interminable soloing and hair tossing, clouds of incense causing sneezing fits among the audience. The Group was also known as having the "biggest strobe-light in the known world." Bob Moore Merlis, who once booked the band for a mixer dance at Columbia University, does not contest the claim: "It was so huge, it was brought in by truck and mounted on a floor crane. It was great, but no one could meet anyone, because people couldn't see each other." (Such college dates were among the first gigs to expose Easterners to West Coast groups. Blue Oyster Cult manager and record producer Sandy Pearlman is credited with putting on the first N.Y. concerts by the Airplane, at the State University at Stony Brook.)

Unfortunately, New York contributed few actual bands to the widening psychedelic circle. The first with the most were the Blues Magoos, who evolved out of the Night Owl folk-rock scene along with such long-lost pioneer psychers as the Headmasters (formerly the Jagged Edge), the all-girl UFO's and the Time (who became the Chicago Loop). The Magoos were both punky and pop, and scored a record deal early—their debut Mercury album *Psychedelic Lollipop* featured the band's concert crowd-pleaser, a five-minute feedback version of "Tobacco Road", as well as their one national hit single from early '67, "We Ain't Got Nothin' Yet". Lothar and the Hand People specialized in slightly more low-fi sounds, relying on Mose Allison material and fewer high-voltage freakouts. They were, however, one of the first pop groups to use the synthetic keyboard instrument, the Theremin, featured on such cuts as "Kids Are Little People" and the "Woody Woodpecker Theme" from their one Capitol album.

Less prominent bands included Autosalvage, whose one RCA album reveals a definite melodic flair but also a knack for overarranging, and Soft White Underbelly (aka the Stalk-Forrest Group), the prototype version of Blue Oyster Cult; the group's unreleased Elektra album is perhaps one of the most successful adaptations and enlargements on Frisco acid-rock outside San Francisco; guitarist Donald "Buck Dharma" Roeser weaves rippling Dead and Quicksilver-influenced leads on "Arthur Comics" and "What is Quicksand."

Discounting the Velvet Underground (whose connection to the scene seems more an accident of timing than anything else) and the Rascals (who flirted successfully with acid-pop in "See" and later singles), New York's biggest contribution to psychedelic music was Vanilla Fudge. Arguably the worst band in recorded history (the competition was to get tougher), Tim Bogert, Carmine Appice, Mark Stein and Vince Martell seized upon a highly lucrative formula approach. Let other bands work that Yardbirds thing to death, rushing here, rushing there with their clanging climaxes; the Fudge would take a pop classic, say the Supremes' "You Keep Me Hangin' On" or "Ticket To Ride" or "Season of the Witch", cut the tempo in half, and ride the beast for 20-30 minutes. The result: just what the emerging stoned-at-any-cost audiences wanted—ponderous "heavy music" packing near-lethal side effects. Nytol.

L.A.: Changin' Times on the Neon Drag

The most active youth-music scene outside San Francisco belonged to the city's traditional arch-rival, Los Angeles. According to northerners, the two towns were separated by more than just 400 miles and a couple of climate zones. To San Franciscans, Southern California has always been "plastic uptight L.A.", a razzle-dazzle backlot whose inhabitants were hooked on looks, insensitive and uncultured. For their part, Angelenos have tended to shrug nonchalantly; if Frisco wants to rant, let it. Nevertheless, in the Sixties, the two cities' "underground" communities had their differences.

"There's a difference between freaks and hippies," Frank Zappa said, defending L.A. to *Rolling Stone* in 1968. "Hippies don't really care what they look like and the freaks care an awful lot. Their packaging and image construction is a very important part of their lifestyle." The remark explains the more anarchic look favored by many of Hollywood's early freaks, like Vito Paulekas and his mad dancers—fluorescent face paint, day-glo, Saranwrap caftans, the sort of calculated outrage approach that yells "Look at me!" loudly.

The Sunset Strip, L.A.'s central artery of hip at the time, was in fact very visible and overground. There was nothing covert about a car-clogged neon dragstrip that had been the center of a flourishing club scene for ten years already. In most cases, acid-rock moved into this existing neighborhood of teenage nightclubs and beat coffeehouses, dispossesing the old tenants. The times were fast a-changing, as writer-actor Richard Blackburn recalls. "Fred C. Dobbs had been, like Ben Frank's coffeeshop, a latenight hip-beat hangout on the Strip. Then, practically overnight in '66, all the bohemians in their cord coats with the big pockets and the knit-ties were suddenly pushed aside by the incoming hippies. You could see Dylan there, Brian Jones."

While some spots, like the Fifth Estate (a coffeehouse with rooms for reading and chess) were reluctant to make the change, most swung gaily with the times. Folk-jazz haunts like the Ash Grove on Melrose adapted, as did the Sea Witch, a Sunset hole-in-the-wall that went from booking the soft folk-pop of Lyme & Cybelle (featuring Warren Zevon) to the

Courtesy Jeff Gold

Arthur Lee of Love

pounding acid-punk of the Seeds. Ciro's featured the Byrds, Sonny & Cher were practically in residence at It's Boss, while Pandora's Box booked younger pop acts—teen hordes milling around outside Pandora's sparked the Sunset Strip riots in November, 1966.

The most popular and long-lived venue was the Whisky-a-Go-Go at Sunset and San Vicente. The "world famous Whisky" had been *the* California discotheque between 1963 and '65, best known as the site of Johnny Rivers' live recordings. By '67 it had jumped into the new freak-fray, more or less. Jim Bickhart, a UCLA student at the time, recalls an early Jefferson Airplane show there: "They were on with the Peanut Butter Conspiracy. It was clearly what you'd call a 'new music' bill, probably with a lightshow and all. But the Whisky still had its go-go cages on either end of the stage and, between sets by the bands, they'd play taped music and the go-go girls would get in the cages in their spangled mini-dresses and start frugging away." Besides giving L.A. its first taste of San Francisco (and England's Yardbirds and Them and Chicago's Butterfield band), the Whisky promoted local talent heavily—the Byrds, Buffalo Springfield, Beefheart, Canned Heat, Love and the Doors.

Love was the creation of Arthur Lee, who'd started the group as the Grass Roots (not to be confused with the half dozen other groups of the same name) in 1965. As Lee told one interviewer, he drew his inspiration from seeing the Byrds at Ciro's, Jagger on the *Ed Sullivan Show* and Jimi Hendrix as an anonymous sideman accompanying Little Richard in a suburban bar. While displaying its influences—particularly Gene Clark's cyclical Byrdsriff which dominated Love's first LP, and Jagger's glottal stops which were all over the second—Lee's music was brazenly original; "Seven and Seven Is", most of the *Forever Changes* album. One of the first hip L.A. bands to score a hit ("My Little Red Book", spring '66), Love was

Psychedelic Sinatra: Jim Morrison

Elektra Records

also one of the first to disband under a cloud of irreconcilable differences late in '67. "Those guys couldn't cut it," Lee told the press. Producer Bruce Botnick told them Lee was "real unusual—he was on acid 24 hours a day."

At the time, "unusual" was considered a mild description of the Doors, who were on their way to becoming one of the most notorious and influential acts to emerge from L.A. and possibly the world—on the strength of a handful of good pop tunes ("Light My Fire," "Break On Through"), ritualistic stageshows and tons of mystique. While the band's history and Jim Morrison's evolution into sex god and the psychedelic Sinatra, his death and resurrection have been well documented elsewhere, a glance at the Doors' pre-history bears some scrutiny.

A scant two years before "The End" was wafting through college dorms across the land, Morrison was a pudgy mascot to his older, cooler classmates at UCLA film school, particularly Phil Oleno and Felix Venable. Richard Blackburn remembers Venable as a crazed post-beatnik high on hustling girls and showing the world where it was at with 16-millimeter weapons. "He came up to me once in May, asking if I knew where he could get a Christmas tree, so he could burn it in one of his films. Felix was just one of Jim's mentors, along with Eliot, Rimbaud and the rest. Morrison soaked up influences like a sponge. He'd read books, passing over the pages like a Geiger counter, finding stuff that supported his world view and filing it for later."

Morrison's file on the seedy underside of Smogville grew thick after repeated visits to the Lucky U, a beer dump on Veteran's Ave. under the San Diego Frwy. Whole packs of film schoolers eager for atmosphere made it to the Lucky U, among them Paul Ferrara (later the Doors' official photographer) and Ray Manzarek. Manzarek specialized in laborious self-films like *Induction* (a short study of his draft physical) and *Evergreen,* which documented a heavy conversation between Ray and girlfriend Dorothy Fujikawa, later the inspiration for the Doors' "Twentieth Century Fox". Blackburn recalled the dialogue as something along the lines of —Ray: "Who do you dig in jazz?" Dorothy: "Brubeck, Ahmad Jamal." Ray: "Oh man, how lame. *I* dig 'trane, Bird, Ornette . . ." And so forth.

Manzarek met drummer John Densmore and guitarist Robby Kreiger through a meditation class, and the Doors swung open. Gigs at the London Fog on the Strip led to bookings at the Whisky, a contract with Elektra and stardom. While it's clear that much of the group's appeal derived from the bloated pretentiousness of Morrison's lyrics and image, it's also clear that there was real ingenuity present in the music, particularly Manzarek's Bach-y keyboard trips and Kreiger's creamy guitar lines. Ultimately, the latter qualities may have contributed more to the Doors' popularity than the former.

It was the Doors, more than the Byrds or the Springfield (who, after all scored with hit singles instead of jaw-dropping stageshows and an underground album), who put L.A. on the psychedelic map. But others had toiled in the same fields; Love, the Sons of Adam, bluesbands like Canned Heat and the Rising Sons (fronted by Taj Mahal and Ry Cooder before he played with Beefheart), the West Coast Pop Art Experimental Band—whose range of cover material was almost as long as their name and included "Louie Louie," the Mothers' "Help, I'm A Rock" as well as songs by Dylan and Van Dyke Parks.

By 1968, the L.A. band roster included Spirit, Steppenwolf, Iron Butterfly, the Electric Prunes and others. The club scene had metamorphized into full, Frisco-size ball rooms—the aluminum-lined Cheetah in Santa Monica, the Kaleidoscope on Sunset plus periodic shows at the Shrine Exposition Hall and Pasadena's Rose Palace.

Beantown's Bus, A Trauma For Philly

Much like Los Angeles, Boston already had an active local music scene by 1965. In many cases, garage or folk-rock bands changed with the times, growing longer hair and guitar solos by '66 and '67. The best known band was the Barbarians ("Are You A Boy Or Are You A Girl?"), but there were also Teddy & The Pandas, the Lost and the Hallucinations (a proto-J. Geils Band that included vocalist Peter Wolf and drummer Stephen Bladd).

The scene itself started in small folk and blues clubs (The Unicorn on Boylston St., Club 47 in Cambridge) and quickly spread to large psychedelic dancehalls. Boston supported three such rooms—the Crosstown Bus, the Tea Party (a theatre) and, later, the Psychedelic Supermarket, a converted parking garage on Comm Ave. that secured its hip credentials in '67 by bringing an unknown British band, Cream, in for an exclusive two-week engagement. Thereafter, Boston became known as a good market for new U.K. acts, among them Procol Harum, Jeff Beck and Led Zeppelin.

Unfortunately, in many minds Boston is best remembered as the source of the infamous "Bosstown Sound" hype, a 1968 marketing ploy designed to sell a series of albums by Boston bands, most of which were on the MGM label. Late in '67 producer Alan Lorber found a mediocre Boston band called Underground cinema, changed their name to Ultimate Spinach and signed them to MGM. The label, whose rock roster at the time was limited to the Animals, the hitless Herman's Hermits and Lainie Kazan, liked what it heard and ordered more. Soon there were derivative, undistinguished albums by the Spinach, Orpheus, Beacon St. Union—even a band called Phluph—and a publicity campaign

The Bosstown Sound of Phluph

for the whole batch of them. "Another revolution has begun in Boston," read the advertisements. "The British and San Francisco are on the run . . ."

The news media eagerly bought the hype, *Newsweek* declaring that "The Boston Sound is as fresh and new as the groups and places that spawned it." *The Wall St. Journal* warned that the music of the Ultimate Spinach "isn't for teenyboppers." Then other labels bought in, ABC grabbing the power trio Eden's Children, Elektra getting Earth Opera (founded by David Grisman and Peter Rowan).

Then it all fizzled like a giant phluph. Despite Orpheus' MOR semi-hit "Can't Find The Time", none of the groups was able to change the face of the Boston rock legacy; the city had not produced a pop act of any consequence since Freddie "Boom Boom" Cannon.

Like mushrooms, scenes sprouted overnight in other regions as well. Philadelphia had its own second story ballroom-with-lightshow, the Trauma, and later (1968) the Electric Factory ("the Fillmore of Philly"). Todd Rundgren fronted the Who-ish Nazz, and there was also Woody's Truckstop, Edison Electric, Elizabeth and the Trauma's houseband Mandrake Memorial, whom some remember for blowing the Doors off the bill one winter night in '69.

Motor City, Chicago, Texas

Detroit had the Grande Ballroom, and a talent roster that included the soul-psychedelic Rationals, the Spikedrivers and the Scott Richards Case (which, like Big Brother, made a rave-up of "Hall of the Mountain King"). The Eagles' Glenn Frey played in the Mushrooms, Suzi Quatro in the all-girl Pleasure Seekers and Ted Nugent headed the scene's sole hit act, the Amboy Dukes, who scored with the Frisco-influenced piledriver "Journey to the Center of Your Mind."

For some reason, Chicago was slow to jump on the bandwagon. While the city had been a hotbed of folk and punk-rock (the Shadows of Knight, Trolls, Cryan' Shames), it wasn't until later '67 that it birthed bonafide psychedelic bands; H.P. Lovecraft went for a full paisley sound, with swirling organ and mysterious lyrics ("White Ship"), while the Illinois Speed Press utilized a less distinguished, guitar-heavy approach.

As if the Thirteenth Floor Elevators weren't enough, Texas produced a whole spate of psychedelic groups which vied with each other for weirdness honors. One was the Moving Sidewalks, Houston's punkish blues rockers whose lineup included Z.Z. Top guitarist Billy Gibbons; the band's opus was the wildly psychedelic "99th Floor." Many of the state's farthest out bands recorded for International Artists Records, the bizarre Houston label operated by Kenny Rogers' brother Lelan. Only the Elevators and Bubble Puppy ("Hot Smoke and Sassafras") enjoyed hits, but that didn't stop IA from churning out acidic wonders like the *Power Plant* album by Golden Dawn or the Lost And Found who wrote songs like "Living Eye." Best of all, there was Mayo

Courtesy Bob Merlis

Moving Sidewalks with fan (Billy Gibbons in white).

Thompson's Red Krayola, whose two LPs, *Parable of Arable Land* and *God Bless the Red Krayola and All Who Sail With It,* set perimeters for freak-rock which frew groups since have crossed.

Everywhere, locals were tripping to the new ultrasound from the Coast, and doing their best to come up with their own version. In Seattle it was the Daily Flash's warped feedback excursions. In Grand Rapids, Michigan, it was the wild abandon of the unforgettable Phlegethon. How far would it go?

Blowing Britain's Mind

Like virtually everything else connected with youth culture in Great Britain, the psychedelic underground was essentially a bastardized version of what was going on in America. Despite that, British youthcult—even from its infancy in the Fifties—possessed its share of original, homegrown elements. By the middle of 1965, the notion of "pop" and Swinging London was gripping the entire nation; a seemingly inexhaustible supply of "fab" records, the thrill of pirate radio, and

Ready Steady Go on TV each week. In the midst of all this, in June a small band of old Beat and not-quite-hippies staged the International Poetry Festival at Albert Hall. The event featured American poets Ginsberg, Corso and Ferlinghetti, Britain's Pete Brown (later lyricist of "White Room" and other Cream songs) together with the first public appearance of hundreds of young people bedecked with flowers and carrying joss-sticks.

Many of the festival's prime movers were in fact American hipsters. One of them, Steve Stollman, brother of ESP Records owner Bernard Stollman (whose roster included New York's infamous Fugs), stayed in London to organize a series of "Spontaneous Underground" events Sunday afternoons at the Marquee Club. The first of these, held in February, featured Pete Brown performing magic tricks, an avant garde orchestra which utilized transistor radios, and assorted weirdness. For the most part, these were somewhat staid, arty affairs—until the March afternoon when an unknown band, the Pink Floyd Sound, tore things up with a loud, wiry brand of freak-rock. Things picked up, and soon the happenings moved to John "Hoppy" Hopkins' London Free School in Notting Hill Gate where lights, films and free-form dancing were added to the Floyd's music.

Motorpsycho Madness

The first *real* coming-out of London's new in-crowd—some 2000 of them—was a massive, Tripfest-type party organized by the Floyd's subsequent mangers with Hoppy and the ubiquitous Miles to launch the duo's latest project: England's first underground paper, *International Times.* On Oct. 15, 1966, the heads filed into the Roundhouse, a former engine shed that had been taken over by the Gilbey's Gin company. The building had wooden pillars, balconies, and a romantic, nineteenth century atmosphere—perfect for the revelry that ensued. On arrival, guests were greeted by Miles handing out sugar cubes (not, however, of the Prankster variety). From there it was a bacchanalia of bizarrely dressed freaks rolling in jellies, dancing, tripping. Paul McCartney showed up dressed as an Arab sheikh. Director Michelangelo Antonioni was there taking a break from the filming of *Blow Up.* Marianne Faithfull showed up in a nun's habit and won the prize for the shortest/barest costume. Onstage, the Floyd went into interstellar overdrive, alternating sets with the Soft Machine, whose instrumentation included a motorcycle with a contact mike attached to the cylinder head; the bike engine was revved up from time to time to augment the group's euphonious wailing. Pink Floyd also brought the lightshow they'd been using at the Free School, a standard projection model that was nonetheless impressive.

Sporadic happenings continued through November, hit-and-run events with names like "Psychedelia vs. Ian Smith" and "Freak Out Ethel." But, as with San Franciscans finding their Fillmore, Britain's underground finally found UFO, a permanent venue located in a basement Irish dancehall called the Blarney Club. UFO's first bash was "UFO Presents Night Tripper," a dusk-till-dawn marathon held on the eve of Christmas Eve, 1966. Like Bill Graham or Chet Helms, UFO's management refined the previous mixed-media shows into a heady brew of sight and sound. Most of all, UFO at the Blarney was a relaxed environment where just about anything could go on—Lennon and Jagger roaming freely, unmolested by autograph hounds; dope deals; shopping for paraphernalia at the on-premises headshop or buying groovy goodies at John Pearce's Granny Takes A Trip stall. In addition to house band Pink Floyd, music was provided by Soft Machine, Arthur Brown (of "Fire" and flaming headdress fame), the Purple Gang (who recorded the UFO anthem "Granny Takes A Trip"), Procol Harum in the heady days when "White Shade of Pale" was shooting chartward, and Tomorrow, which featured the young Yes guitarist Steve Howe. (Just before UFO secured the Round-

Music from exhaust pipes: Soft Machine Courtesy John Platt

house, Chet Helms had flown over and attempted to lease the building for a "London Dog" operation. He failed but hung around long enough to open the Family Dog Shop off Portobello Road, which sold Avalon posters to budding British heads.)

With the scene now so visibly overground, trouble was afoot. There was abusive coverage from the press and in April of 1967 the police raided the *International Times* offices in an attempt to shut the paper down. The ensuing *I.T.* benefit attracted 10,000 people and presented some 41 acid-rock groups. Despite the money it raised and the impressive turnout, the benefit marked the end of the London underground. Within weeks, scene-chief "Hoppy" Hopkins was in jail on drug charges and UFO was forced to find new, more expensive quarters to cater to the swelling crowds coming to see Jeff Beck, Eric Burdon's Animals and others. But increasingly the club's original freak clientele was being displaced by trend-bent weekend hippies, drunken sailors and even hippie-bashing skinhead punks. UFO stick it out till October then folded.

The slack was taken up by other clubs—the more commercial Happening 44, Middle Earth in Covent Garden (which persisted until fall of '68 and presented Captain Beefheart, the Byrds and other American bands) and the Temple, a seedy Wardour St. dive that ran briefly in 1969. By that time, the counterculture appeared to have more adherents than ever before, but in reality the bloom had been off flower-power for a good year already. As in the States, the party had grown so large that its original hosts got lost in the crowd.

Tabs and Defecting Gray

As for the music itself, British rockers took two routes to psychedelia. On the one hand, plenty of blues-based pop musicians like Clapton, Bruce, Jeff Beck, John Mayall and Fleetwood Mac's Peter Green flirted with the style, dropping their tabs then beating it back to the barracks to play their South Chicago licks. (Some of the best examples of this type approach were provided by the Stones-ish Pretty Things; "Defecting Gray," "Talking About the Good Times".) On the other hand, the majority of English psychedelians actually came from soul music backgrounds. Even Pink Floyd and Soft Machine had started off performing Stax and Motown numbers (though the early Softies mixed that with equal parts of Coltrane and Terry Riley). Tomorrow had been a soul outfit called the In Crowd, and Britain's most zealous convert, Eric Burdon, knew nothing but R&B until he met the girl named Sandoz. The Who came from similar roots and, in their 1966 op-art phase, provided the most influential model for U.K. bands wanting to psyche out; younger groups such as the Creation, Eyes and John's Children (which included T. Rex's Marc Bolan) simply grafted Who-like arrangements and electronic effects onto a basic soul sound.

While 1967 marked the start of the scene's decline, it was a good year for British acid-rock—Pink Floyd's "Arnold Layne", Tomorrow's "My White Bicycle", Soft Machine's "Love Makes Sweet Music", and "I Can Take You to the Sun" by expatriate Californians the Misunderstood. The year also gave the world its foremost electric guitar technician in Jimi Hendrix, who'd been discovered by Animals' bassist Chas Chandler in New York and brought to London the year before. With a name change, two British sidemen, and a quickly earned a reputation as a Continental crowd-pleaser, Hendrix made his initial impact on Americans—on the handful of FM rock stations and at the Monterey Pop Festival (where he'd been added to the bill at Paul McCartney's request)—as "the biggest thing in England." Hendrix's claim could only be challenged by Cream, rock's first "supergroup" who had to first make it in the States (San Francisco, Boston, New York) before they were awarded honors.

Despite tours by the Dead, Airplane and the Doors, West Coast psychedelic had little if any effect on the British. The exceptions were Fairport Convention, whose early music revealed a healthy dose of Airplane influence (as well as Kaleidoscope and the Youngbloods at times), and Mighty Baby. The latter evolved out of the mod-soul band the Action in early 1968; helmed by guitarist Martin Stone, they relied on an electric, improv approach that bore more than a little resemblance to the Dead's. In the Seventies, Deke Leonard's Welsh group Man openly declared their Quicksilver roots, recording an entire lp (*Maximum Darkness)* with John Cipollina. Like most British followers of pop, music historian John Platt was "bowled over" by the first rush of psychedelia in 1966. "It was almost as though all the musical styles I'd grown up with merged into something new. It was the music I'd been waiting for without knowing what it was, since it didn't exist." While he became an inveterate scene-goer, attending many of the historic gigs earlier described, it was the California variety of acid-rock that first grabbed his ear: "Throughout '66, reports were filtering through to England about these strange bands with weird names who played all night long. It was all very confused and it was hard to tell whether Love were from San Francisco or the Dead were from L.A. Gradually it all sorted itself out . . .

"It really wasn't until early 1967 that we heard all the new bands. An English deejay, John Ravenscroft, had returned from California and joined Radio as 'John Peel'. His 'Perfumed Garden' show singlehandedly turned us on to Country Joe, Beefheart and all the rest . . ."

With what seemed like the whole world now alerted to the spectacle of San Francisco's psychedelic subculture; with every middlesex village earnestly emulating the sights and sounds that were rocking the Bay; with the whole wiggy adventure now a certified phenomenon—the time was ripe to take the music out of the ballrooms and onto the profit margins of record business ledgers. It was inevitable that, sooner or later, the vinyl entrepreneurs would beat a path to Frisco from the pop citadels of Tin Pan Alley and the Sunset Strip. They'd built their business, after all, on a knack for recognizing What's Happening and there was no 'what' that was happening more than the noises exploding from the Fillmore and Avalon.

When they got there, wraparounds gleaming and contracts thirsting for ink, the pop-moguls were in for a bit of a surprise. San Francisco's music establishment was, by and large, no gullible bunch of gee-whiz amateurs; on the contrary, their exalted status as counter-culture heroes was quite sufficient, thank you; they were not about to jeopardize their credentials by collaborating with known commercial interests. It was, of course, one more holdover from the scene's early affinity with folk music's political conscience. The us-against-them'ism had been aggravated by such counter-culture quenchers as outlawing LSD and hassling runaway pilgrims in the Haight-Ashbury. The music biz slicks suddenly coming out of the woodwork were suspiciously sized-up as more emissaries from the Military Industrial Complex.

"We were playing regularly and making good money," Jerry Garcia recalls. "We didn't have any tremendous need to make a record." "The group was incredibly paranoid," says Country Joe & the Fish manager Ed Denson. "They were sure some record company was going to rip off their music and use the profits for God-knows-what evil scheme."

Yet even when San Francisco's ballroom bonanza was at the raging apex of its popularity, the groups who were packing them in had already had a long and checkered history with the platter industry. It was a tragi-comic chain of events that no doubt contributed the bands' studied air of seeming indifference.

Ironically, the scene's first brush with exploitation was not at the hand's of visiting sharpies. The sharpie was right in their own midst. In 1964, when Tom Donahue brought the Rolling Stones to the Civic Auditorium to help kick things off, he was already the established kingpin of San Francisco's bush league music business: a very large fish in a very small pond. Any group interested in cutting wax had one of two choices—leave town or deal with Big Daddy. Most, whether they liked it or not, took the Donahue option.

Which meant, invariably, cutting a demo for Donahue's flagship label, Autumn Records. "We started out with a music tip-sheet," Donahue told one interviewer. "It was a great business. You got records for nothing and culled through them for hits. Radio stations subscribed for 50 bucks a month because they didn't have their own staff to figure out what to play. We built up a sheet called *Tempo* with the top 30 or 40 tunes and various comments about each of the records. We were also doing a lot of concert production."

From tip sheets and Cow Palace extravaganzas, the next move was unavoidable. "We got into the recording business," Donahue continued. "It was ridiculous because none of us had ever been in any of these businesses. We thought we could handle it all by hiring expensive accountants and expensive attorneys."

'Coattail Parties'

Autumn Records' first foray into the pop mainstream was "I Taught Him," by Gloria Scott, produced by an up-and-coming East Bay youngster named Sylvester Stewart. Born in Texas and bred on the factory streets of Vallejo, Sly Stewart had taken a music course in high school and attracted enough attention to pique the interest of Big Daddy. Donahue associate Pete Marino recalls: "We used to do these 'coattail parties.' We'd go to Sacramento or some suburb on the Peninsula, throw a little party and invite the student body presidents and school paper editors from all the local high schools and junior highs. We'd tell them we were going to throw a dance and we wanted each school to provide us with their *best* talent. The bands would then battle it out and the winner would get a prize, a trip or something. It was a scam, but it really worked. In Vallejo, the group that won was the Viscaynes, with Sly as the lead singer."

The talented teen was recruited by Donahue to process the scores of hopefuls attracted to Autumn. "He was on salary," recalls Carl Scott. "We made him part of the company." It was a sound investment. Sly went on to produce a string of local hits by Bobby Freeman, the Beau Brummels, the Mojo Men and others. "He had a way of getting what he wanted from musicians," recounts Jan Erico, who sang

Courtesy Hamerschlagg Archives

for both the Mojo Men and the Vejtables. "If we weren't as energetic as he wanted us to be in the studio, he would jump up and down inside the control room. If something wasn't right, he would sit in and play on the session."

Autumn was quickly becoming attuned not only to prevailing Top 40 tastes but to the sounds of San Francisco's emerging underground as well. Aside from such local phenomena as George and Teddy, a duo whose dance steps the Righteous Brothers later studiously copied, and the Spearmints, who died their hair green for Cow Palace shows, Autumn had the song stylings of Dino Valenti, artist on a number of unreleased sides for the label including the anthemic "New Wind Blowing In My Mind." The Valenti connection was, however, no help at all for John Cipollina's fledgling Quicksilver crew. "Donahue would never return our phone calls," the guitarist asserts.

"We had incredible potential," Donahue recalled. "The whole thing was just beginning to happen. We had cut demos on the Charlatans and the Grateful Dead, back when they were called the Emergency Crew . . ."

Donahue, through his partner Bob Mitchell, had indeed caught wind of the Charlatans' ongoing Virginia City wingding back in the summer of '65. "We got some free time from the Red Dog and took a train down to San Francisco," explains George Hunter. "We were in the studio for one day and cut four tracks with Sly. That was it."

It was also the first in what proved to be an extensive screening of San Francisco's new bands by Donahue. Shortly after his biliously-hued nightclub Mother's opened its doors, Big Daddy hit upon an ingenious scheme for culling the best from the rest of the city's brand new musical crop, searching, as always, for likely hitmakers. Using a stint at Mother's as bait, he auditioned all comers; any group that caught his fancy was booked into the club and invited to cut a demo for Autumn. The Grateful Dead, fresh from the Peninsula pizza circuit, came down the assembly line, recording six tracks as the Emergency Crew for Autumn at Golden State studios; among them, "Can't Come Down," "Mindbender," "Caution—Don't Stop On Tracks," and Gordon Lightfoot's "Early Morning Rain" with Phil Lesh singing lead. The band's only previous studio experience: a session at a friend's home studio had resulted in a single "Stealin' "/"Don't Ease Me In" on Scorpio Records.

Next up was the Great Society. "There was an ad in the paper," recalls Darby Slick. "It said, 'Get a job at Mother's and a recording contract.' It was a complete cattle call. Sly was there and he was the one to impress; he decided whether you got to play the club or not. Also there were a lot of Autumn's successful acts—the Beau Brummels and the Vejtables—who were hanging around for the fun of it. They fell over laughing when they heard us, but we got the gig."

After playing at the club for a few weeks, Donahue was impressed enough with the Great Society to move on to the next step in his master plan. "I remember

Courtesy George Hunter

The Charlatans wait for Autumn

Tom announcing out of the blue that we were going to manage this band and we had to talk them into it," Carl Scott remembers. "We had a lot of meetings with Grace and Darby and they kept asking what we were going to do for them. There was also a lot of tap-dancing on our part, trying to figure out whatever it was we were supposed to offer them as managers and having no idea."

Too Many 'Somebodies'

"Donahue sent us down to record with Sly," continues Darby. "It was part of the process. I remember he wanted us to do 'Summertime,' and put patches on our clothes. We ended up cutting 'Somebody To Love.' It was a real disaster. We got set up and did a perfect take of the song. But the engineer wasn't ready and we lost it. Sly made us do it 50 more times. We kept arguing with him about the arrangement, telling him we were creative types and eventually he just gave up."

About that time, things weren't going too well for Autumn Records either. Despite a respectable chart showing with the Beau Brummels, the Vejtables and others, the company was deeply in debt. For a short time they moved from their garment district headquarters to the closest thing San Francisco had to a Brill Building—an ornate flat-iron antique in the heart of North Beach called Columbus Towers. "It had tiny little offices," Carl Scott laughs, "and this ancient elevator. The only plush office in the place was the penthouse and that belonged to Frank Werber, who managed the Kingston Trio and was a really weird guy. He had gold fixtures in the office bathroom and put his desk up high on a platform surrounded by mirrors. When you talked to him, you always talked up and his reflection was everywhere."

Whether Frank Werber's elevated office furniture served as an object lesson for the struggling Donahue isn't known. The Kingston Trio's svengali certainly wasn't going broke overestimating the tastes of the American record buying public, while Big Daddy was facing foreclosure trying to promote bands like the Great Society, whose idea of ultimate fulfillment was 20 minutes' worth of raga-rock. "We got into desperate trouble," Donahue admitted. "The studio had locked us out for the $10,000 we owed them and they were holding all our tapes. So we made a deal with Warner Bros. Records and sold them all our acts. Sly wasn't part of the deal because he was part owner in the company, but they got the Great Society. The band's option was up with us and Warner Bros. never picked up the deal."

For Tom Donahue, Autumn Records was simply a failed attempt to capitalize on the promotional flair that had already made him a name in local music circles. For the bands shuttled through the label's revolving door, it was an early taste of what it meant to be a 'property'. The Autumn experience was positively benign compared to what would shortly follow, but it accentuated the essential difference between the music establishment and the Frisco freak alternative. Carl Scott recounts: "Connie DeNave, who was a publicist for Herman's Hermits and lots of teen singers, had given us a list of one hundred questions we should ask any band we wanted to manage. It was like a scientific way of giving you 'complete knowledge' of what the artist was all about. We gave it to the Great Society and they couldn't figure it out. 'What is this shit?' Grace said. 'Why do I have to tell you my favorite color?' 'You gotta do it,' we were saying. 'It's for publicity.' They just thought it was stupid." Grace and Darby and all the rest of their free-form comrades were positively hostile to 'playing along', putting on a palatable public front. Why bother?

Why indeed? One good reason was

the tantalizing prospect of success; big success; Beatlesque success. It was, after all, George Hunter's intent from the very beginning that the Charlatans give the Fab Four a run for their money. And even someone of Luria Castell's ideological purity couldn't help but catch a gleam in her eye at the thought of that particular pay-off.

On her early exploratory foray to Los Angeles, Luria had met an up-and-coming young producer named Erik Jacobsen. A midwestern folkie who relocated to Greenwich Village, Jacobsen had landed a production job at Kama Sutra Records where his first assignment was an LP for some local talent named the Lovin' Spoonful. *Do You Believe In Magic* rocketed straight to the top. Strange rumors from San Francisco had, meanwhile, filtered cross country to Jacobsen, who was searching for the next likely production prospect. On a trip to Frisco for a look-see, he was sought out by Luria with that gleam in her eye and a very intriguing proposition.

"It was in the elevator at Columbus Towers," Jacobsen relates. "Luria kept telling me about this fantastic band she'd heard and then she takes out this Polaroid of a bunch of guys dressed like characters in a Jules Verne novel. I couldn't believe it. I'd started getting into old time clothes a little myself from hanging out with the Spoonful, but these guys were taking it to the limit. I just kind of stared at the picture and in the meantime Luria started playing a cassette. It was the Charlatans doing 'Alabama Bound.' It was recorded live and I don't see now how it could have sounded like anything at all, but right then, it was just incredible—the most amazing thing I'd ever heard. I couldn't believe it." Jacobsen flew back to New York, convinced he'd heard the future of rock & roll, returning a few weeks later to meet the band and close a recording contract for his Sweet Reliable Productions. It was a measure of how anxious the Charlatans were for a shot at the big

Courtesy Erik Jacobsen

Erik Jacobsen

time that they agreed to record their first LP for no advance money. "George put the deal together without really being too aware of all the implications," is how Dan Hicks kindly recalls the negotiations.

"They picked me up at the airport," Jacobsen recalls. "Hunter met me at the gate and he seemed real mysterious, kind of aloof. We got my bags and he took me out to the parking lot to this truck." It was, to be precise, the band's 1941 Langendorff Bread truck, used as a conference-hall-on-wheels. The group had just returned from their stand in Virginia City, feeling fortunate not to have been strung-up by the citizenry after word of Wilhelm and Laughlin's pot bust had leaked out. "George opened the back of the truck and this enormous cloud of smoke rolls out. I could just barely make out some figures inside, sitting around on overstuffed chairs. There was a Tiffany lamp hanging inside the truck and these guys, dressed to the nines, staring back at me. I climbed in and sat next to Wilhelm. On the way back to their apartment, I kept looking at his hair. It had the weirdest kinks and curls. Later I realized it was a wig. When he'd been busted, they'd shaved his head and he was wearing it until his real hair grew back."

Courtesy George Hunter

Co'dine and Kama Sutra

Once in the recording studio, things went from bizarre to abysmal. "They really weren't any good," Jacobsen asserts. "They could play alright, but they really couldn't sing." Nine songs were eventually cut, including "Alabama Bound," "By Hook Or By Crook," "32-20 Blues," and two numbers with Lynne Hughes, a folksinging barmaid the band had met at the Red Dog.

The band's plan was to release "Co'dine" as their first single: a bigger mistake it would be hard to imagine. Kama Sutra backpeddled from the song faster than a cycling race in reverse. The band's liaison at the time was an old-line music biz pro—another of Alan Freed's ubiquitous one-time gofer's who'd lately hit with Jay & the Americans—by the name of Artie Ripp. "There was a lot of controversy about how to make a record that dealt with the drug experience," Ripp recalls. "How were we going to say something without it being rejected out of hand by young people, just because we were adults? I concluded that it was totally necessary to make this record. Unfortunately that wasn't how it was perceived by the radio stations. They didn't believe me when I told them that this was an anti-drug song that kids could relate to. They thought I just wanted to sell records. I liked the song because it came right out and said, 'Hey, kids, no one can ride this buffalo.' "

Ripp, who was to loom large in San Francisco's love/hate relationship with the record industry, may be indulging in a bit of buffaloing himself in his account of "Co'dine's" supression. The fact was, Kama Sutra wouldn't touch the record with a ten-foot stylus. The Charlatans, in the process, began to look like more trouble than they were worth. Hunter had designed an advertisement for the single's release with the motto "Remedy For A Drugged Market," which sent the label brass into an apoplectic tizzy. Jacobsen returned to New York with the master tapes and after a huddle with Ripp, emerged with a re-mixed version of "The Shadow Knows." Subsequently released through Kapp Records, the tune died

Artie Ripp, 1966

Courtesy Artie Ripp

without a whimper.

It was also, effectively, the end of the Charlatans. Unhappy with their Kama Sutra contract, they demanded an audience with Artie Ripp. "They invited me to their house and gave me something to smoke," the Ripper recalls. "Before I knew it, there was some guy standing over me with a shotgun saying 'Listen, we think it's best for your personal health if you sign this form releasing us from our contract. You'll be making us very happy.' "

Shortly afterwards, the band played a show at Winterland. George Hunter: "Just before the second set, Ferguson disappeared and didn't come back. Graham is yelling at us and personally hauling our equipment off the stage. It turned out Mike had gone out to eat and spilled barbeque sauce on his white pants. He wouldn't come back out looking like that." To the very end, the image, unsoiled . . . In September of '67, Ferguson left to take a job at the post office.

"I Can Get You On Shindig"

The handwriting was getting clearer for another original aggregate as well. As early as the spring of '65, the Mystery Trend had decided it was hopelessly out of step with the freeform foolhardiness of most San Francisco bands. The only other option was to go mainstream, which meant landing a recording contract, which meant taking a trip to Sunset Strip. Manager Mike Daly and guitarist Bob Cuff were designated as ambassadors to Lotusland, taking with them a demo of the band's best pop material.

"The first place we went was Sonny and Cher's office," Daly recalls. "We didn't have an appointment or anything. People in L.A. didn't really care about bands from San Francisco. So we just sat on the couch and eventually Sonny and Cher actually walked in. For some reason it seemed like a big deal. Eventually, this guy with a Lancelot beard comes out and plays our tape. He listens to the whole thing and then tells us we're totally unprofessional and we'd never get signed. So we went down the street to White Whale Records and the same thing happened." Far from getting discouraged, the pair dropped by The Trip hoping to catch another glimpse of Sonny & Cher. Outside the club they met an agent named Howard Wulfe who, according to Daly, "took one look at our hair and clothes and said, 'Hey, I can get you on *Shindig.*' I thought, this is it! We've made it."

They hadn't. Returning home empty-handed the band resolved to tighten its vocal approach and, on the advice of Marty Balin, began taking lessons from a singing coach named Judy Davis. Davis—who had worked with Streisand, Vickie Carr, even Carol Doda—liked what she heard and pointed the group in the direction of Frank Werber—the same Frank Werber perched atop Columbus Towers in his mirrored penthouse. Werber agreed to take on the Trend and sent them down to the Columbus Towers basement to cut a demo. At the time Werber's Trident Productions had a pack-

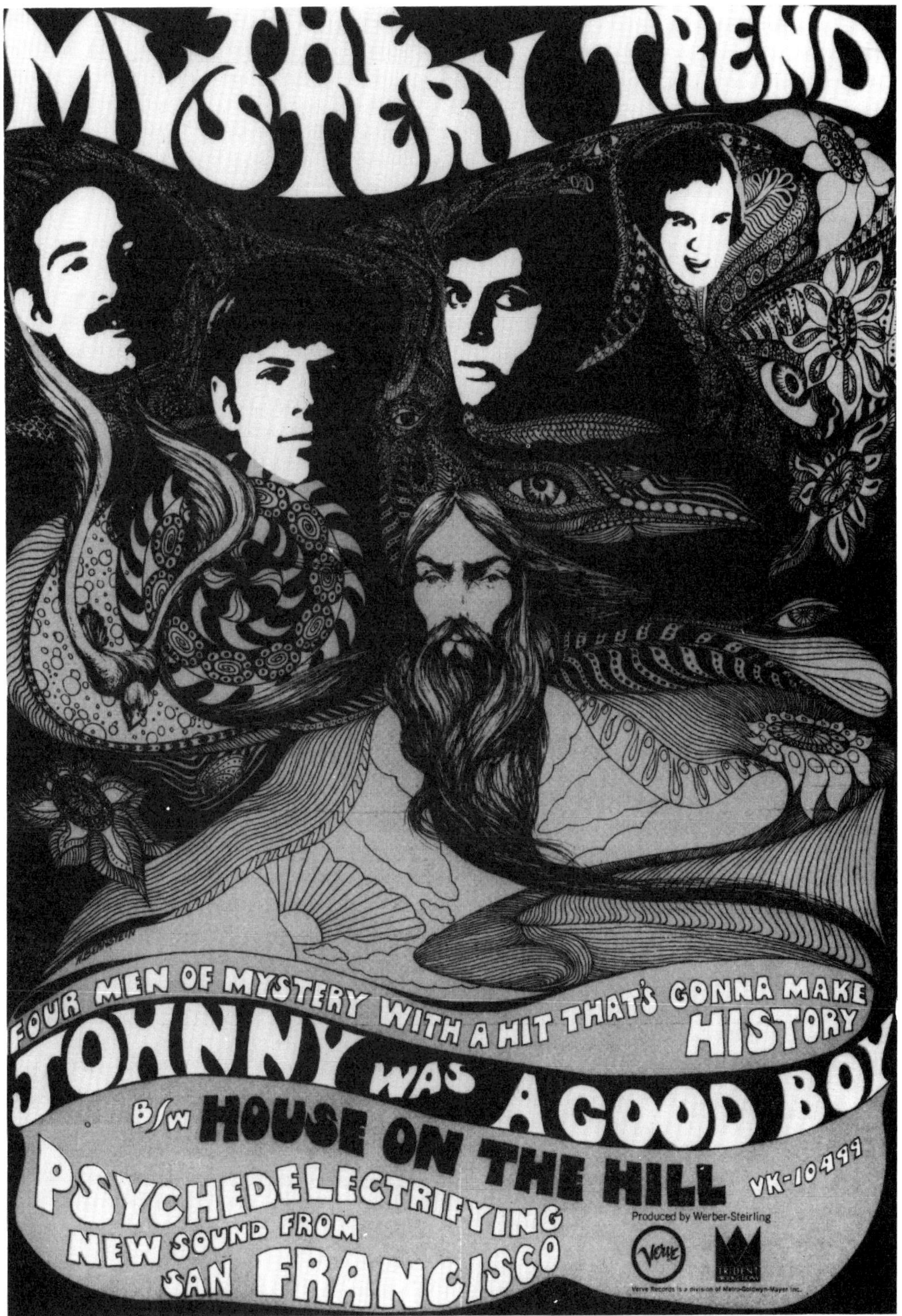

Courtesy Gordon Skene

age deal with Verve Records and Nagle and company could certainly be excused for thinking they had at last arrived. They cut nine tunes, including a version of the Who's "Substitute." Verve settled on one, a hot-wired Nagle original called "Johnny Was A Good Boy," and released it in April of '67. An ad for the single in *Cashbox Magazine* read, "Four Men of Mystery With A Hit That's Gonna Make History; Psychedelectrifying New Sounds From San Francisco." Verve had also taken it upon itself to speed up the original version for airwave consumption.

By this time, the band had replaced guitarist Larry 'Way Out' West after his traumatic duel with Darby Slick at the Gate Theater. With new axman John Gregory they waited with baited breath for their debut single to rocket up the charts. It was a long wait. "We weren't playing much," Nagle recalls. "And after a while we realized that the record had stiffed. By then I was going through a divorce and everyone was pretty tense. We started hating each other." In the early summer of '67, when Frisco's ballroom frenzy was reaching its peak, the Mystery Trend quietly disbanded.

It was back in the spring of '65, a happier, more hopeful time for Nagle and his band, when Marty Balin dropped by the Trend's Gough St. digs with some startling news. Ron Nagle: "He said, 'Man, you're not gonna believe this but we just got $25,000 from RCA.' We thought he was lying."

If it was a lie, it was a pretty outlandish one. $25,000 was a staggering advance for any group, particularly one in the midst of a scene that snubbed the very concept of play-for-pay with the big boys. But if, by virtue of the Airplane's palpable musical skills and ready-for-market pop sensibilities, the sextet was the natural choice to attract the attention of a major label, its attitude was only too typical of time and place. "The band was cautious," recounts Neely Plumb, RCA's West Coast A&R man. "They were suspicious and fearful of big business."

Plumb's background in the big business of music went back to the big band era where he had played saxophone and clarinet for Artie Shaw and others. Later, as a producer, he'd put together soundtrack albums for Broadway plays like *The Sound of Music* and *Bye Bye Birdie*. After becoming RCA Records' A&R Director on the coast, he made an early foray to San Francisco to sign, then produce, The Limelighters as well as Hugo 'Good, Bad & Ugly' Montenegro. In 1965, he was lodged in L.A. as RCA's regional ears, putting together, in his spare time, an extension course at UCLA on the music industry. He caught wind of a "weird-named group in San Francisco called Jefferson Airplane. I was really intrigued. The next morning I got on a plane and flew up."

He found the Airplane at the Matrix where they'd been playing regularly ever since Balin had first pulled them together. "I just walked in and introduced myself. I chatted with them between sets in the kitchen. I really liked Signe, but I think what impressed me the most was their precision as a group. It took me back to my tenure with the big bands—they took the same sort of care. I really flipped over what I heard. When I came back to L.A., I told Al Schmitt, an engineer and producer who worked for me, to go up for a second opinion. He flipped too."

Precision and big band memories are one thing: $25,000 is quite another. Plumb began tortuous negotiations with the band's manager Matthew Katz. "The bottom line was, they needed money for equipment. Katz demanded this enormous advance, which at the time was outlandish. I agreed. RCA thought I was out of my mind. Shortly after I'd signed them, the company had a convention in Bermuda and the chief financial officer backs me against the wall and says 'What do you think you're doing? Are you crazy?' 'No,' I told him, 'and you won't have to ask me that after we start having hits with them."

Plumb's Kid Gloves

With twenty-five G's in their pocket and a once-in-a-lifetime opportunity staring them in the face, the Airplane winged down to Hollywood and walked into RCA Victor's Music Center of the World to begin work on their first album. Having put his reputation—and the company's money—on the line, Plumb did all he could to insure that the Airplane would indeed deliver. He hired producer Tommy Oliver to oversee the band's first album. Matthew Katz, in turn, appointed himself to oversee Tommy Oliver. "Tommy'd been a music director for lots of TV shows—*Name That Tune* and later *Laugh-In,*" says Plumb. "I had confidence in him, but the main thing was that it was absolutely essential for the group to have a producer they could relate to."

Plumb's kid-glove treatment of his latest discovery was only partially due to the huge chunk of money he committed to the project. It was clear he heard genuine potential in the band and when RCA held its annual sales convention in Monterey in '66, it was arranged for the band to appear at the famed Monterey Jazz Festival. It was a risky venue—these folk-rock adventurers playing loud electric instruments for the staid box-lunch crowd—but it was an indication of the faith Plumb and other RCA insiders had in the band's future. Even the most sacred commercial credos were set aside in an effort to let the Airplane do its thing. "I would have sooner taken a meatball away from a tiger than to ask those guys to shorten their songs," is how Plumb explains it. "I was under a lot of pressure from New York to do it, but I resisted. I had one boss who found it painful to release any single over two minutes. But I knew the band would resent it if I interfered and they'd be right if they did."

Marty Balin remembers it a little differently. "We had great trouble with the first recording," he told Ralph Gleason. "We never think of time. We think of putting down an idea and when it's done, it's done. We had a six minute song and they were flipping out. So on the album we had to cut down quite a bit. We had great battles . . . Neely Plumb would say, 'Well, take out this verse,' and I'd say, 'Oh, but that explains the idea of this and that . . ."

This and that notwithstanding, the Airplane was not above gnawing on the hand that fed it. "Plumb was pretty straight," Kantner says. "I'm not sure what his taste was. He seemed to come out of the Lawrence Welk age. He thought we were a little crazed and wanted us to cut our hair. Eventually that attitude was translated into the recording process. We had to go into the janitor's closet to smoke a joint."

There was, in fact, a not-insubstantial in-studio set-to about some purportedly "questionable" lyrics in the song "Run Around." "I got into a huge argument with the group," admits Plumb. "The song had a line about 'blinded by colors that sway as you lay under me.' That probably sealed my fate with them."

In September of '66 *The Jefferson Airplane Takes Off* was released. The album was a clear and engaging representation of the band's folk-rocking charm, but despite a major push from RCA, it made a disappointing first impression on the public. "It's No Secret," the LP's debut single, failed to make a dent in the charts outside Frisco and the album's sales were meager. Plumb wandered off to greener pastures, repairing his tarnished reputation by signing the Monkees. In one respect, however, *Takes Off* was a resounding success. The infant profession of "serious" rock criticism gleaned from the LP all manner of portents for the future of music. Waxing euphoric over Casady's bass-playing, Tim Jurgens, in *Crawdaddy* observed that it was "the most advanced bass work in pop recording history. Casady's lines come, it seems to me, not to much from rock or jazz as from classical music. His bass becomes an electric cello . . ." San Francisco bands were going to hear a lot of that sort of talk before long.

Whatever the fate of the Jefferson Airplane's maiden flight into commercial spheres, conventional wisdom has it that *Takes Off* laid the groundwork for the industry's dealing with underground rock bands forever after. "Their contract broke the ice," declares Neely Plumb. "It broke the ice for bands to be seen as their own entities," echoes Jack Casady.

Tell it to Country Joe and Big Brother.

In the fall of '66, the Fish had agreed to record their debut effort for prestige folk label Vanguard for a miserly $5,000. For many psychedelic neophytes, *Electric Music For The Mind And Body* did more to ignite the eerie, transcendental fires of acid rock than the Airplane's big budget extravaganza. The LP was recorded, according to Fish manager Ed Denson, under very tense conditions, not all of it generated by Vanguard's leery approach to its first rock flirtation. "The band had these tremendous, continuing fights in the studio," he reports. "They'd argue for hours about an arrangement, finally exhausting themselves and then going back and recording something that incorporated the best of what everyone wanted." The end result sold well but did little to ease the intense suspicion between the group and their record company. Denson sums up the band's feeling best by recalling that one of the talent scouts sent to Frisco to sign the band, looked, under the influence of LSD, "just like the devil."

Microscopic Royality Rates

Big Brother's particular version of Beelzebub was Bob Shad—another A&R man from a Chicago jazz label called Mainstream. Peter Albin: "Chet Helms heard about an audition Mainstream was holding in San Francisco and got us into it. Two other groups were trying out—Final Solution and Wildflower. Shad was there and he had a long talk with Chet. Shad told us to come with him to Chicago where he'd sign us and get us gigs playing in local clubs." Once in the Windy City, the band was at the mercy of a host of sleazy shysters, including one club owner who booked the band for a one month stand. "After three weeks," recalls Albin, "he told us, 'I can't pay you what I owe you. I don't know what to do about it, but I'm open to suggestions.' " The band's suggestions are better left unrecorded . . . besides, they had other worries. Since their arrival, Shad had been slurring Chet Helms in no uncertain terms. "He said Chet tried to sell us down the river,

Janis Joplin and Jim Gurley

and that he was the only one who could insure that we got a good deal with the record company," continues Albin. "We said, 'Well, we don't have representation,' and he got us a lawyer . . . *his lawyer."*

Before it was over, Big Brother had signed a deal with Mainstream for no advance and a microscopic royalty rate. It was, it turned out, only the beginning of their troubles. "The whole thing was cut in two evenings in Chicago and two day sessions in L.A.," Albin sighs. "Shad produced. We weren't allowed into the mixing booth and he never let us do any more than thirteen takes. He said it was unlucky to go past thirteen."

The ten resulting cuts were released as an eponymously-titled album in the fall of '67. It succeeded, against almost impossible odds, in capturing much of the band's quirky, makeshift exuberance and was compelling evidence of Janis Joplin's considerable vocal skills long before her fame as a blues banshee. *Big Brother & the Holding Company* was a mild Bay Area hit and a national nonentity, despite the insistence of the liner notes that "you will be amazed at the gamut of emotional sounds this group produces."

As San Francisco's heaviest hitters, it was inevitable that the Grateful Dead's encounter with the record industry would embody the whole culture-clash surrounding the signing of the psychedelic pioneers. When their turn came, it wasn't with any of the hit-seeking minor labels that flocked to the Bay Area like ticks to a dog's ear.

"Our name had impact. *Sinatra's* name had impact. He was a real star, even though he was light years removed from what was happening in San Francisco. And we were a real record company." Which made Joe Smith a real record man. A former deejay from Boston, Smith had become national promotion director of Warner Bros. Records back in 1961, climbing the corporate ladder as the company gained a foothold in the middlebrow music market with acts like Petula Clark, Peter, Paul & Mary, Dean Martin and, of course, Sinatra. By the mid-Sixties, thanks to his longtime association with

Joe Smith,
Warner Bros. Records
Courtesy Warner Bros. Records

Donahue and Mitchell, he was the company's Bay Area connection, paying regular visits at the behest of Big Daddy, who was urging the label to buy into the new sound for reasons of his own. And the group Donahue pushed the hardest was the Dead.

"They were playing this weekend at the Avalon and I was supposed to meet them late, after the gig," Smith recounts. "So my wife and I were having dinner at Ernie's and I was all dressed up in what I called my Bank of America suit and she had on basic black with pearls." The Smiths barely had time to peruse Ernie's hundred-dollar-entree menu when Big Daddy summoned him by phone to the Avalon. "He said the band was getting off in a half hour and I should come right down. I remember he told me not to worry about how I was dressed. So there we were, walking up the steps of this startling place and there were these kids, lying around painting each other's bodies and all these lights and smells everywhere. Somebody wanted to dance with my wife. I told her 'Don't come with me to meet the band. You must understand.' The

Grateful Dead. Even the name was intimidating. What did it mean? No one knew."

No one indeed. But it didn't take a clairvoyant to figure out that the music throbbing through the hall was not "Strangers In The Night." Tom Donahue: "Joe told me that night. 'Tom, I don't think Jack Warner will ever understand this. I don't know if I understand it myself, but I really feel like they're good.' I told him, 'You've got to sign them, because this is where it's going.' "

Like a wise man leading the seeker to clear light, Donahue escorted Smith backstage. "He was telling them that I was okay," Smith laughs. "I was talking to all of them. They always moved in a phalanx and the ones I really remember were their managers, Rock Scully and Danny Rifkin. Those two were scammers from eight miles back. I could figure them out . . . the others were out in space somewhere. Garcia was the most visible, but he refused to speak for the group. Pigpen never said ten words and Lesh was very nasty, constantly negative, because I was a record company guy and he was a serious musician. We had this conversation about the right kind of equipment to record with and I later found out that the stuff they wanted hadn't been invented yet. Lesh felt they were selling out by not getting it."

Before things got any further out of hand, Smith laid his cards on the table. "I was pumped up by what I'd seen," he admits. "I felt it was really going to be something. Music had been in a holding pattern up until then. I told them I wanted them, that we were a good record company. That was before I found out that to them, every record company was square. They lived in terror of being ripped off."

Package Deals and Doses

Reeling, Smith retrieved his wife and left the Avalon, convinced he had unlocked the sound of tomorrow. It was time for Big Daddy to make his play. "He told me he could deliver every other band up there for $25,000 apiece. Country Joe, Quicksilver, maybe five or six bands. If I could come up with it, I could have the town. So I went back to L.A. and told Mike Maitland, the president of Warner Bros. He said, 'Gee, I don't know. Let's see how we do with the Dead. In retrospect, I don't blame him."

Working through Donahue, Smith finalized the deal and returned, a few weeks later, to sign papers with Rifkin and Scully. "We had this meeting at my house on Telegraph Hill," Donahue recounted. "Joe walks out on the porch and Rock and Danny say to me, 'Listen, man, we gotta take acid with this cat, then he'll really understand what it is we're doing.' "

"They told me I couldn't really understand their music until I dropped some acid," Smith confirms. "I informed them that under no circumstances would I do that." The Dead, it seems, had a thing about dosing their business associates. For a time Bill Graham was in such fear for his brain cells that he took to bringing

Editors' Archives

his lunch to work in a sack, sealed with wax. The band finally got to him by injecting a dose of LSD into a 7-Up can with a hypodermic.

Warner Bros.' next move was to bring the band down to Hollywood, to cut their album. Joe Smith was not about to play the role of Neely Plumb, however. "I pretty much left them alone," he admits. "I didn't like to be around them much. They seemed so weird, there were so many drugs . . ."

Clyde Bakkemo, Smith's assistant at the time, recalls that "the band literally had to live at the studio for awhile to get used to the environment before they could record."

"We were pretty comfortable because we didn't feel pressure one way or the other," recalls Jerry Garcia. "We were one of the last groups to sign and we were doing fine without any record at all. We went in and said 'Let's see what'll happen.' We didn't even use all the freedom we had built into our contract. We went in and let them tell us what to do. They had no idea."

The Grateful Dead's *Grateful Dead* was an uneven sampling of the band's ballroom fury, an album that oscillated from short, snappy poppish tunes—such as their first single "The Golden Road (To Unlimited Devotion)"—to the band's extended blues epics like the ten minute version of "Viola Lee Blues." As the first permanent representation of what the band did live—of the whole San Francisco jamming ethic, in fact—the song captured little of the streamroller weight of being there, sounding instead sluggish and aimless. Surprisingly, it was the short stuff—originals like "Cream Puff War" and "Cold, Rain and Snow"—that caught and held. "We had to do something for a record that was conventional," admits Garcia. "So we did shorter songs. Recording back then was a very conventional thing."

Somewhat less conventional was Warner Bros.' attempt to market the Dead. For a time the company ran a "Pigpen Look-Alike Contest" and started a fan club for the band. It wasn't working. The album repeated the now established pattern of local acceptance and a barely stifled yawn from the rest of the country. "We started selling records in New York," recalls Smith, "which I never understood because we couldn't get radio play." "Golden Road," a Frisco chart item, stiffed everywhere else and the company's attempt to get the band interviewed on radio was foiled by the Dead themselves. "They refused," is how Smith remembers it.

No matter. By late '67, Joe Smith had hung up his Bank of America suit and was fully into the swing of the Summer of Love. "I was up in San Francisco twice a month trying to sign other stuff," he says. "I'd hang out at the Dead's house in the Haight with a cast of thousands. It was a wonderful scene. Everyone was trying to get Quicksilver and couldn't. I ended up signing the Only Alternative and His Other Possibilities, but they could never get it together to make a whole LP . . ."

It hardly made a difference. Advances had been paid and contracts called for three album deals. Sooner or later, RCA, Warner Bros., even Mainstream, knew they'd get lucky. They had to.

Jefferson Airplane at the Fillmore
Courtesy Paul Kantner

The March Of The Hip Capitalists

Having made its initial investment in the San Francisco sound, the record industry felt a little like the sailor's wife who goes down to the docks to see her husband off; she's never sure just when her John Riley will return, or if he'll come back at all.

Unlike the heroines of the sea chanties, the record companies didn't have long to wait. The ship came in, loaded with treasure, during the Summer of Love, 1967. Earlier in the spring, the Sopwith Camel had taken their perky single, "Hello, Hello," Top 30 nationally—which made some hipper-than-thou San Franciscans cringe; when the followup single stalled, they were able to write the whole thing off as a fluke. But by June, the new music was openly consorting with the masses. The Airplane's hypertense version of the Great Society's "Somebody To Love" was Top 5, the Doors' "Light My Fire" was headed for No. One, and the Buffalo Springfield—those feuding fringe-leather cats from L.A.—had got themselves a hit singing about the Sunset Strip riots in "For What It's Worth." In the Bay Area, Top 40 stations were even playing things like Big Brother's "Blindman" and "Not So Sweet Martha Lorraine" by Country Joe & the Fish. What's more, thanks to the spread of hip FM stations in the wake of Tom Donahue's KMPX and KPPC, and the burgeoning concert circuit, rock & roll *albums* were starting to sell like hot singles.

As surely as the mode of the music was changing, so was the marketplace. Since the Fifties, rock acts rarely released albums until they'd saved up enough singles to justify a greatest hits collection; either that, or they'd toss their latest smash onto an lp rounded out by soundalikes and filler. Sure, the Beatles and the Beach Boys had had successful albums, but they were always tied to 45's. Now, all of a sudden, there were these LP's—Country Joe's *Electric Music For The Mind and Body,* Cream's *Disraeli Gears* and this *Are You Experienced?* thing by that wild-haired guitarist, with its songs about purple hazes. Only weeks before, Joe Smith had been holding regional sales conferences in the Midwest, trying to get his

Editors' Archives

KFRC PRESENTS THE BIG 30

ISSUE NO. 63 - - - WEEK ENDING AUGUST 9, 1967

This Week	Last Week	TITLE	ARTIST	LABEL	Weeks On Big 30
1	1	ALL YOU NEED IS LOVE	BEATLES	CAPITOL	3
2	6	ODE TO BILLIE JOE	BOBBIE GENTRY	CAPITOL	3
3	2	WHITE RABBIT	JEFFERSON AIRPLANE	RCA	9
4	4	SAN FRANCISCAN NIGHTS	ERIC BURDON/ANIMALS	MGM	3
5	5	PLEASANT VALLEY SUNDAY/WORDS	MONKEES	COLGEMS	5
6	3	LIGHT MY FIRE/CRYSTAL SHIP	DOORS	ELEKTRA	13
7	11	COME BACK WHEN YOU GROW UP	BOBBY VEE	LIBERTY	4
8	7	PURPLE HAZE	JIMI HENDRIX	REPRISE	7
9	21	BLINDMAN	BIG BROTHER	MAINSTREAM	3
10	16	OMAHA	MOBY GRAPE	COLUMBIA	3
11	8	WINDY	ASSOCIATION	WARNER BROS.	12
12	12	MASKED MARAUDER	COUNTRY JOE AND FISH	VANGUARD	6
13	HB	THE LETTER	BOX TOPS	MALA	1
14	13	CAN'T TAKE MY EYES OFF YOU	FRANKIE VALLI	PHILLIPS	8
15	15	GENTLE ON MY MIND	GLEN CAMPBELL	CAPITOL	5
16	9	TRAMP	OTIS AND CARLA	STAX	6
17	10	I WAS MADE TO LOVE HER	STEVIE WONDER	TAMLA	7
18	20	FAKIN' IT	SIMON AND GARFUNKEL	COLUMBIA	3
19	HB	REFLECTIONS	DIANA ROSS / SUPREMES	MOTOWN	1
20	14	SILENCE IS GOLDEN	TREMELOES	EPIC	4
21	HB	THERE IS A MOUNTAIN	DONOVAN	EPIC	1
22	17	LOVIN' SOUND	IAN AND SYLVIA	MGM	5
23	28	HEROES AND VILLIANS	BEACH BOYS	BROTHERS	2
24	26	COLD SWEAT - PART 1	JAMES BROWN	KING	2
25	29	BABY I LOVE YOU	ARETHA FRANKLIN	ATLANTIC	3
26	HB	BROWN EYED GIRL	VAN MORRISON	BANG	1
27	27	A GIRL LIKE YOU	YOUNG RASCALS	ATLANTIC	4
28	30	HA HA SAID THE CLOWN	YARDBIRDS	EPIC	2
29	19	SOUL FINGER	BAR-KAYS	VOLT	4
30	HB	LET'S GET TOGETHER	YOUNGBLOODS	RCA	1

distributors fired up about Warners' new releases: "I'm in Minneapolis, with our most powerful distributor, the Heilecher Bros., and I'm giving a speech about how the Dead and Hendrix represent the future of music and 'Something's happening here, Mr. Jones', etc. When I finished, Amos Heilecher orders *seven* copies of the Hendrix album! If you ordered seven, you got one free. That's how confident they were about this music. I said to myself, '*This* is the future?' "

Gold and Plastic

By summer, the future had been sighted in all its amplified, paisley glory. Responding to all the chart activity, the record industry went on a binge; San Francisco became a boomtown once again as a new breed of argonauts rushed to get in on the action. If Neely Plumb and Smith and Jacobsen were finding gold, there must be more. Ahmet Ertegun showed up, Mr. Atlantic Records himself, scouting talent from his Fairmont Hotel suite, bubbling on about the "mystical quality" of San Francisco rock. And the head of A&R for Liberty Records, home of Julie London, Kay Starr and Gary Lewis & the Playboys, flew up from L.A., telling the trades "We can't be complacent and just sit and watch the S.F. scene."

Who could? Certainly not Kama Sutra Records, Artie Ripp's feisty little New York label that had already connected with the Camel and fumbled with the Charlatans. One of Ripp's more memorable projects was a co-op recording label involving most of the major Bay Area groups. Ideally, the bands would all record for Ripp's 'umbrella' company, sharing equally in the profits and contributing a specified percentage of their take to "the community." Country Joe's Ed Denson recalls "a big meeting, at Moe Moskowitz's apartment in San Francisco. Musicians and managers from all the bands were there, plus Chet Helms and some other people." In high record biz fashion, Artie Ripp had the affair catered, and arrived in a chauffeured limousine. "It was a full gross-out," Ripp remembers, "like out of *Caligula* or something." The stage was set for a showdown.

For Ripp, the idea was "for us all to get together and say, 'Look, we have a certain power among us, an influence if you will. The question is: we've all been talking about this unity, that we're all one and so forth.' *I* say, 'I think you're all full of shit.' *I* think everybody's saying that they're wearing the same badges, but really everybody's running their own show. If you really mean all this, let's form a corporation, put everybody's bread into it. Let's get down to it, take it public, use our income, our power and intelligence, jointly. Let's do it just like the thirteen states and say, 'This is the U.S. Fuck the guys with the wigs over on the other side of the pond!' "

Understandably, Ripp's proposal didn't set well with the San Franciscans, who were leery of pooling their profits and equally suspicious of Kama Sutra Records; in a controversial dope bust that had only recently occurred in the Bay Area, two members of the label's big act, the Lovin' Spoonful, had fingered other members in an attempt to beat charges. Ripp spent most of the meeting defending his label against Zal Yanovsky's actions, and the afternoon ended in acrimony. "It fell flat," says Ripp, "because, despite all this b.s. about flower power, love and unity, it still came down to the same old bit; 'I love you till I get my dick into you and I come, then after that I'm finished. See you later.' Basically, that's where it was at. It was hypocritical and immature. I wanted it to be like the Beatles tried to do with Apple—take all our capitalistic circumstance and try and recycle it back into the community. Every time I suggested that to any of them, they were either scared to death of me, or scared of themselves—'Oh, God, what will I *lose* if I do this?' "

Warriors in the Courtyard

While the communistic record label flopped, Ripp couldn't resist a grand finale. Like the hip Nazarene himself, he ended the powow at Moskowitz's by gathering up all the catered food, stashing it inside his limo, and ordering his chauffeur to drive straight to the Golden Gate Park Panhandle. Then, Ripp put his money where the San Franciscans' mouths were; with his chauffeur, he stood there on Oak and Masonic, passing out apples, oranges and finger sandwiches to derelicts and threadbare hippies, a regular Digger in Hollywood drag.

Ripp next took a less lofty, more pragmatic run at the issue, attempting to found a Family Dog Records label with Helms. "By 1967, we had a library of tapes from the Avalon," explains Helms, "and we were looking for a record contract. I had talked with Mercury and Liberty. Our connection with Kama Sutra was the Spoonful, since Luria Castell knew John Sebastian."

Ripp envisioned the deal as a "sort of magnet", a focal point which would attract local talent: "We talked about building a studio inside the Avalon, marching the bands in and auditioning them, one after another, and being able to say 'Oh, *that's* great' or "No, let's wait before we sign that one.' " The idea was pure Fifties rock & roll entrepreneurial genius; like George Goldner hustling groups through his Manhattan studios—processing dozens of Teenagers, Cleftones and Mello-Tones daily—for his Gee Records label, Artie Ripp would set up shop inside the Avalon and pick and choose psychedelic groups for his label.

Artie Ripp (right), Billy Joel (left)

Courtesy Artie Ripp

An unlikely team, Helms the hippie with shoulder-length hair, and Ripp the savvy rock exec, became fast friends. They took meetings, tripped back and forth between Frisco and L.A.—where Helms stayed at Ripp's pad on Doheny Drive, a huge house done in pseudo-Egyptian style, painted flat black with a gold roof. It had a black, kidney-shaped pool and statues of Chinese warriors in the courtyard. Songwriter Tony Bruno was there, and a parade of show biz in-crowders whose antics made even Helms' eyes pop. "Some of these guys could eat more acid than anyone alive," he remembers. "I saw them take three hits then turn around and negotiate a three-million dollar deal with Lucille Ball." And there was the MGM Records convention in Vegas—Helms and assorted Kama Sutrans taking off for California from McCarran Field, the plane already taxi'ing down the runway and Ripp showing up late, snapping his fingers and getting the airline to call the plane back so he could get on.

Wild times and optimistic press releases aside, the deal soured before either partner could usher their first group in front of a four-track. While Helms remained friends with Ripp, he was less than happy to read in *Billboard* of "Kama Sutra's Plans to Tie Up S.F. Scene." Without apprising anyone, the label's local promotion man had gone public with details of Helms and Ripps' hitherto private conversations for their joint venture. Worse still, the proposed label's name had been changed from Family Dog Records to Hippop Records. "I read that article," says Helms, "and thought 'So this is how these guys are going to screw me.' "

Ripp too was disappointed. Not only had his plans for cherry-picking the best of the local bands gone awry, but the writing was on the wall for the scene at large. "My intuition at the time was that the real *creme de la creme* of San Francisco talent was finding its own way into the major leagues. They now knew enough to say, 'Hey, *I* want to be with the big guys, on Columbia or Atlantic or whatever.' " Ultimately, Helms and Ripp signed a deal to distribute Avalon posters through the wholesale distribution arm of Capitol Records. "Get Hip to Where it's At!" read the trade advertisements. "Dig the Capitol Psychedelic Shop!" Thereafter, Helms returned to dance promotion while Ripp went on to develop more new talent, including songwriter Melanie ("Candles In The Rain," "Brand New Key"), the Lemon Pipers and the Hassles, a Long Island group which featured Billy Joel.

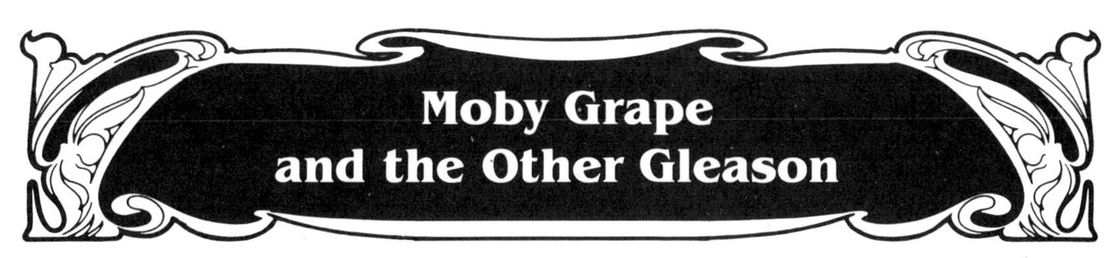

Moby Grape and the Other Gleason

If Ripp envisioned dropping a bundle on a deal that would potentially net Kama Sutra a dozen new Deads or Airplanes, Columbia Records was prepared to spend just as much on one band. In the same issue of *Billboard* that singled out the Airplane's "White Rabbit" as a pick-to-click ("intriguing lyric content and driving beat"), there were reviews of *five* singles by a band nobody'd heard of, with one of the dopiest names imaginable: Moby Grape.

Actually, plenty of those in the know had heard of Moby Grape; at least everybody who'd run into David Rubinson in the last six months. Rubinson was a

The Jordan Collection

Moby Grape at CBS signing; Skip Spence, right

young, smart staff producer for Columbia. Having apprenticed to CBS' legendary Goddard Lieberson, co-producing classical records and documentaries, he was allowed to take a few "flyers"; for some odd reason, Rubinson's flyers—classy singles like "Hey Joe" and "Morning Dew" by Tim Rose, and "Creators of Rain" by Smokey & His Sister, scored in Frisco but punked out elsewhere. The action was enough to bring him to the city regularly in '66 and '67.

"I saw all the original San Francisco bands," Rubinson remembers. "I thought they all sucked, every one of them. Awful musicianship, couldn't play or write." Then, one night at the Ark in Sausalito, he saw Moby Grape. They changed his life. "They had four-part harmonies, Peter Lewis' country-western influence, plus Mosley's R & B approach, three guitars. They were unbelievable." Getting Columbia interested in the group was anything but easy. "Their A&R department didn't want to know about hippies and long hair," Rubinson continues. "Paul Revere and the Raiders was a heavy duty rock band for them. The Cyrkle ["Red Rubber Ball"] was far out." Ultimately, Rubinson and Columbia's S.F. promotion man, Bill Keane, wound up bankrolling the Grape as negotiations went on, and on and on.

"Bill and I were buying them meals, paying Skip Spence's dentist bills. Columbia made me cut a demo with the band; we did 'Omaha' and 'Sitting By the Window.' Then we talked. Then Columbia's lawyers talked with Matthew Katz, who was manging the Grape, but the Grape didn't want him to manage them . . ."

When Columbia learned that Atlantic's Ertegun and Elektra Records' Jac Holzman were after the group, Moby Grape was signed, for a $5000 advance. Rubinson cut their first album, mostly live, in Los Angeles; it took three weeks and cost a meager $11,000. Columbia heard the tapes, smelled a winner, went wild—devising a marketing plan that called for the simultaneous release of five singles from the LP, thousands of Moby Grape press-kits in fuzzy purple binders, a major push. The topper was a lavish party to launch the album in the band's hometown.

"We took over the Avalon," Rubinson explains. "And this is where it became like something out of Jackie Gleason. If Ralph Kramden was going to be a rock star, this would've been his story. You turn him around, walk him to the pot of gold and say, 'Ralph, go five feet, make a left turn, there's the pot of gold.' He goes right, bumps into a wall, breaks his ankle and winds up in the hospital. Here were the Grape, with three singles on the charts, the Monterey Pop Festival coming up, the album starting to sell. Columbia had flown out all their heaviest execs. Radio station KFRC donated 10,000 orchids—they were all over the floor. Columbia's serving specially bottled Moby Grape wine. Everybody's there, San Francisco society, Haight St. hippies, 2000 people going nuts. What a party. Janis got up and sang with the band . . ."

That night, Rubinson took the redeye flight back to New York, where he was awakened at five in the morning by a call from California: three of the band members had left the party and been busted, up on Mt. Tamalpais in Marin County, for dallying with some underage girls. "The next morning, the front page of the *Chronicle:* 'Rock Band Arrested for Impairing Morals of a Minor'. Boom! The singles come off KFRC. When they get off the morals charge, they go on tour. They're behaving so nuts, that every city they go to, they get thrown out of and their records come off the radio. I've got CBS promo guys calling me up, yelling 'Get these fucking guys out of my city!' In Philadelphia, they were driven to the airport and put on a plane out."

But nothing could change the shape of things to come. Despite the debacle, *Moby Grape* sold over 200,000 copies, staying on the charts much of the summer—along with the Doors, Hendrix, *Sgt. Pepper* and the Airplane's *Surrealistic Pillow* which was turning gold (by August, its second single, "White Rabbit," was bettering "Somebody To Love"). And the San Francisco groups, all of them, were rehearsing for the Monterey Pop Festival, to be held June 16–18 at the Monterey County fairgrounds, about 100 miles down the coast from San Francisco.

Courtesy Ken Barnes

The Jordan Collection

Talking to the Enemy

The featival, billed as "three days of music, love and flowers" and organized by Lou Adler and Alan Pariser—with help from the Mamas & Papas' John Phillips, Beatles publicist Derek Taylor and others—meant a lot of different things to a lot of different people. Columbia Records president Clive Davis, as he reports in his self-congratulatory autobiography, "sensed change" at Monterey. For the Byrds' David Crosby, Monterey was a chance to sound off onstage on the issues that concerned him—war, JFK's assassination and why everyone should take LSD. For D.A. Pennebaker's crew filming the *Monterey Pop* documentary, the festival was work. For Ralph Gleason (described in the program booklet as the "trench-coated conscience of San Francisco rock"), Monterey was "a beautiful thing" that resonated with good vibes, raised half a million bucks for charity, and left the 175,000 people who attended in high spirits.

One thing Monterey surely signified was a cessation of hostilities betwen the new musicians and the record business per se. If Clive Davis was slow to pick up on the change, it was nonetheless a powerful, inarguable fact; despite their trench-coated conscience, San Francisco bands were now doing some serious talking with their old enemy. One measure of the psychedelians' newfound readiness to do business was the number of managers, business managers and lawyers they brought with them to Monterey. When the checkbooks came out, there'd be no shortage of endorsers.

In effect, the festival served as a showcase for the Davises, Erteguns, Holzmans and the rest—a combination trade show and shopping spree where they might browse till they saw something they liked, then inquire about the price. Contracts were being drawn up, it seemed, before the bands finished their sets, and the list of acts who arrived in Monterey as contenders and left as superstars is well known. Making his American debut, Jimi Hendrix was panned by both *Billboard* ("bombastic . . . his chicken choke handling of the guitar doesn't indicate a strong talent") and Gleason ("like the Who, show biz . . . he ended *his* set by pouring lighter fluid on a cheap guitar and kneeled on the stage while it burned. I yawned"). Warners' Joe Smith did not yawn. In fact, he gaped at the Hendrix Experience onstage. Their performance was riveting, but so was the fact that, up there flailing away on drums, was the burr-headed Brit to whom Smith had delivered a fresh knuckle-sandwich just minutes before. "We had these box seats, and when we got to them, there are these two guys sitting in them. I politely asked one of them to move, so the pregnant wife of one of the members of the Association who was with us, wouldn't have to stand. The guy says to me, 'Fook off, mate!' and I went after him. It wasn't until I saw him onstage that I realized it was Hendrix's drummer Mitch Mitchell. We had already signed the band but none of us had ever met them before. I thought 'Oh, my God.' "

It was a weekend for historic introductions. American got its first in-person look at the Who, the hippies got turned on to Otis Redding and Ravi Shankar, and Clive Davis introduced himself to Big Brother's manager, Jules Karpen, who introduced Davis to the band's attorney. No less fatefully, the members of Big Brother met Albert Grossman, the heavyweight, silver-locked professional manager whose clients had included Dylan, The Band, Paul Butterfield and Peter, Paul & Mary; Grossman's latest find, the Electric Flag, was playing Monterey. "We used to refer to Albert as the Gray Cloud," recalls Peter Albin with a laugh. Less than a year later, the Grey Cloud had helped Big Brother negotiate their cut of the profits from *Monterey Pop*, replaced Jules Karpen as the group's manager and signed them to Columbia Records (through Clive Davis). Per Albin, Grossman "helped us get out of our Mainstream contract." The deal called for Columbia to pay Mainstream $200,000 out of Big Brother's advance and forthcoming royalties. Not bad for a band that was bashing away in a Page St. basement barely two years previous.

An Eight-Track in Every Contract

Even as the Summer of Love turned to fall, the signing frenzy continued. Capitol shelled out over $100,000 in advances to the Steve Miler Band and Quicksilver Messenger Service; through options and bonus arrangements, the label's long-term commitment to the two bands totaled more than $700,000. Both groups were holdouts who'd passed up numerous offers to record, until Capitol's hip, thirty-ish president Alan Livingston made them offers they couldn't refuse. "We had no reason to sign a contract," explains Quicksilver's John Cipollina. "We were working a lot, but we did want to get out of town and work, and for that a record deal would help." Negotiating from a position of strength, neither band was afraid to make demands. Quicksilver asked for, and obtained, complete control over the graphics and packaging of their records, as well as the right to pick their own producers. And, while less demanding groups might have settled for less, Quicksilver demanded they be allowed to record their first album on an eight-track machine, hardly standard procedure in '67. "Now, Capitol didn't know about eight-tracks, and *we* didn't know a thing about them either, but we'd read in *Billboard* where they were the coming thing. So we told 'em we had to have one and they got it."

Less auspicious signings included Berkeley's Notes From the Underground (to Vanguard), and Morning Glory, a colorless folk-rock outfit, to Mercury. Mercury may have inadvertently made history when it inked the world's first heavy-metal power trio, Blue Cheer—who were managed by a Hell's Angel named "Gut" and took their name from an especially potent batch of Owsley acid. (A few labels declined the offer to psychedelicize. A & M general manager Gil Friesen told the trades his company would do quite well, thank you, with the Tijuana Brass, Brasil '66 and Claudine Longet: "There are five or six acid records brought here every day. We turn them down. It's just not our bag."

The flood of new groups and records continued. While it contained no hits, *A Whole New Thing* promised greatness for Sly & the Family Stone. Having ditched Autumn when the label went into a tailspin a year before, Sly had put in time as a deejay on KSOL and KDIA (where he bravely mixed a healthy percentage of Beatles/Stones/Dylan into the predominantly R&B formats), and formed a band around his brother Freddie, Larry Graham and Cynthia Robinson. When they were ready, Sly trouped them down to Winchester Cathedral (a singles bar on the same Peninsula strip where the Warlocks debuted) and auditioned for record company talent scouts; Epic won out, signed the band and went with *A Whole New Thing.*

Before the year was through, Jesse Colin Young's quartet, the Youngbloods, moved out from New York, and enjoyed a huge local smash with a cover of Dino Valenti's anthem "Get Together." And on New Year's Eve, somewhere in the East Bay, John Fogerty's decidedly unpsychedelic band, the Golliwogs, took the stage for the first time as Creedence Clearwater Revival.

From around the world came endorsements—George Harrison bestowing an unofficial Beatle blessing on the scene when he strolled through the Haight one afternoon, pressing the flesh; in England Eric Burdon backing "San Franciscan Nights" with "Gratefully Dead." Donovan told listeners to "Fly Jefferson Airplane . . . gets you there on time" in the middle of "Fat Angel." The Dead complimented him by nicking a riff from his "There Is A Mountain" and inserting it into one of their rambling new originals, "Alligator."

In November, Ralph Gleason, photographer Baron Wolman and an unemployed 21-year-old writer named Jann Wenner scraped together $7500 and began publishing *Rolling Stone,* a sharp tabloid devoted to the local and international pop scene. The first issue included coverage of the Grateful Dead's dope bust, an inquiry into what became of the profits from the Monterey Pop festival and advertisements for the Fillmore, several mail-order psychedelic poster firms and Sonny Bono's new album.

In short, things never looked better.

Reverberations

It wasn't only the Flower Children whose heads were being turned by the San Francisco rock bonanza. In 1968, recognition was coming from some of the most unlikely quarters. A Bank of America Vice President, analyzing the Bay Area's financial future, saw rosy profits in "hard rock." By 1970, Michael Phillips predicted that rock & roll would become San Francisco's fourth heaviest industry. Taking a bottom line look at concert grosses, radio station revenues and projected studio bookings, Phillips calculated that the four million dollars plus that the "acid rock business" was now generating would balloon to ten times that amount by the mid-Seventies. Which would make Pigpen and Jim Gurley among the city's most prominent captains of capitalism. Why, with a little stretch of the imagination, it wouldn't be hard to imagine them sipping bubbly from crystal goblets at the Bohemian Club, trading bon mots with the cream of the social register.

If it was up to the record industry, Phillips' rosy forecast would come to pass sooner than later. "There were A&R men everywhere," Joe Smith recalls. "It was getting out of hand. Warner Bros. had plans to open up an A&R office in the city." They weren't the only ones and among the busiest was Chicago-based Mercury Records. Encouraged by the success of their first psychedelic signing, Blue Cheer—whose *Vicebus Eruptum* LP yielded the Top 20 hit "Summertime Blues"—the label pulled out all the stops. They hired ex-KMPX deejays Abe 'Voco' Kesh and Milan Melvin to scout likely talent. The only problem was, it was hard to tell real natives from recently arrived hopefuls. Mercury quickly signed such practitioners of the "San Francisco Sound" as H.P. Lovecraft, Linn County and Harvy Mandel, all from Chicago, and Texans Doug Sahm, Melting Pot, pianist Wayne Talbert and Mother Earth, whose Janis Joplin-sponsored vocalist Tracy Nelson once summed up San Francisco bands as "garbage" for their lack of blues purity. A reformed Charlatans was added to the Mercury roster, revived by Richard Olsen and Mike Wilhelm (Dan Hicks having long since departed to form Hot Licks while Mike Ferguson was assembling Tongue & Groove with singer Lynne Hughes). George Hunter designed the cover, one of the first projects for his new graphics venture, Globe Propaganda.

While Warner Bros. stopped short of hanging out its shingle, its presence was felt in the person of producer Erik Jacobsen, the label's point man ensconced in Columbus Towers and bankrolled to the tune of $250,000. Hits were hard to come by for Jacobsen until '69 when he scored with the fuzz-tone spiritual "Spirit In The Sky," by Norman Greenbaum. Not to be outdone, Columbia's Clive Davis struck a deal with Bill Graham for studio space in the Geary Temple, an empty synagogue next to the Fillmore that Graham had purchased to record the overflowing sounds from his ballroom.

Hardly a week passed without the opening of some new recording venture being announced, not all of them landlocked. Ex-Airplane and Grape manager Matthew Katz, seeking the elusive "free" sound, planned to record this latest finds—Tripsichord Music Box, Puddin' N' Pipe and Black Swan—at sea. From the bounding main to the bucolic charms of the country: Elektra President Jac Holzman unveiled plans for a philanthropic recording "retreat" a hundred miles above Sacramento and housed in a former alcoholics' sanitarium. Dubbed variously The Recording Farm, Fantasy Orchestra Ranch or Operation Brown Rice, making records at the studio sounded more like a no-holds-barred encounter weekend at Esalen than the usual sing-and-splice session. The ranch, he explained to *Rolling Stone*, was an experiment which would "make it possible for people to move around in various combinations without being bound by highly restrictive recording arrangements." Holzman aimed to capture "an organic feeling" by allowing artists to "get their heads, their bodies and music together," freeing them from "urban pressures" and "permitting emancipated music to pass through them back into the city." Two of the first artists-in-residence were to be Essra Mohawk and newly signed singer/songwriter Jackson Browne.

As induction centers the Fillmore and Avalon, by '68, were processing more applicants for the Aquarian Age than they could handle. That summer the Fillmore swung into a full six-night-a-week schedule, mixing local talent with such imports as Ike and Tina Turner, Richie Havens, Jeff Beck, The Staple Singers, Steppenwolf and others. Citing overcrowding and increased racial tensions in the Fillmore ghetto, Graham closed the doors of the auditorium on July 5th, relocating to more spacious accommodations across town at Market and Van Ness. The newly christened Fillmore West was situated above a car dealership in another old dance hall, the Carousel Ballroom. "The owner was married to the Irish singer Carmel Quinn," recalls Graham who winged to Ireland to negotiate the deal. "I flew over with a planeload of nuns, drank bourbon and had breakfast at the airport, cut the deal and came home that afternoon."

Between the Carousel and a cavernous ice skating emporium near the old Fillmore named Winterland, Graham maintained his thriving dance/concert empire. Four months earlier, he'd paid $425,000 to renovate the old Village Theater on New York's Second Ave. The Fillmore East opened with Big Brother, Albert King and Tim Buckley on March 8th.

Police in Denver, White Birds on Radio

Chet Helms was doing his best to keep up. In an old industrial warehouse near the University of Colorado he launched The Denver Dog, an enterprise that resulted in pitched battles with, Helms asserts, "the absolutely fascist police." Practices such as strip-searching 300 patrons at a time resulted in a restraining order, a suit against the city and a song celebrating the battle called "My Crime (Police in Denver)" by Canned Heat. The Family Dog also mounted a short-lived venture in Portland's Crystal Ballroom and a handful of shows in the L.A. suburb of Irvine.

Back in San Francisco, meanwhile, there was no shortage of bands to fill the bills. It was getting hard to tell the groups without a program: among the best, and ultimately most successful, of Frisco's Third Wave was Creedence Clearwater Revival. John Fogerty's tight little traveling band had first attracted attention at a benefit for the striking KMPX staffers in March of '68. A tape of the band's lugubrious eight-minute version of Dale Hawkins' "Susie Q" had been in heavy rotation on the station and subsequently surfaced as the set piece of the band's first Fantasy album, released in June. Tom Donahue's former boy wonder, producer Sly Stone and his Family, catapulted into prominence with the first in a string of huge hits, "Dance To The Music," followed by "Stand," "Everybody Is A Star," and "Everyday People"—all part of a body of work that would eventually establish him as the most influential black artist since James Brown.

Matthew Katz' final sleight-of-hand was an assemblage fronted by an electric violinist named David LaFlamme. It's A Beautiful Day precipitated a bidding war that ended when Columbia's Clive Davis beat out Apple for the honors. Their debut album hatched one enormous FM radio hit, "White Bird." A Mexican-born guitarist named Carlos Santana ditched his Chicago-styled Santana Blues Band in favor of a latin/rock hybrid that became one of the city's biggest draws by 1969. Percussion-heavy jams overlaid with nominal psychedelic guitaring, Santana was snapped up by the voracious Columbia Records and scored almost at once with "Black Magic Woman." The original band contained Gregg Rolie and Neil Schon, the founders of a future Frisco

Courtesy Epic Records

Sly Stone

rock institution, Journey.

Mad River, a Berkeley-based band with Quicksilver influences, boasted speedy metal moves and a pair of Capitol albums. The first featured tunes with such intriguing titles as "Amphetamine Gazelle" and "High All The Time," while the second, *Paradise Bar & Grill,* highlighted hip poet Richard Brautigan intoning his work. Former Charlatan Dan Hicks had parlayed his quirky songwriting talent into a recording contract with Epic Records. The music of Dan Hicks and His Hot Licks owed much to the frontier efforts of his former band, with loving reworkings of such Charlatans classics as "How Can I Miss You When You Won't Go Away?"

Championing a kind of rude back-to-basics aesthetic, two bands—Clover and the Flamin' Groovies—earned small but loyal followings with, respectively, their country and Fifties-style rock approaches. Clover at one time included singer Huey Lewis while the Groovies, fronted by Cyril Jordan, released their own independent LP, titled *Sneakers.*

All this was only the tip of the iceberg. After an extensive examination of the San Francisco scene in early 1968, in which it named literally scores of new groups, *Billboard,* in the following issue, was obliged to print an article naming still more bands it had neglected to include in the round-up—including such up-and-comers as the Hajibabs Band and the Rear Exits. In a 1969 book on the San Francisco scene, Ralph Gleason printed a compendium of Frisco bands that ran to over 400 names. It is perhaps the only time such groups as Black Shit Puppy Farm, the Drongos and Hofmann's Bicycle ever saw their names in print.

While hordes of latecomers clamored for a place in the psychedelic sun, the city's handful of original bands were being sucked into a cyclone of adulation, avarice and artistic license that was laying waste to established music industry norms. "It blew my mind that all these guys were huge successes," Ron Nagle admitted, years later. "Sure, I begrudged every one of them their fame and their money."

Cheap Thrills

The days, not so long before, when the originators had to go, cap-in-hand, to the business big shots for a chance to 'Please sir, cut a few sides,' seemed as long ago and far away as the rent parties and basement jams that had started it all. The crucial chores of management were no longer relegated to old friends; for Big Brother & Holding Company, Chet Helms had been decisively displaced; first, by the mysterious Chicagon Jules Karpen, and eventually, Albert Grossman. "He had a lot of solid pop bands," Albin explains, "groups like the Paupers and the Pozo Seco Singers. We were nothing like that. We were psychedelic rangers." Janis Joplin was, however, being touted as the closest thing to Billie Holliday the white race would ever produce, and Grossman was hardly the first to try and pull her away from the ranger corps. Back during Big Brother's Lagunitas tenure, when

Janis had first been recruited, she had been approached by Elektra's Paul Rothchild. "He told her he wanted to talk with her, that he thought he could get something going for the band," says Albin. "It turned out he wanted to put together a supergroup around her with Taj Mahal and some other people. She was two months out of Texas and here he was offering the world on a platter. She didn't know what to do; she started crying. She was really torn; you know, we were all living together, we were a family. That's one of the reasons we took the

Mainstream deal. We thought it would lock Janis into the group."

It was a lock being picked with subtle skill by Grossman. "He didn't like the band," Albin states flatly, "especially Dave and me. We started recording our CBS album and he'd say, 'I hope this doesn't offend you guys, but I think we ought to bring in some other people for the recording.' We'd say, 'As a matter of fact, it does offend us.' But Grossman kept working on Janis. 'Even if Dave and Peter don't play on the album, they can still make a lot of money,' he told her."

Cheap Thrills, Big Brother's trumpeted debut on Columbia was originally

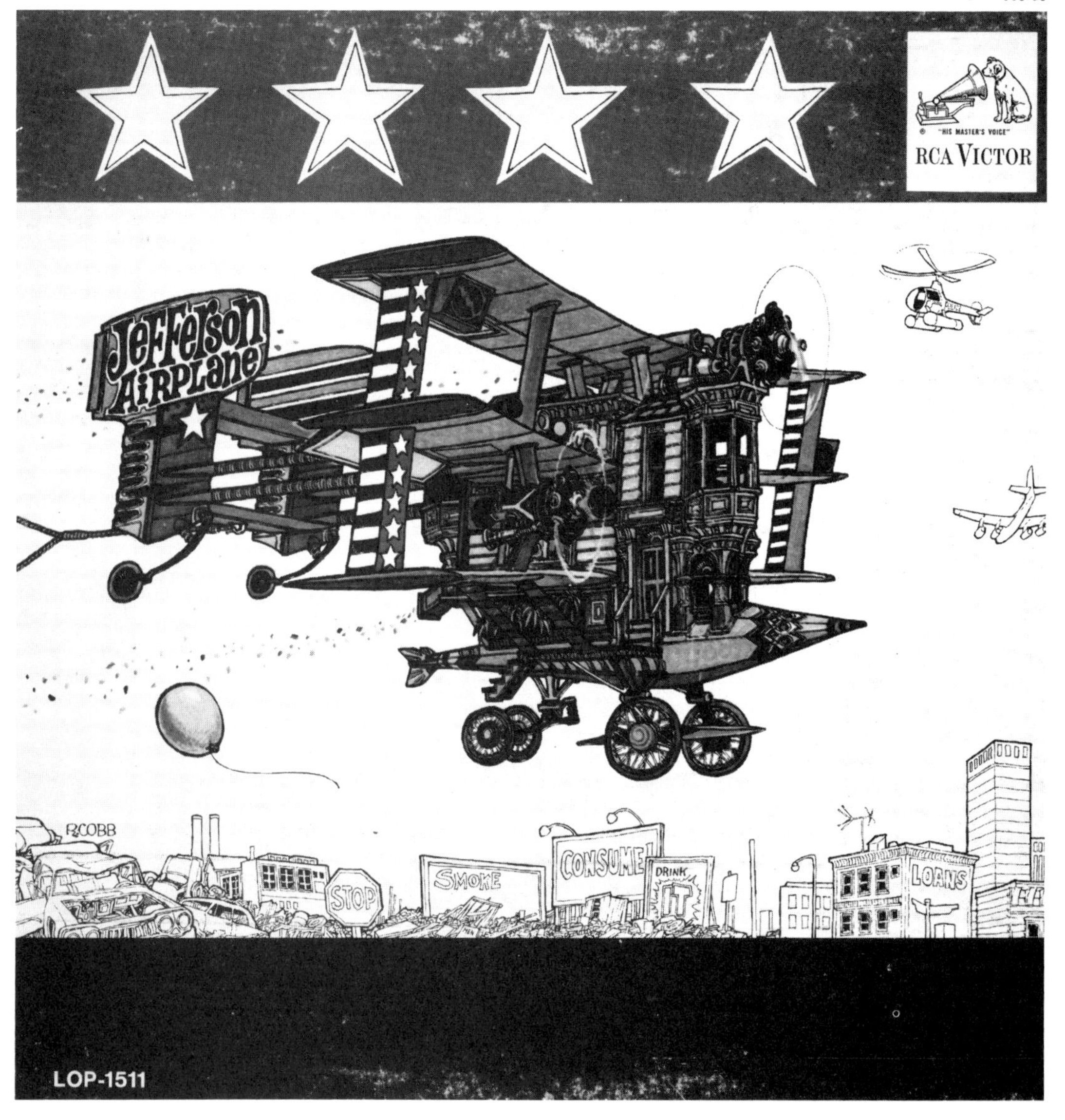

planned as a live recording. The band had played a three night stand at the Grande Ballroom in Detroit, recorded by Elliot Mazur and John Simon, the producer Grossman had hired for the sessions. "It didn't sound so good," recalls Albin, "so we tried to get a 'live' sound in the studio by keeping the overdubs to a minimum." Eventually, Simon mixed in ballroom ambiance and an introduction by Bill Graham. Released in September of '68, *Cheap Thrills* sold a million copies as fast as they could be pressed. As a musical document it chronicles Joplin's rapid overshadowing of the group—with her unvarnished vocals pushed way to the front on blues workouts like "Ball and Chain," and "Summertime," the group sounded shoved into a corner, tinny and ineffectual against the unrestrained energy of their singer's performance. It was a telling symbol of the band's rapid disintegration. By early the following year Janis had left the band, following The Grey Cloud to certain stardom.

Since the nearly unanimous and critical success of *Surrealistic Pillow,* the Jefferson Airplane found itself hurled headlong into the netherworld of ego clashes, non-stop performing and overheated creative impulses. As their manager, Bill Graham had toured the group nationally to the point of exhaustion, prompting Spence Dryden to scream, "Your brain is made of money," during one particularly nasty confrontation. Due to record their third RCA album, the group exercised its increasing clout with the label by rejecting the company's choice for producer, "a big swarthy type," group aide Bill Thompson told Grace Slick biographer Barbara Rowe, "with a big cigar in his mouth. His big thing was that he had produced the song 'I Left My Heart In San Francisco,' and he told you about it all the time." With engineer Al Schmitt, the group began a six-month recording ordeal, struggling against itself and public expectations to come up with a winner. "There was some definite indulgence in the studio," Jack Casady allows. "We had a much bigger budget than previously and complete artistic control."

"They recorded the album by trial and error," Schmitt told one music reporter. "They wanted to experiment with new dimensions in sound." Or, as it turned out, new heights of folly. Slick began trying to imitate the sounds of Kaukonen's guitar for no apparent reason. "She would turn her head from left to right," Schmitt continues, "to create weird but interesting nasal noises. On other days, she would keep changing her position from left to right in front of the microphone to see what changes she could create in her own tonalities."

Pure LSD & 13 Other Things

Living in a $5,000 a month Beverly Hills mansion, the group returned day after day to the studio, pushing the limits of the recording art to their post-logical extremes. "We were trying to become Einstein without ever having studied physics," Grace told her biographer. "We figured we were going to create the most brilliant album ever released in the field of rock. Instead we came up with probably the most obscure and chaotic one." The eleven song assortment, dubbed *After*

Bathing At Baxters, was released in November of '67. It was, according to Paul Kantner, "Pure LSD, among thirteen other things." "I can't remember a song that came off that LP," laughs Casady. "After a while it was just six strong egos. We were always either on the road or in the studio. It takes its toll."

One of the first albums ever to be recorded on an eight-track machine, *After Bathing At Baxters* caught RCA executives off guard. Nonplussed by such in-bred exercises as "Two Heads," and "Rejoice," a four-minute incantation of updated passages from *Ulysses,* the label was nevertheless reluctant to interfere with

Warners publicity shot of the Dead

Courtesy Warner Bros. Records Photo: Herb Greene

the mysterious creative processes of San Francisco's premier hit-makers. They shipped the lp without meddling and it climbed to the Top 20 on national album charts. It was hardly a good showing for a band that was remaking rock in its own image. The group's immediate solution to the album's lack of success was to fire Bill Graham and replace him with long time associate Bill Thompson. According to Thompson, the band reached a parting of the ways when Graham refused to provide them with a bottle of Southern Comfort before every show. The Airplane felt totally justified in their request after hearing that the Grateful Dead had dumped a plate of spaghetti on Graham's head after he refused to buy them steak for dinner.

Speaking of the Dead, they too were becoming fully acclimatized to their new role as scientist/priests of the recording ritual. For *Anthem of the Sun,* their second Warner Bros. release, they hit upon the novel idea of recording "heavy air,"— 3 to 5 minutes of the sound of L.A. smog to contrast with a "clean air" recording cut in the high desert. The two would then be mixed together with added lyrics for a new aural sensation. "They wanted a budget for fruits and nuts to hand out at concerts," Joe Smith recounts. "Then they got into animal sounds. They were going to bring recording equipment to the San Diego zoo, wait until it closed and then come out and, like, communicate with the animals. You know, get the monkeys and lions to sing with them. I mean one minute you'd be talking rationally about radio promotion and the next they'd be wanting to record air."

In preparation for a live LP, the band recorded concerts all over the country, firing engineer Dave Hassinger halfway through the project, because, according to Smith, "they wanted to learn how to record themselves. It was costing a tremendous amount of money. We were $100,000 into this album and we finally came to the agreement that we'd release a double LP package so we could make more money and recoup the costs. The Dead had been stiffing on record, the music was always overintellectualized or something, but this stuff sounded good; more like their live sound. The problem was, they wanted to call it *Skullfuck."*

Skullfuck! So much for commercial potential. "We called a meeting at the Continental Hyatt on Sunset Strip," continues Smith. "There was about a hundred of them; family, friends, hangers-on, in this enormous conference room. It went on forever and I got nowhere. Everytime I made a point some baby would start crying or something. Finally I told them, 'Look. You guys worked a year to make this record. If you call it *Skullfuck* you'll sell 15,000 copies out of headshops. Sears and Wards aren't going to touch it. If you change the name you might have a gold record.' Finally they agreed." *Live/Dead,* released in 1970, did only marginally better than its predecessors despite capturing the genuine excitement of a Dead concert on cuts like "Dark Star" and "The Eleven."

For Moby Grape, recording had become a kind of strange coda to the general decay that had infected the once-promising band. After the mammoth hype of their first lp had subsided, the band flew to New York to begin work on a second with producer David Rubinson. "They were falling apart," recounts Rubinson. "Skip was nuts on acid. He and his girlfriend had gotten hold of some batch called Blue Cheer and were holed up in the Albert Hotel. One night I showed up at the studio and Stevenson and Miller were crazed because Skip had gone beserk in the hotel, taken a fire ax off the wall and tried to chop them up. The cops showed up, but he escaped and was on his way to the studio in a taxi with his ax. I locked the rest of the band in the room and called the security guard, telling him not to let anyone in. Then I went to the police station and told them a guy was coming over with an ax to kill people.

David Rubinson & Friends Photo: Kaz Tsuruta

David Rubinson

They told me I had the wrong precinct, so I went to the right one, but they wouldn't do anything unless someone got hurt. So I went back to the studio and there's Skip, waving his ax in the air out on the street in front of CBS. The cops showed up, but I was the one who had to ask him for the ax. He was very contrite."

Scared for their lives, the rest of the group broke it as gently as possible to Spence—then at residence in Bellevue—that his services would no longer be needed. "He wanted to do a solo record in Nashville," recounts Rubinson, "and believe it or not, he got the budget. As soon as the sessions were over, he told me he was going back to San Francisco on his motorcycle. He kind of disappeared into the sunset, wearing a pair of pajamas."

Wow, the band's second album, held together well enough for a group on the precipice of meltdown, but failed to make any substantial impact. Manager Matthew Katz was dismissed and, claiming he owned the name, assembled another Moby Grape that played a date at the Cheetah on Santa Monica pier even as the ill-fated originals were in L.A. cutting a third album. "We all went down to see them," recalls Rubinson, "and they were doing all our songs. It was the first real clone band I'd ever seen. When they saw us in the audience, they put down their instruments and walked off stage."

Doctors With Flashlights

Before Quicksilver Messenger Service, the last of Frisco's unsigned original bands, signed with Capitol Records, they had had more than a few offers. "For a while Vanguard had been interested in us," John Cipollina recounts. "Sam Charters came out to talk with us. I had pneumonia at the time and was lying in bed, like dying, covered with furs, and there were all these young girls and the room was full of god's eyes and people burning incense and a doctor who was trying to check me out using a flashlight to see what he was doing. And there was Sam Charters, talking about making records."

Quicksilver first hired Electric Flag bassist Harvey Brooks to capture their steely sound and almost at once, there was trouble. The band completed two full albums with Brooks in San Francisco that were rejected either by the label or the group. Brooks was sacked and his bandmate, Chicago writer and blues singer Nick Gravenites, was recruited. Gravenites, in turn, called on Capitol staff producer and former *downbeat* editor Pete Welding. "He asked if I'd work with him on it because he really wanted someone to act as a buffer between him and the group and the Capitol executives.

"They had a pretty clearly defined idea of the material they wanted to do," continues Welding. By this time, they certainly should have. Having cut versions of such live staples as "Back Door Man" and "Walkin' Blues," the only evidence that now remained of the group's San Francisco sessions were some uncharacteristic horn tracks that had been grafted onto "Pride Of Man." It was obvious that by the time Quicksilver had reached Capitol's studio "A" in Hollywood, they had shaped up considerably. Pete Welding: "I was amazed at them. We were hard pressed to do versions of tunes on the basis of solos because the solos were all top-notch. I was gassed by the way Gary and John played off one another with two very contrasting styles." John Cipollina: "We put $45,000 in that album before it was all over."

Released in May of 1968, *Quicksilver Messenger Service* was a tame but serviceable substitute for the group's live fire. Sales were respectable but the critical response was something short of overwhelming, despite the fact that cuts like "The Fool" were as tightly arranged and performed as anything that had emerged from the San Francisco scene. On a subsequent national tour, they recorded tracks that would end up on their second album, 1969's *Happy Trails.* Here, the attempt to capture the band's live sound was considerably more successful, as evidenced by "Mona" and the side-long "Who Do You Love."

At a time when most groups were inflating their own talents, Quicksilver consistently made the most of what they had. Hampered by the lack of a single, strong vocalist and virtually no songwriting skills, the band depended on their considerable performance and arranging talents. Unlike the amorphous jamming that defined the music of so much of the competition, QMS buit a bonfire out of extended explorations like "Who Do You Love" by carefully arranging their kindling.

In the midst of completing *Happy Trails,* Gary Duncan quit, a loss from

George Hunter's Quicksilver cover

which the band did not recover. To compensate, they picked up English session pianist Nicky Hopkins, who appeared on 1969's spotty *Shady Grove*. By then, for all intents and purposes, the spark had gone out of the group. Even an eleventh hour appearance by Dino Valenti two years later could not revive the music. Cipollina was shortly to depart. "By then it had changed. I certainly couldn't throw the blame on Dino. He was in it for different reasons. By that time, it was just a whole different attitude and direction."

San Francisco had been ground zero for the psychedelic music explosion. In 1968, the shock waves were being felt around the world. Sweeping commercial success and a chorus of critical acclaim from scores of newly founded music magazines, as well as established critics, elevated rock & roll to very high art. "It blew my mind," says Cipollina, "the first time Ralph Gleason came to see us at the old Fillmore. I mean, I'd read him in *downbeat*, and now here he was, looking at *me?*"

Eight-Tracks on the Roof

The open-ended studio experiments of the *After Bathing At Baxters* variety were now becoming commonplace. In New York, London and Los Angeles, meditation sessions and incense rituals were an indispensable warm-up to the work day. Musicians could be found laying on studio floors in pitch darkness to insure the vibes were at the perfect pitch for creativity. Recording their never-to-be-released *Smile* album, the Beach Boys sent budgets skyrocketing as Brian Wilson experimented with everything from banging forks and spoons together for percussion tracks to outfitting an entire crew of session musicians with firemen's hats to get them in the mood to perform his "Elements Suite." Artists hauled portable eight-tracks into empty swimming pools, up on roofs and into forests to capture some ever-elusive ambience.

For their part, having heard the sound the future was making, the record companies were hardly playing the stern taskmasters. RCA raised industry eyebrows by signing the Airplane for $25,000. Two short years later, Atlantic Records hardly batted an eye when forking over $200,000 for an English quartet named Led Zeppelin.

No label worth its grooves could afford to be without a piece of the acid-rock. Both Columbia and Warner Bros. launched major campaigns to talk to the new audience in a language it could understand. Warner/Reprise took to *Rolling Stone* and the burgeoning "underground press" with a bold series of ads conceived by copywriter Stan Cornyn. Aside from the "Pigpen Look-Alike Contest," the label ran a "Win A Fugs Dream Date" competition, various one-cent album sales and an offer for a free bag of Topanga Canyon dirt to anyone who bought Neil Young's first LP. Columbia's bid for "relevance" was an ad campaign depicting an assortment of alternative types openly passing a joint under the head "The Man Can't Bust Our Music." MGM threw its entire product line into the fray with a campaign titled "Psychedelia—The Sound of the Now Generation." Beethoven's 5th Symphony and madrigals by Monteverdi were peddled as "Mind—Expanding Classics," while its children's line was hawked as

The Jordan Collection

Enter now! The giant

Pigpen look-alike contest

MR. PEN

Normally, a contest like this one doesn't happen along. But this is an honest-to-God real contest. Honest. With real prizes.

The winner is the lucky guy or gal whose photo looks most like Pigpen of The Grateful Dead. So, send in your pictures to our Box Top and Party Games Dept.

Do not, please, send in the actual people. We got troubles of our own.

How to enter. First off, you should be hip to The Dead's two albums on Warners, which are:

THE FIRST ONE and THE SECOND ONE

These albums, in case you've been in solitary for the past 38 months, are very, very good. So good, in fact, that of them it has been said:

"This album is possibly the finest yet by a group in the general area of white blues-rock. Those who prefer another sort of rock may disagree with the Grateful Dead's predeliction for the blues, but no one could deny after hearing the record that the band is superb." — *Downbeat*

Now that you've waded through the ad copy, back to fun! Here are *The rules*. Send in a photograph of the Pigpen Look-Alike, with his or her name and address on the back of the photo, *PLUS* a reasonable facsimile of either of the two Grateful Dead album covers.

(We ask for the album cover picture because we hope you'll buy or steal an album to draw from. We do that because if we don't move those records, friends, there's no more contests).

So, send in the stuff, and we'll let you know who won.

The prizes. First prize is $200 worth of our grooviest albums (Jimi Hendrix, Van Morrison, Joni Mitchell, Van Dyke Parks, etc.). Second prize is $100 worth. Third-through-tenth prizes: $50 worth.

The fine print:

All entries become the property of Warner Bros.-Seven Arts Records, Inc. Entries must be received no later than March 15, 196[illegible]. None can be returned. If we feel like it, we may use these photos in an ad later on, so fair warning. If this contest is illegal somewhere, then skip it where it is. Your facsimile of the album cover doesn't have to look terrific. We already know what the album looks like. What we want to know is what you look like. Sort of.

Send in your things to:

Box Top and Party Games Dept.
Room 208
Warner Bros.-7 Arts Records
Burbank, California [illegible]

And please hurry. You have no idea how games like this break up the day here in Burbank.

One more thing: if you can, buy a Grateful Dead album. After all, can you afford in this life to go without an album that *The San Francisco Express* said was "... as though we were hearing for the first time in our lives"?

Shove your entry in the mail. We'll get back to you.

W7

If you won't listen to your parents, the Man or the Establishment...

Why should you listen to us?

Because of the power of Rock, the shriek of the Blues, the doubt of Country-Folk.

Because of the sound of love and anger and confidence and hope.

The sound of a search.

Because of a white chick belting black Blues and wiping you out—Janis Joplin

three greats together for the first time feeding each other's souls—"Super Session"

brothers signing their vibrations with peace—The Chambers Brothers

a young songwriter who got tired of other people singing his songs—Gordon Alexander

the sensation of seven guys creating a new direction for Rock—The Millennium

the greats of British Blues brought together in one album

the sound track of the image of our time—"You Are What You Eat"

a musical accompaniment to the agonies of heroin—"Chappaqua"

an album that's as different as it looks—Small Faces

an imported sound with a macabre name—The Zombies.

Because it's you.

And that's why you might want to listen.

COLUMBIA RECORDS

KCS 9700*†

CS 9701*

CS 9522*

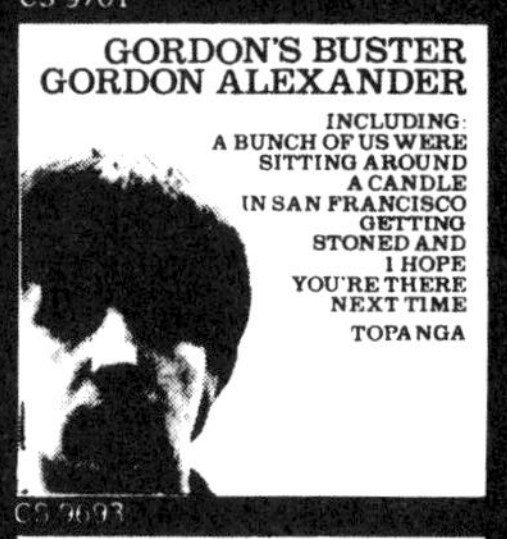

CS 9693

CS 9663*

Z12 52006* Immediate Records

OS 3240*†

OS 3230

Z12 52008* Immediate Records

TES 4013 Date Records

"Electric Lollipops for Little Love-People." "Switched-on sales" were promised for all.

1968 was the year that such hitherto square labels as Musicor and Dot took the plunge as well; the former with signings that included Federal Duck and the Tingling Mother's Circus, the later with City Zu, Peppermint Trolley and the Chuck Barris Syndicate. Psychedelic jargon even seeped into the nuts and bolts aspects of the industry. ABC livened up its August '68 distributor's confab with the catchy theme "Turn On to Profit Power."

It wasn't only in music that the tremors were making themselves felt. On television, *Laugh-In* and *The Smothers Brothers* offered diluted dope humor and occasional rock acts to millions of middle Americans. Virtually every product with even the most marginal youth appeal was being marketed with unmistakable psychedelic overtones—Wes Wilson calligraphy, flower petals and paisley motifs—everything from soft drinks to amplifiers. For those unable to reach to temples of acid rock, an in-home lightshow was offered to millions courtesy Mind Reels Productions.

Coast to coast, Teen-age Fairs lured thousands of eager disciples into a wonderland of psychedelized merchandise.

Editors' Archives

A label gets hip: Capitol merchandising display, circa 1967

Amidst blaring rock bands and fashion shows, the kids wondered through a maze of booths. On display: Maharishi Mahesh Yogi posters, Sears "Sock It To Me" buttons and Dog Tags for Doves.

The Price of Levi's

Where would it all end? Dog tags and day-glo decals might come and go, but something much more fundamental and permanent had altered the record industry. For one thing, profit margins had ballooned beyond anyone's wildest expectations. The lasting result of the San Francisco music revolution was a drastic change in the currency rate of pop. Since the days of Elvis, the 45 rpm single had been the coin of the realm; an under three-minute A-side packed in a brown paper sleeve and selling for around a dollar. Suddenly, the long player was the medium for rock's message—40 minutes of music for $5.98. This shift virtually

Editors' Archives

Amplifier advertisement, 1968

Hamerschlagg Archives

Lick my decals, 1968

created the modern record industry, with its cradle-to-grave systems of career development. Overnight, FM underground radio grew into a hand-in-glove partner for the new album market. By the mid-Seventies, with a few modifications it had become the dominant format, AOR—Album Oriented Radio. The ballroom experience would develop geometrically into the stadium experience, dancehalls giving way to superdomes. "Dance Loses Footing As Halls Go Concert," reported one music trade in August of '68. "Young people are not dancing, just digging," the article announced. Bill Graham would go on to create a concert promotion empire from his bi-coastal Fillmore operation, but for Chet Helms, it was just about all over. After losing his lease on the original Avalon, Helms opened up shop for a time in a rundown hall along a stretch of forlorn ocean drive at the edge of town. It was the Light Artists Guild strike for more pay that, according to Helms, "broke us in one night. I remember Robert Elliott, from the Garden of Earthly Delights Light Show, Jerry Garcia and myself sitting in a van one night outside the hall. We were all singing the same tune; each of us was $60,000 in debt and none of us knew how to do anything else."

Anyone could tell you: the revolution had been won. But not without a price: "We were just another refrigerator, only with paisley on it, as far as the music industry was concerned," says Paul Kantner. The lines between commerce and creativity had gotten blurred. In 1967, the Airplane did a series of ads for White Levis. "We had a certain code of honor; we'd never do commercials, but Levi's came to us and made us an offer." Three years later, the band became their own executives, founding Grunt Records and releasing a string of unprofitable vanity albums along with the annual Airplane/Starship offering.

Charlatans soulmate Mike Prichard saw the conflict as inevitable, fundamental. "The Charlatans started as a happen-

Courtesy Artie Ripp

Nothing lasts

ing," he recalls, "but as they got closer to the music establishment they had to define themselves, make it clear. Janis was the same way. It was fine as long as she was just a person 'doing her thing.' As soon as she defined herself, that put her into the nexus of show-biz. That move had implications nobody expected."

Least of all Family Dog founder Luria Castell. When she returned from Mexico in early 1966 to the thriving scene she'd helped birth, it was barely recognizable. "Part of me said I want to be involved, but then I realized, like the Stones said, you can't come back and be the first in line. Later I went to Winterland and it was packed, but there were no vibes, it was a vacuum. It was crazy, with all that energy and none of it being released. It had nowhere to go."

Jerry Garcia: "It started out going in a much more interesting direction than it ended up. I could never understand that. For me, the Trips Festival was as good as it got."

Bill Graham: "The absolute best weekend was the 13th and 14th of August, 1967. It was Pigpen's birthday. Everyone was onstage singing 'Dancing In The Street'—the Airplane, the Dead, Joan Baez and her sister Mimi. The cops wanted to close us down. 'Don't you feel that?' I asked them. 'It's Pigpen's birthday!' Back then when it was right, it was an inner sanctum. I was older. I knew how lucky I was."

Interviewer on the *Acid Test* album: "Would you say this trip is deliberately self-destructing?"

Ken Kesey: "This is about as deliberately self-defeating as anything has ever been in history. The people involved in this realize that there's nothing to be gained, that every time you try and lay your hands on something and get hold of it, that you've sold yourself down the river. The first Prankster rule is that nothing lasts."

AFTERMATH

George Hunter operates a furniture design studio in Sonoma, California, and is planning to release an album of vintage Charlatans material.

Charlatans pianist Mike Ferguson died of diabetes in 1979.

Ron Nagle is a world class ceramicist, and has scored sound effects for the soundtrack of *The Exorcist* and written or produced music for Barbra Streisand, The Tubes, Michelle Philips and John Hiatt. He has also released solo albums.

Luria Castell works as a para-legal in Albuquerque.

Chet Helms owns and operates the Atelier Dore art gallery in San Francisco.

Bill Graham continues as an international concert promoter.

Peter Albin of Big Brother & the Holding Company and John Cipollina of Quicksilver Messenger Service, perform as the Dinosaurs with former Airplane drummer Spencer Dryden and ex-Fish Barry Melton.

The Grateful Dead continue. Ron "Pigpen" McKernan died in 1973.

Paul Kantner left the Jefferson Starship in June of 1984, although Grace Slick continues with the group.

Ralph Gleason died in 1975.

Darby Slick teaches school in Marin County.

Tom Donahue was general manager of KSAN when he died in 1975.

Janis Joplin died in 1970.

Jim Gurley lives with his wife and children in Palm Desert, California.

Erik Jacobsen continues to produce records in the Bay Area.

Artie Ripp is still active in the music industry and lives in Los Angeles.

David Rubinson produces Herbie Hancock and other contemporary artists in San Francisco.

Marty Balin lives in Mill Valley and performs occasionally.

Joe Smith is active in film and soundtrack production.

Rick Griffin lives in Orange County and continues working as an artist.

Acid Rock Consumer Guide

AMBOY DUKES

Flower-power comes to Detroit and leaves with a busted jaw. Ted Nugent also starts here, sans loincloth and Cro-mag table manners. As lead guitarist, he's the mystic eye behind the screeching *Journey To The Center of Your Mind* and *Migration* (both Mainstream). Stretched-out Sixties punk forms the bottom, but them Dukeboys often reached for the ether when it came to word-slingin'. Inspirational Verse: "Leave your cares behind, come with us and find/The pleasures of a journey to the center of your mind."

ANIMALS

Once psychedelicized, Eric Burdon's soul was never quite the same. On "Monterey," "Sky Pilot" and "San Franciscan Nights," he mixes equal parts bombast and Owsley blue to good effect. His masterpiece, though, remains an overlooked single from the Summer of Love, "When I Was Young" b/w "Girl Named Sandoz": bells, bedouin chants and mind-melting lyrics reach new heights in stupid, plus you can meditate to it. Various greatest-hits collections, on Abkco and MGM.

THE BEATLES

Sgt. Pepper's Lonely Hearts Club Band, Revolver, even *Rubber Soul*—the sounds of San Francisco loomed large in the Fab Four's best work and vice versa. Fame kept them from the stage where they might have stretched out, but studio isolation yielded some splendid acidic experiments. To psychedelians the music sounded stoned; to everyone else it just sounded good. A neat trick.

BIG BROTHER & THE HOLDING COMPANY

Big Brother's 1967 Mainstream album is still the truest representation of the group's special and fragile charms. Thin and slapdash as it is, the eponymous lp shines with some of Janis' best, most controlled singing and the band's funniest, most idiosyncratic writing and playing. '68's *Cheap Thrills* annoys more often than it entertains; Janis was already the main attraction, too far out front, and her flayed voice is a ghastly omen of the looming tragedy. The band sounds nervous and out-of-sorts and the histrionic pseudo-live atmosphere sets your teeth on edge. A recently re-issued 1966 live recording, *Cheaper Thrills* is a sweet echo from happier times.

BLUE CHEER

Years ahead of its time. The band's 1968 debut *Vincebus Eruptum* (with liner notes by Stanley Owsley) prefigured every wretched excess of heavy metal years before the term was invented. "Summertime Blues," with a sound like Dueling Foghorns, was a Top 20 hit. Plain awful.

BLUES MAGOOS

Pure, escapist early psyche-rock wasn't made to withstand New York winters, but the Magoos made a gallant attempt to grow their own. Get their first Mercury LP, *Psychedelic Lollipop,* for "We Ain't Got Nothin' Yet" and "Tobacco Road." Get their second, *Electric Coloring Book,* for the title.

BUFFALO SPRINGFIELD

On record, always more pop than psyche. The first one, *Buffalo Springfield,* reveals them as peppy, song-oriented, refreshingly original synthesists ("Nowadays Clancy Can't Even Sing", "Hot Dusty Roads"). *Second Time Around* has its moments, most notably "Broken Arrow," Neil Young and Jack Nitzsche's aural cloudscape which really does resemble "Phil Spector on acid."

THE BYRDS

The Byrds' best attempts at mind-expansion reside on mid-period classics like *Younger Than Yesterday* and *5D.* Their psychedelic impulses were sharply divided between McGuinn's brilliant twelve-string techniques ("Eight Miles High") and Crosby's absurd poetic pretenses ("Mind Gardens"). The proof was in the hits.

CAPTAIN BEEFHEART & HIS MAGIC BAND

To lift a copy line used to sell his former Reprise stablemate, "In all the world there is none so rare" as Cappy Don. *Safe As Milk* (Buddah) is psychedelic pioneering and remains the album of just about any decade it's bought, played or taped in. *Strictly Personal* (Blue Thumb) *is* horribly overproduced, but its blabber 'n' smoke is also overpowering, as demonstrated by "Mirror Man" or the spiked Halloween confection, "Kandy Korn." Days of future passed: *The Legendary A&M Sessions,* punky blues from '65.

CHAMBERS BROS.

One story has it these gospel ploughboys cut "Time Has Come Today" as a jerkoff between takes in the studio—which may or may not explain the non-song's Top Ten success in 1968 or its popularity as a cover item for punks (Ramones, Angry Samoans) in the Eighties. Unlistenable then, unbearable now.

CHARLATANS

Sometimes misrepresentation is better than no representation at all. Parties curious about Frisco's legendary Red Doggers are directed to the recently re-released Phillips import, *The Charlatans.* It's just not the same without Hunter's autoharp, Hicks' wry writing or Ferguson's bawdyhouse piano, but Mike Wilhelm picks pretty and uses the same arrangements for "Alabama Bound" and "Wabash Cannonball." Until the real thing comes along.

CHOCOLATE WATCH BAND

With the Seeds, Standells, Magic Mushrooms and others, these garage greats comprise the tip of the fire and iceberg known as acid-punk. What we have here are snot-nosed teens too young to get into the Fillmore, figuring out their own version of the New Sound. To the Chocs, that meant adding a little vibrato or wah-wah to their impersonations of the Stones ("Sweet Young Thing"), Kinks ("I'm Not Like Everybody Else") and Van Morrison ("Baby Blue"). Bonus: the openly hostile "Are You Gonna Be There (At the Love-In)?" Get the *Best of the Chocolate Watch Band* (Rhino).

COUNTRY JOE & THE FISH

Electric Music For the Mind and Body, released in 1967, is an enduring document of the real thing—swirling organ, lanquid melodies and mysterious, intriguing lyrics. The LP may well have been better than the band—it was certainly better than most recorded efforts from Frisco groups of the period. What followed was only painful elaboration on the band's lack of direction.

CREAM

Despite the squirrely experimental charm of their debut *Fresh Cream,* easily the most overrated band in recorded rock history. Evidence of the band's near-total worthlessness is as close as a copy of *Wheels Of Fire;* Jack Bruce's constricted soul-caterwauling ("White Room") set the standard for generations of pompous Brit vocalists, while Clapton committed sins in the name of the blues which may never be erased ("Spoonful"). To say nothing of Ginger Baker's 15-minute drum solo, "Toad." The road (and the band's influence) went on forever, leading to such milestones as Blind Faith, Ginger Baker's Air Force and Clapton's persistent career as an MOR featherweight. Saints preserve us.

CREEDENCE CLEARWATER REVIVAL

Before they rose to mythic heights on a string of stripped-down smash singles, establishing the work-shirt and faded-jeans rock ethic in the bargain, Creedence flirted briefly with psychedelia on their first Fantasy LP with the hit "Suzie Q" and its follow-up "I Put A Spell On You." The urge to jam re-appeared from time to time, most notably on "Born On The Bayou" and a reworking of "Heard It Through The Grapevine," but the band knew which side the bread was buttered on and remains, rightfully, famed for its three-minute gems.

DOORS

The first album's the one; a moody-hued song cycle thick with fugue-in' and groovin', and a kind of creepy crawliness that, if not always appropriate, was once highly original. "Break On Through", "Crystal Ship" and the "Fire" that won't go out still impress. The followup, *Strange Days,* subverts music to the ever-widening image of Jimbo the Shaman, who takes the reigns completely on successive LPs. "Father, I want to . . ."

ELECTRIC PRUNES

"Too Much To Dream" and "Get Me to the World On Time" stand up best (see the band's debut LP, on Reprise), but the Prunes' legacy may finally rest on their third album, *The Mass in F Minor.* The brainchild of arranger-producer David Axelrod, this holy terror of a record is a mind-boggling mix of chimes, chorales and fuzz-tone, as the band transubstantiates its way through "Kyrie Eleison", "Agnus Dei" and the "Gloria." Not content to rest on their pews, the Prunes next tackled the *Kol Nidre* with similarly astonishing results. Axelrod himself went secular, for two Blake-built instrumental LPs on Capitol, *Songs of Innocence* and *Songs of Experience,* which took the studio-acid genre still farther.

THE BARRY GOLDBERG REUNION

A lost gem, one of the real sleepers of psychedelic pop. After his honky first album (*Blowin' My Mind),* organist Goldberg got melodic, airy, wistful, with the help of guitarist Harvey Mandel, drummer "Fast" Eddie Hoh and friends. The result: tasty, shook-up takes on Lazy Lester's "Sugar Coated Love" and the unclassifiable originals "Another Day" and "Hole In My Pocket." From Buddah Records, somewhere between Captain Beefheart and the 1910 Fruitgum Co.

GRATEFUL DEAD

In a long and brutally uneven recording career, the band has never equalled the occasional flashes of brilliance evidenced on their first four LP's. A genuine artifact from Frisco's Golden Age, their debut *The Grateful Dead* was followed by a series of live and in-studio efforts that underscored the frustration of trying to translate ballroom ecstasies to wax. *Anthem of the Sun, Aoxomoxa* and *Live/Dead* were often interesting excursions that rarely arrived at their promised destinations. From 1970 and *Workingman's Dead* on, the group returned to its folk/country roots, dallied endlessly with lyricist Robert Hunter's obtuse sagas and even came up with a pair of quasi-hits, "Truckin' " and "Casey Jones." The Dead's recording career reached a nadir in the late Seventies via horrendous flirtations with disco and formula pop on *Shakin' Street, Go To Heaven,* etc. With some precious exceptions, the band's dilemma has remained substantively the same for almost 20 years—they can't put it in a groove. Instructional.

GREAT SOCIETY

As artifacts go, both *Conspicuous Only In Its Absence* and *How It Was* (Columbia) aren't half bad. Recorded live at the Matrix in 1966, the Slick family and friends work out on Dylan's "Outlaw Blues", a tribute to Lenny ("Father Bruce"), plus the hits "White Rabbit" and "Somebody to Love". Lots of gnarly guitar from Darby and David Minor.

HAWKWIND

Notwithstanding a complete lack of musical talent, this gaggle of genial frauds earned a cult following by dressing up funny and playing freeform galactic symphonies with titles like *Space Ritual, Hall of the Mountain Grill* and *Doremi Fasol Latido.* A rich, if unintentional joke, on English rock progressivism.

JIMI HENDRIX

The lush glow of legend obscures the fact that Jimi Hendrix, at his best, was more than an *ubermensch* guitar technocrat—he was a lot of fun. Back when a black on LSD was an eye-popping anomaly, Hendrix took full advantage of his pioneer status with a Barnamesque flair for showmanship. As impressive and influential as his recorded work may be for all its (sometimes excessive) virtuosity, Hendrix' freak flag flew highest when he was reveling in the sheer wigged-out joy of making noise. For the record: *Are You Experienced?, Electric Ladyland* and parts of *Axis Bold As Love,* along with most early singles best capture the excitement. *Cry Of Love* is memorably sad, *Band Of Gypsies* the low point.

IRON BUTTERFLY

For about 17 minutes, the Sixties' premier "heavy" band. That's the recorded length of the 'fly's lumbering downer-classic "In-A-Gadda-Da-Vida". Performed live throughout '67 and '68, the song often ran longer, assuming Torquemadan proportions. Still available: *Heavy,* and *In-A-Gadda* (Atco).

IT'S A BEAUTIFUL DAY

A bad forecast of what was to come for San Francisco music; rampant eclecticism, gussied up middle-of-the-road arrangements and—worst of all, a violin as a lead instrument, a smart move immediately copied by such likewise memorable outfits as the Flock (from Chicago) and Pavlov's Dog (St. Louis). If one must: *It's A Beautiful Day* (Columbia).

JEFFERSON AIRPLANE

Surrealistic Pillow is surely the most consistent, but *Takes Off, Crown of Creation* and even *Volunteers,* 1970's up-against-the-wall epic, manage to shine in spots. *Early Flights* offers pre-first LP tracks and assorted rarities.

KALEIDOSCOPE

Eclecticism triumphant. This nifty L.A.-based quintet featured future Jackson Browne guitarist David Lindley back when he mattered and a repertoire of material that dipped deeply from an international cornucopia. '66's *Side Trips* dished up everything from jug band blues to middle-eastern ragas to credible acid-rock ("Pulsating Dream"). '67's *Beacon From Mars* threw in Scottish folk reels and some engaging originals ("I Found Out" and "Life Will Pass You By"). Some of the best of both is currently available on an Edsel Records English import. A lot of fun.

KING CRIMSON

No matter how he cuts his hair, guitarist/theorist Robert Fripp can't escape the deadly implications of his own music. Art-for-art's sake poseurs, King Crimson gives progressive excess a bad name. Psychedelic—as in a bad acid trip.

LED ZEPPELIN

"Whole Lotta Love" probably qualifies as psychedelically-derived. After that, it's all a blur.

LOTHAR AND THE HAND PEOPLE

This New York band's claim-to-fame was a Theremin named Lothar and a repertoire that included "The Woody Woodpecker Song" and an original titled "Kids Are Little People."

LOVE

Arthur Lee's singing and songwriting vehicle, Love—along with a handful of other savvy L.A. bands—did what most Frisco aggregates could never pull off; taking the quirky, skewered energy of psychedelic rock and making it work for radio. The band's first four Elektra LP's are punky, idiosyncratic state-of-the-art collections, brimming with catchy hits that sacrifice none of the band's formidable eccentricities. "Signed D.C.," Burt Bacharach's "My Little Book" and the landmark "Hey Joe" together displayed the band's wide-ranging musicality as did, much less successfully, their magnum opus, the 20-minute plus "Da Capo." A band that made its own breaks.

THE STEVE MILLER BAND

Children of the Future and *Sailor* are both enduring contributions to the psychedelic lexicon—full of light and freedom and lithe maneuvers. The blues-rooted group seemed ill at ease among San Francisco's acid-rock heroes, but when it came time to record, they gave an eloquence and grace to the music that few bands were capable of delivering. Moments of *Brave New World* and *Your Saving Grace* hold onto the memory—after that it's all pop formulas, for better or worse.

MOBY GRAPE

The band's first eponymously-titled 1967 album remains one of the very few psychedelic masterpieces ever recorded. A brilliant piece of playing and writing, every tune reveals another facet of this hugely underrated band—from the furious joys of "Hey Grandma" and "Omaha" to polished ballads like "8:05" and "Sittin' By The Window" to the epic "Indifference." The follow-up, '68's wildly overhyped *Wow* (including the forgettable 'bonus' LP *Grape Jam),* caught the band in the throes of distintegration, but still cuts much of what was set to vinyl that year. The six albums that followed need not detract from the band's glory. A great group, a tragic history, an indispensable album.

MOODY BLUES

The line between excusably naive psychedelic and truly dopey has always been a fine one. In the days since their soulful "Go Now" single, this Brit fivesome has steadfastly walked the latter side of the line. For many middle-brow young Americans, the closet they came to acid-rock was the magnificent Moodies' *On the Threshold of a Dream, Our Children's Children's Children* or *In Search of the Lost Chord*—which contained the sublimely silly "Timothy Leary (Legend of a Mind)."

MOTHERS

When *Freak Out* was released in August of '66 it was so far ahead of its time that it seemed to be emanating from another dimension entirely. Zappa and his aggregate made fun of the psychedelic mandate and created anthems for the weird-at-heart everywhere. "Trouble Every Day" can still raise hackles, while almost everything on *Absolutely Free* and *We're Only In It For The Money* falls on the far side of inspired. Sadly, Zappa subsequently revealed himself as a surly curmudgeon with classical pretenses; the music got deadly and stayed that way. Still, the high humor and unabashed pride of freakery of those first three albums can never be equaled. Wowie Zowie.

THE MOVE

Roy Wood's thundering herd of hard rockers, The Move's bottom heavy sound was leavened by a keen sense of humor and a equally sharp songwriting skill. Their best effort, 1969's *Shazam* features a forgotten classic of English psychedelia; the baroque-tinged "Fields Of People." Also noteworthy: a lush rendition of Tom Paxton's "The Last Thing On My Mind."

NICE

One of many English R&B bands who sought to exchange new togs and topics for their sweaty soul rags circa 1967. *Thoughts of Emerlist Davjack* was inoffensive enough, but when keyboarder Keith Emerson ascended, on 1968's *Ars Longa Vita Brevis,* all was lost. The man wrote the book on Anglo pomp-rock, then published second and third editions as founding father of Emerson, Lake & Palmer. Enough already.

PEANUT BUTTER CONSPIRACY

After spotting the Byrds at Ciro's, this is what well-attuned talent scout Billy James came up with next. A sort of Sunset Stripped-down Airplane, the group made passable, fuzz-tinged folk-rock, and featured vocalist Sandi Robison. *It's A Happening Thing* and *The Great Conspiracy* (Columbia) play well ("Twice Is Life," "Captain Sandwich"), but oh those lyrics; "Firecracker sky, filled with roots of fusion/Trash cans floating by, we're so far ahead we're losin' . . ."

PINK FLOYD

Official band of the British underground in its heady first days, the Floyd were best in the hands of guitarist-singer Syd Barrett, a true psycho-bud who flowered on such tunes as "See Emily Play," "Lucifer Sam" and "The Scarecrow." Their Tower Records debut, *Piper at the Gates of Dawn,* contains same plus the space-needling "Take Up My Stethoscope And Walk." Barrett departed an album later, turning things over to David Gilmour, a singularly colorless chap who walked the madcap band first into grating progressivism *(Atom Heart Mother)* then later into mundane commerciality *(Dark Side of the Moon)*. Syd, we hardly knew ye.

PROCOL HARUM

The band's underrated second LP, 1968's *Shine On Brightly* was their most successful stab at mind-expansion. Graduate school rockers, they loaded the songs with arcane references that surprisingly succeeded in creating the requisite atmosphere of musty mysticism. "Magdalene (My Regal Zonophone)" casts a sleepy spell. Life is a bean stalk, isn't it?

QUICKSILVER MESSENGER SERVICE

If their Capitol debut (*QMS*) seems a bit cautious, it's an album that wears better than some hairier artifacts of the era. David Freiberg transforms the folkie "Pride of Man" into a sort of electric torch-song, while Duncan and Cipollina's dual leads, ever circling and stinging, make Side Two's "The Fool" one of the more articulate "long forms" in the acid-rock canon. *Happy Trails* (Capitol) gets the repertoire right ("Who Do You Love," "Mona") but sounds flat next to *Maiden of the Cancer Moon,* released last year on the Psycho import label. Taken from Fillmore East board tapes in 1968, *this* is the way the band sounded at their apex, for better or for worse.

ROLLING STONES

To their credit, the Stones have never had much use for jamming or any structural deviation from da blues. When they "went psychedelic," they did it within the confines of pop ("Dandelion," "We Love You") or laced it with humor (most of *Their Satanic Majesties Request*). As their big psyche move, though, *Majesties* was one of their most uneven sets—"Citadel" and the whirling "2000 Light Years From Home" being the standout cuts.

SANTANA

If anyone must bear the responsibility for the shotgun marriage of rock and latin music, it is guitarist Carlos Santana and his band, who parlayed turgid rhumbas and screeching guitar solos into a string of hit solos including the deadly "Black Magic Woman," and a sacreligious reworking of Tito Puente's "Oye Como Va." A misbegotten musical-hybrid sprung from the Pandora's box of psychedelia, Santana was not latin, not rock and not good.

SLY & THE FAMILY STONE

An excess of wah-wah and a determined need to get and stay "on the one" characterized some of Sly's live shows (see *Woodstock*), but nothing could obscure the fact that brilliant compositions breathed beneath all the noise and beat-beat. From the period, *Stand!* and *Dance To The Music* (Epic) still throw off "life-affirming" vibes and lotsa heat.

SMALL FACES

Reformed mods, Small Faces had a brief but fruitful psychedelic interlude with the single "Itchycoo Park" and the concept album *Ogden's Nut Gone Flake.* A slight, but pleasant footnote to the times.

SOFT MACHINE

An early corps of English psychedelic cadets, Soft Machine applied for its improvisation license early and kept it long after the expiration date. Avant Garde with a vengeance, the band's most interesting incarnation was during the tenure of drummer Robert Wyatt and guitarist Kevin Ayers who gave the band a much needed rhythmic anchor. Best albums are *Soft Machine* and *Volume Two* on Probe.

SOPWITH CAMEL

More than an ersatz Spoonful ("Hello Hello"), Peter Kraemer's bunch looked, and sounded, like they'd just jumped off the pages of the funny-papers; their tunes splashed with bright color, their playing tight and focused like a field of Ben Day dots. "Postcard From Jamaica" floats like a toy boat, and "The Great Morpheum" waltzes stately and mysteriously nearly 20 years after its appearance on the group's debut album (*Sopwith Camel,* Kama Sutra).

STEPPENWOLF

Bay Area-based as the Sparrow, John Kay and his Canuck crew cut one sharp single for Columbia, "Green Bottle Lover" b/w "Down Goes Your Love," then changed their name. *Early Steppenwolf* (Dunhill), recorded live at the Matrix in '67, offers honkoid blues and buzzsaw soloing. It also features twenty minutes of Hoyt Axton's "The Pusher", reprised on the *Steppenwolf* LP alongside "Born To Be Wild." "Magic Carpet Ride" shows up on the less energetic *Steppenwolf The Second.*

THEM

Early Them yielded two certified psychedelic landmarks—"Mystic Eyes," a blues howler, and a reworking of Dylan's "It's All Over Now, Baby Blue," delivered with passionate anguish by Morrison. 1966's *Them Again* qualifies as the band's best and most adventurous album.

TRAFFIC

Traffic 1967's debut *Mr. Fantasy* stands as a minor masterpiece of note-perfect English acid pop. What passion the band laid claim to was furnished by Winwood's trebly blues warbles, while Dave Mason's obtuse but tuneful writing was to make its presence felt in the gilded age of singer/songwriters. Other Traffic LP's of passing interest: *John Barleycorn Must Die* and *Shoot Out at the Fantasy Factory.*

UNITED STATES OF AMERICA

Psychedelic for sure, but much less rock & roll than haywire eclecticism performed by a bunch of academics—namely Joseph Byrd (whose subsequent term project was Joseph Byrd & The Field Hippies). These States used lots of synthesizers, "electric drums" and ring modulators to create what is essentially a humorless version of the Mothers' *Only In It For The Money,* though Dorothy Moskowitz's witchy vocals almost make it worth it. From the inspiring "Garden of Earthly Delights"; "Blackening mushrooms drink in the rain/Sinister nightblooms wilt with the dawn's welcoming pain."

VANILLA FUDGE

Everything the name implies. A great sludge of groaning organs, anguished vocals and incessant thuds, the band's 1967 Atlantic debut still stands as the best example of what went wrong with psychedelia. It includes dirge-tempoed renditions of "Ticket To Ride," "Eleanor Rigby," "People Get Ready," and their uproarious hit "You Keep Me Hanging On." Four subsequent releases were highlighted by '68's *The Beat Goes On* with a cut that encapsulated the entire history of music in twelve insufferable minutes. Nightmarish.

VELVET UNDERGROUND

More psychodramatic than acidic, since their drug of choice was not lysergic. Still, there are those who claim to have seen God standing on the corner, suitcase in hand, ready to trip uptown to the whitenoise outback. For those who dare: "Heroin" off *The Velvet Underground and Nico* (Verve), the 18-minute "Sister Ray" and title track from *White Light/White Heat.*

WEST COAST POP ART EXPERIMENTAL BAND

Liner notes on their first Reprise album *(Volume One)* describes the band as "the weirdest, most original man-made sensation ever experienced." Whle they may not live up to the hype, these three surfers-gone-to-pot were nothing if not experimental, covering songs by Van Dyke Parks, Zappa, Sonny Knight and the immortal P.F. Sloan—all on their debut LP. Less diverse and less hectic, *Volume Two* salutes groupies ("Queen Nymphet"), puffs up the "Smell of Incense" and philosophizes ("Suppose They Give a War and No One Comes").

THE WHO

'66's *Happy Jack* and '67's *The Who Sell Out* about sum up the band's psychedelic flirtations unless one counts (unwisely) the windy heights of *Tommy.* The group's best contributions to the genre—"I Can See For Miles," "Rael" and "Armenia City In The Sky."

YARDBIRDS

After exporting electric blues improvisation to America, the Yardbirds dallied briefly with some nicely textured oddities, earning hits like "Shapes Of Things" and "Over Under Sideways Down." But the group's finest psychedelic moment remains the awesome "Happening Ten Years Time Ago," an excursion positively scary for its intensity.

YOUNGBLOODS

Sure, "Get Together" was *the* countercultural theme song, and yes, they were one of the first groups to form their own label (anyone remember Raccoon Recors?). And Jesse Colin mellowed out in Marin, contemplating nature and probably the buttons on his bib overalls. But the band was better in New York, where they recorded that first one (*Youngbloods*, RCA). Real songs, powerful singing, and on "Four in the Morning" and "Other Side of This Life", blistering a-rock guitar from Banana—with nary a wasted note or nuance.

Filmography

Fillmore (1972)
Documentary on the final week of concerts at Fillmore West. Includes the Grateful Dead, Jefferson Airplane, the Dino Valenti version of Quicksilver Messenger Service, plus Hot Tuna, Boz Scaggs, Santana, It's A Beautiful Day, others.

GAS! (1970)
Skewered Corman flick features Country Joe in a prominent role, plus four songs by Country Joe & the Fish.

Gimme Shelter (1971)
The Maysles' brothers infamous Altamont documentary, featuring the Stones, Tina Turner and a performance by the *Volunteers*-era Jefferson Airplane.

The Grateful Dead Movie (1977)
An entire, two hour-plus Dead concert documented in detail. Performances from 1974.

Janis (1975)
Full-length study of Janis Joplin, featuring a good deal of concert footage (mostly from later, post-Big Brother shows). Soundtrack LP still available (Columbia).

Monterey Pop (1968)
D.A. Pennebaker's somewhat brief but fairly comprehensive festival documentary, which helped make stars of Janis and Big Brother, Hendrix and Otis Redding. Along for the ride: Country Joe & the Fish, the Airplane, Animals, Who, Canned Heat, Who, Simon & Garfunkel, Ravi Shankar.

Petulia (1968)
Highly atmospheric film concerning an affair between Julie Christie and George C. Scott. Frisco during that certain Summer is the backdrop. Watch closely or you'll miss cameos by Big Brother (Janis wailing "Roadblock") and the Dead (performing "Viola Lee Blues" at a society party).

Psych-Out (1968)
Dick Clark's intensive look at the hippie scene. Some good street footage, plus sounds by those old Frisco favorites the Strawberry Alarm Clock ("Incense and Peppermint").

Revolution (1969)
Another documentary on the same subject, this one centering on a forlorn flowerkid named "Today Malone." Fleeting footage from inside the Avalon at its peak (where a barely distinguishable 5-man Quicksilver are seen onstage), and a better-than-average soundtrack on United Artists, which features a pair of tunes each by Quicksilver, Steve Miller and Mother Earth.

Woodstock (1970)
Michael Wadleigh's muddy meditation on whatever it was that went on Upstate that weekend. San Francisco is represented by Country Joe & the Fish, Sly & the Family Stone and Santana. Plus: John Sebastian, Sha-Na-Na, Joan Baez, etc.

Zachariah (1971)
So-called "hip Western" starring members of the comedy group Firesign Theatre and Country Joe & the Fish. Whoa, pardnuh.

Index